Social Environments and Human Behavior

Contexts for Practice with Groups, Organizations, Communities, and Social Movements

T. LAINE SCALES
Baylor University

JON SINGLETARY
Baylor University

H. STEPHEN COOPER
Stephen F. Austin State University

BROOKS/COLE
CENGAGE Learning

Australia • Brazil • Japan• Korea • Mexico • Singapore • Spain • United Kingdom • United States

BROOKS/COLE
CENGAGE Learning

Social Environments and Human Behavior: Contexts for Practice with Groups, Organizations, Communities, and Social Movements
T. Laine Scales, Jon Singletary, and H. Stephen Cooper

Executive Editor: Jaime Perkins

Acquisitions Editor: Seth Dobrin

Assistant Editor: Alicia McLaughlin

Editorial Assistant: Suzanna Kincaid

Media Editor: Elizabeth Momb

Marketing Manager: Tami Strang

Content Project Manager: Michelle Clark

Design Director: Rob Hugel

Art Director: Caryl Gorska

Print Buyer: Judy Inouye

Rights Acquisitions Specialist: Don Schlotman

Production Service: Teresa Christie, Macmillan Publishing Services

Photo Researcher: Bill Smith Group

Text Researcher: Pablo D'Stair

Copy Editor: Debbie Stone

Cover Designer: Caryl Gorska

Cover Image: ImageZoo Illustration/Veer

Compositor: MPS Limited, a Macmillan Company

For product information and technology assistance, contact us at **Cengage Learning Customer & Sales Support, 1-800-354-9706.**

For permission to use material from this text or product, submit all requests online at **www.cengage.com/permissions.**
Further permissions questions can be e-mailed to
permissionrequest@cengage.com.

Library of Congress Control Number: 2011930527

ISBN-13: 978-0-495-17172-0

ISBN-10: 0-495-17172-7

Brooks/Cole
20 Davis Drive
Belmont, CA 94002-3098
USA

Cengage Learning is a leading provider of customized learning solutions with office locations around the globe, including Singapore, the United Kingdom, Australia, Mexico, Brazil, and Japan. Locate your local office at **www.cengage.com/global.**

Cengage Learning products are represented in Canada by Nelson Education, Ltd.

To learn more about Brooks/Cole, visit **www.cengage.com/brookscole**

Purchase any of our products at your local college store or at our preferred online store **www.CengageBrain.com.**

Printed in the United States of America
1 2 3 4 5 6 7 15 14 13 12 11

We dedicate this work to our teachers,
Diana Garland, Mary Katherine O'Connor, and Linda Morales:
Social workers and educators who inspired us to write
for the generation of professionals to come.

Contents

Preface

This book developed from the experiences of teaching our courses in human behavior and finding that the textbooks available to us and our students were not adequate for our students' needs. We found ourselves struggling to supplement texts with primary and historical readings that were difficult to access. As we spoke with other social work educators we learned that we were not alone in our frustration. As we talked with our students about what they might appreciate about a textbook, we learned that students at both undergraduate and graduate programs had difficulty connecting Human Behavior and the Social Environment content to their other courses. In addition, they wanted more opportunities to apply theory to practice. We also noticed that students were unaware of how current theories evolved historically within the social work profession. These discussions drew our attention to the need for a text that would bring together theoretical information with practice application, highlight historical foundations with accessible primary documents, and help students make curricular connections.

After some discussion, we decided that the best approach to addressing this need was to produce a textbook that incorporated primary documents along with artistic and literary pieces to help students tie their human behavior content to a liberal arts base, a historical foundation, and to the practice behaviors outlined by the revised Educational Policy and Accreditation Standards (EPAS) from the Council on Social Work Education. We sincerely hope that our readers, both students and instructors will find this book useful for their learning.

ACKNOWLEDGEMENTS

We have enjoyed our work together as partners, and we thank our respective institutions, Baylor University and Stephen F. Austin University, for their support. Special thanks go to the graduate assistants who helped us research the

Curriculum Connections and Competency Connections sections and provided general help with research and formatting: Kyna Baskin, Karen Birech, Michael Ormsby, and Everett Smith. We appreciate the students in our classes who read our chapters and gave us feedback to improve our work. In addition, we are grateful to Dr. Terry Wolfer, College of Education, University of South Carolina, and the other decision case writers, and the artists who allowed us to publish their original creations. We owe much to the late Lisa Gebo, who encouraged us to pursue this project; we will remember her always as "the queen of social work publishing." Finally, many thanks to Brooks/Cole and CENGAGE, particularly Seth Dobrin, as well as the reviewers who provided helpful feedback to improve our text: Nancy Amos, Bradley University; Frances Bernard Kominkiewicz, St. Mary's College; Nancy Keeton, Brescia University; Nancy Kelley-Gillespie, University of Nebraska – Omaha; Juanita Mansell, Carolina State University; Erin Olson, Dordt College; Adelle Sanders, Governor's State University.

Human Behavior and Your Social Work Curriculum An Introduction

As social work educators, we hear many stories about how students come to the decision to study social work. What is your story? Why are you reading this book? Some of you are reading it because you learned about social work from a social worker who made an impact on your life through an agency where she was helping your family get through a difficult situation. Some of you are reading this because your friends at school convinced you social work is a place where you can learn the skills you need to serve children struggling at school, older adults adjusting to living in a new environment, women whose lives have been shaped by violence, or men who are striving to overcome an addiction. Some of you are reading this because you love it all and still cannot decide what you want to do or where you want to make a difference, but you know you want to be a part of a helping profession or that you want to work for social justice in our world.

As we think about how we came to this place, we can recognize that the lives we lead are rich and complex. We know the impact that family and friends have on us. As students, fellow classmates impact us, and as we enter the workforce, our colleagues are just as influential. Just as individuals and small groups shape our lives, so do the communities where we live, whether this be your neighborhood or your entire city, and in the organizations where we spend our time, whether they be schools, businesses, or nonprofits. This is a book about these factors that influence our lives. These social factors make up the social environments that influence our behavior as humans.

MAKING THE CONNECTIONS BETWEEN
ENVIRONMENTS AND BEHAVIOR

This book recognizes the multiple social environments that influence our lives and the many different ways that we can learn about these influences. In particular, we are focusing on groups, communities, organizations, and social movements as factors in the social environment that are particularly influential. In the chapters that follow, we will define each of these and discuss what they mean to us and what they can mean to you as you explore social work. As a part of learning about them, we want you to recognize the ways these four factors interact with each other and with you to shape who you are and how you live—that is, to shape human behavior. We describe these four factors in the social environment as social systems. Sometimes these systems overlap and interact in ways that are helpful and sometimes in ways that are hurtful. Sometimes it seems we cannot tell the difference between these systems; other times it seems they are not related at all.

An example of a group can be as simple as the friends you had in high school who were as influential as family at times. You spent time together, made decisions together, shaped each others' lives and probably shaped the lives of others who knew you. A professional function of a group is in operation when a social worker organizes a gathering of people who have all left loved ones behind and who come together for support as they share stories of being immigrants. They teach one another, learn from one another, and shape each others' lives as they cope with the opportunities and challenges of being in a new place.

An organization for you to consider might be the school where you came to meet your group of friends. It might be the church that hosts the support group. These organizations, a school and a church, are quite different, but they share some similarities, as they involve people who have come together for a common purpose or for similar reasons.

The groups found in these organizations can also be described in terms of where they are found in communities. Perhaps the school where you met your friends was the only high school in your rural town; students from all around the county would have come together at your school. Chances are, you knew most of the people in your school, and you knew of the similarities and differences in your group of friends and among all of the kids—in part, because you knew your community. In our other example, the church offering the support group may be one church among many in a large urban setting, but it is a church from a Latino tradition. The families in this church know each other well and are tightly knit because of the strong Latino community they have formed. They are quite aware of the commonalities and the differences they share with African Americans, Asian Americans, and Caucasians in their city, but they experience community in the relationships they share in common based on their ethnicity and their common experience as immigrants.

Social movements influence our groups, our organizations, and our communities. The education movement in United States has built strong schools that foster the relationships you experienced. We know that strong families and strong communities need strong schools in order to nurture and develop our young people. We may take our education system and the time we have with friends for granted, but it has taken a movement of people working together to make our education system possible. Likewise, immigrants coming together for support experience that need because of changes happening right now in our nation's immigration policies. Our country is wrestling with how supportive we will be of immigrants and Latino communities are working together to ensure that immigrants are not persecuted or oppressed. As people come together collectively to organize for change, social movements are born.

As you learn more about ways that social environments shape human behavior, we want you to understand the theory and the research related to understanding human behavior in social environments. We want you to see the ways theories have changed throughout history. Some theories are based on ideas that assume that all groups or organizations function in the same way and other theories focus much more on the differences between communities or social movements. Research can be used to compare the ideas found in these theories to help determine the extent to which they hold true. For example, in a later section of this book you'll read the history of collective action theories of social movements. You'll see how some efforts to work for change could be sustained because of common experiences of conflict or marginalization. This theory of collective action held true for years, but then researchers (some of them social workers) began asking questions about how and why people work together for change. From this research we learned that resources had to be mobilized in order for change to be sustained. Theories are created, research is conducted, and ideas change. Parts of theories shift and change the way people think and how social workers practice. At the same time, when research suggests a shift in a theory, then practitioners are encouraged to shift as well. The chapters ahead are full of examples of theory and practice to help you make sense of these things and to shed light on how you practice social work, first in your field placement and then in your career.

But, there are other ways besides theory and research that we learn. Stories and art influence our understanding of human behavior and our practice. They help us learn and to make sense of the world around us. Humans have always been inspired by art and we can each think of favorite poems or songs that have shaped us. We can identify photos that change how we see the world or plays that alter our understanding of life's meaning. As a result, we have chosen poetry, music, and photo essays to tell the stories of groups, communities, organizations, and social movements. For each brief artistic expression you see here, there are hundreds of thousands of expressions that help us understand the social environments that are important in our lives. We intentionally chose unknown artists (in fact, two of them are college students) to illustrate the point that anyone can use art to explore human behavior. Our hope is that you will be inspired to create something original to express what you are learning about human behavior in these larger systems.

ORGANIZATION OF THE BOOK: MULTIPLE PATHS TO LEARNING

Each of the environments we have been discussing—groups, communities, organizations, and social movements—forms a unit of this book. Each unit includes four very different types of readings to allow you to explore the topic from multiple perspectives.

The first reading in each unit presents the core content related to that system. This is an overview chapter that describes relevant theories and research and provides examples for thinking about the system. To help you connect theory to practice, we end each core chapter by discussing ways that each social environment functions as a context for practice.

As a second reading in each unit, we offer a historical reading from an earlier period in our profession's history. By seeing how social workers used to think about the system and comparing it to contemporary views, you will gain a deeper understanding of how social work thinking has evolved over time.

We draw upon a liberal arts base so important to social work education and encourage "right-brain thinking" by including selections from poetry, music, and photography. We do this in order to encourage students and teachers to apply the content in a creative manner. This artistic expression can help us understand these systems more clearly. Our hope is that these inspire you and at the same time help you better understand the issues relevant to the system being studied in the unit.

Finally, in a fourth reading, we give you foundation students opportunities to apply behavior principles in practice situations by closing each chapter with a decision case related to larger systems. These are open-ended cases that may be used for class discussion, small group work, or written exercises. These cases, reprinted from the Wolfer and Scales series *Decision Cases for Generalist (Advanced) Social Work Practice: Thinking Like a Social Worker*, are not fictional; they actually happened and were reported by social workers. Cases may be used to prepare you for the chapter or to serve as a touchstone for instructors and students to discuss key concepts after reading the chapter.

SOCIAL ENVIRONMENTS, HUMAN BEHAVIOR, AND EPAS

In creating this text, we have taken as our beginning point the revised Educational Policy and Accreditation Standards (EPAS) from the Council on Social Work Education. These are the policies and standards that shape the core content of what we teach, and they continue to tie human behavior to its practice applications and to field education. In addition, as educators, we recognize the need to help students connect human behavior and social environment foundations to other parts of their curriculum, such as research, policy, practice, and history of social work; our Curriculum Connections and Competency Connections sidebars will reinforce this integration called for in the EPAS.

Here are some of the EPAS and ways that our text engages them:

Apply knowledge of human behavior and the social environment.
This EPAS is addressed throughout the text as we continually require to the reader to apply knowledge about social environments and human behavior through examples, scenarios, and decision cases.

Respond to contexts that shape practice. Addressing this EPAS, our text goes beyond understanding to practical application in the contexts of practice where social workers find themselves.

Engage, assess, intervene, and evaluate with individuals, families, groups, organizations, and communities.
The areas of practice in which social workers serve include the groups, communities, and organizations, as well as the social movements, addressed in this text.

As educators, we often hear concerns about students' struggle to tie together knowledge and skills from their classes into an integrated picture of social work. Students express frustration during the final capstone course if a professor is unable to explain how theories from human behavior courses tie to policy or practice. Instructors are mystified when entire pieces of the curriculum seem to "disappear" as some students focus on discrete bits of learning that they are unable to integrate. One of the foundational ideas of the new EPAS, first proposed in 2007, is that the curriculum will be more integrated around a practice focus and our signature pedagogy, field experience. We are convinced that students must regularly practice thinking about how one course ties to another so that this integration becomes a natural process for them. Instructors can help, and textbooks like this one can address this concern as well. This book is focused on making those connections, and we believe it will be a helpful guide as students apply their understandings of human behavior in social environments, particularly in the four contexts of practice that comprise our four units: groups, communities, organizations, and social movements. Let us turn to each of these now.

EPAS and Competency Connections

In creating this text, we have taken as our beginning point the revised Educational Policy and Accreditation Standards (EPAS) from the Council on Social Work Education. These are the policies and standards that shape the core content of what we teach, and they continue to tie human behavior to its practice applications and to field education. For more explanation of the EPAS, see http://www.cswe.org/Accreditation/2008EPASDescription.aspx

Unit	Page #	EPAS competency	Competency Connection
1	4	EP 2.1.1	Groups and the History of Social Welfare
1	6	EP 2.1.4, 2.1.5, 2.1.10	Groups in Practice
1	12	EP 2.1.3, 2.1.4, 2.1.9	Groups in Research
1	18	EP 2.1.2	Ethics in Social Work
2	45	EP 2.1.5	Organizations in Social Welfare History
2	58	EP 2.1.6	Organizations and Research
2	64	EP 2.1.5, 2.1.8	Organizations and Policy Issues
2	66	EP 2.1.3, 2.1.4, 2.1.5	Organizations and Social Work Practice
2	not in paper	EP 2.1.2	Ethics and Social Work Organizations
3	113	EP 2.1.5, 2.1.8	Communities in Social Welfare History
3	107	EP 2.1.5, 2.1.8	Communities and Policy Issues

Unit	Page #	EPAS competency	Competency Connection
3	98	EP 2.1.5, 2.1.6, 2.1.8	Communities in Social Work Practice
3	119	EP 2.1.2, 2.1.3	Ethics in Community Practice
4	148	EP 2.1.5	Social Movements & Social Welfare History
4	153	EP 2.1.6	Social Movements Using Research
4	156	EP 2.1.8	Social Movements & Policy
4	160	EP 2.1.2, 2.1.3	Ethical Decision Making

About the Authors

T. Laine Scales is Associate Dean of Graduate Studies and Professional Development and Professor of Higher Education at Baylor University, Waco, Texas. She served for 12 years as a faculty member in social work at Baylor University and Stephen F. Austin State University, Nacogdoches, Texas, where she taught human behavior with individuals, groups, communities, and organizations. Dr. Scales has published in the areas of social welfare history, spirituality and religion in social work, and rural social work. She has authored, edited or co-edited seven books, including *All That Fits a Woman: Training Southern Baptist Women for Charity and Mission, 1907–1926* (Mercer University Press, 2000), *Spirituality and Religion in Social Work Practice: Decision Cases with Teaching Notes* (Council on Social Work Education, 2002)*, Rural Social Work: Asset-Building to Sustain Rural Communities* (Brooks/Cole, 2004), and *Decision Cases for Generalist Practice: Thinking Like a Social Worker* (Thomson Brooks/Cole, 2006). Dr. Scales earned her BA at the University of North Carolina, her MSW at the Carver School of Church Social Work, Louisville, KY, and her PhD at the University of Kentucky.

Jon E. Singletary is Diana R. Garland Chair of Children and Family Studies and Associate Dean for Baccalaureate Studies in the School of Social Work, Baylor University, Waco, Texas. Receiving his MSW and PhD degrees from Virginia Commonwealth University, Dr. Singletary's interests are in community organizing and social movements, particularly as they involve congregations and faith-based organizations. He also holds a Master of Divinity degree from Baptist Theological Seminary of Richmond and served as pastor of a Mennonite congregation in Richmond, Virginia, supporting nonviolent initiatives in the local community. In addition, he practiced with an agency providing health care to people who were homeless. Dr. Singletary has published over 20 peer-reviewed articles and over 35 presentations on communities and congregations. He teaches in the BSW and MSW programs in the areas of human behavior with groups, communities, organizations, and social movements, as well as practice courses.

H. Stephen Cooper is Assistant Professor of Social Work and Associate Dean, College of Liberal and Applied Arts, at Stephen F. Austin State University in Nacogdoches, Texas. He has also served as the Coordinator for the School's Initiative for Rural Research and Development. Dr. Cooper teaches both BSW and MSW courses, primarily in the areas of human behavior, research, policy, and community/organizational theory and practice. He earned a BS in Psychology and an MSW from Stephen F. Austin State University, and a PhD in Social Work at the University of Texas at Austin. His work experience includes law enforcement, child/adolescent community mental health, adolescent residential treatment, therapeutic wilderness programming, administration, and network planning/development. Dr. Cooper's research interests include child and adolescent mental health, juvenile delinquency, rural social work, community practice, and civic engagement.

Small Groups

LEARNING OBJECTIVE

To expose students to the basic concepts needed for a foundational understanding of human behavior and groups, including concepts and theories about types, structures, mutual aid traditions, leadership, diversity, and conflict within groups. Students will have opportunities to apply theories and concepts about groups to a practice case and connect knowledge about human behavior in groups to other areas of the social work curriculum.

INTRODUCTION

The purpose of Unit 1 is to assist you in deepening your understanding of human behavior in small groups. Social workers work with groups in a variety of contexts: they are members of committees and task forces, they are in work groups within the organizations that employ them, or they may use treatment or mutual aid groups in practice. Unit 1 begins with an overview of small groups and an opportunity to connect theory to practice.

We have included three additional elements to supplement and illustrate the key aspects presented. First, we draw your attention to group theory as it developed in history. Tuckman's presentation of stages of group development, created when group work was peaking in the 1960s and 1970s, became a classic framework adopted widely by social workers, psychologists, and others interested in how groups develop and change over time. The poem "The Caregivers" encourages you to view small groups through an artistic lens as you visualize this support group and their emotions and behaviors. A decision case, *Larry Steele's Group*, will engage you in applying the theories and concepts presented in this unit and give you practice thinking like a social worker about human behavior in groups. Throughout the chapter, the *Curriculum Connections* commentaries will assist you in understanding how the topic of groups relates to other pieces of your social work education.

We hope that through your interaction with this unit you will have an opportunity to deepen your understanding of human behavior as it relates to small groups and begin applying your theoretical knowledge to practice situations. Groups are found everywhere in social work practice and a thorough understanding of group behavior will be essential to effective practice.

Reading 1

Human Behavior in Small Groups

Prior to reading this chapter, take a moment to think about the groups of which you are a member; these may be groups that gather for a formal purpose, such as a committee or a support group, or less formal groups, such a group gathering weekly for a religious purpose, or a social group of friends and acquaintances in which people come and go as they make more or less time for the group. While reading this chapter, consider how the concepts presented apply to these groups. You may be asking "Why do I need to know about groups?" People of all kinds are tied to a variety of groups, both formally and informally. If you are working with people, you can be assured that they are connected to groups of some kind. In developing social work skills, an understanding of behavior in groups will serve as an important foundation to understanding humans socially.

As you integrate your observations of a group's behavior with your social work skills, you will draw from the various theories and concepts about group behavior that you have learned. While reading and digesting the material from this chapter, try to practice observing the behaviors of various groups and applying these concepts. What groups can you see within your own classroom? By building a foundational understanding of group behavior, you are preparing to assess quickly and accurately a group's behavior and to intervene (or empower others to intervene) in ways that influence that behavior. In other words, it is important to know what an effective group is and to have the skills to shape a group to be effective in your role as a member, a facilitator, or perhaps a consultant to a group. Our purpose in this chapter is to facilitate understanding of how groups behave as well as how individuals behave within groups.

TWO STREAMS OF KNOWLEDGE ABOUT GROUP BEHAVIOR IN SOCIAL WORK

Social workers have used small groups to improve lives since the profession was emerging in the late 19th and early 20th centuries. For example, early settlement houses used democratic group participation to teach skills and values of developing citizenship and democratic participation. In this spirit, the field of social group work emerged to emphasize work with groups of children, youth, women, adults in immigrant communities and other neighborhoods of oppressed populations. Social workers formed the American Association for the Study of

Group Work during the 1930s and later the retitled organization of American Association of Group Workers (AAGW) merged with others to form the National Association of Social Workers in 1956 (Ephross & Vassil, 2005). This tradition of social group work focused on vulnerable populations and democratic ideals while providing a voice to those who were often silenced. Unfortunately, while focused on action, social workers in this tradition sometimes neglected to record their experiences and observations of human behavior. In other words, the social workers were busy practicing group work, but often neglected to capture their practice wisdom in writing. Therefore, social work education has often defaulted away from the group work tradition to draw from other disciplines, like psychology, that did document behavior. Today, some social workers are trying to recapture this important tradition of social group work with vulnerable populations and incorporate it more explicitly.

At the same time in history, a second stream of knowledge about groups was emerging among social scientists particularly psychology, education, and business, but spanning several disciplines. This body of knowledge came to be known as "group dynamics" or "group processes." Much of this research on group behavior was conducted by social psychologists with temporary groups of college students paid to participate in experiments, rather than by studying natural groups (Ephross & Vassil, 2005). The contributions of the group dynamics studies may be valuable to social workers, but we have to critically examine the information through social work lenses. Is our purpose to empower groups of people in vulnerable populations in a democratic spirit, through task groups? Is our purpose therapeutic, to serve a small portion of the population by addressing particular issues, but with very important outcomes? In reality, social workers do both of these types of work. We esteem the social group work tradition that will involve task groups such as neighborhood organizations, religious congregations, school boards, and others in democratic change. Yet we recognize the essential role of

---

Competency Connection

Groups and the History of Social Welfare: The American Association of Group Workers (AAGW)

The American Association of Group Workers, founded in the 1930s, was one of the first organizations that practiced group work. The members represented a wide range of professions, such as "recreation workers, volunteer workers, and street workers, etc." (Ramey's 1998 interview, as cited in Andrews, 2001). For many years, the AAGW was set apart from the social work profession. In fact, the history of the AAGW, and group work in general "was seen as a movement before it became a field" (Andrews, 2001). The AAGW was a powerful coalition that rallied alongside immigrants and other oppressed groups to improve social conditions and social problems within communities. They focused on issues such as housing and education, and

they organized recreational and leisure activities. Group work became more closely linked to social work in 1935, when the National Conference on Social Work (NCSW) included a session on group work. It was out of the NCSW Conference that about 15 to 20 group workers began to meet, and they eventually formed the National Association for the Study of Group Work. Group work then began to branch out from the neighborhoods to practice in "various types of institutions, in hospitals, in clinics, and in extracurricular activities of schools" (Andrews, 2001).

Andrews, J. (2001). Group work's place in social work: A historical analysis. *Journal of Sociology and Social Welfare, 28*(4), 45–64.
Ramey, J. (1998, June). Interview with the author, New York City.

groups serving therapeutic purposes as well. You, the next generation of social workers, must have knowledge, skills, and values to equip you to work with a variety of groups. Both of these streams of knowledge will be addressed in this chapter while introducing some key concepts social workers have used with groups. However, we anticipate that after this brief overview, you will explore more deeply one or both of these very different streams of knowledge, social group work and group processes, according to your purposes and the needs of your client groups as you continue in your career.

Group Definitions, Types, and Environments

What Makes a Group?   It may not surprise you that social scientists have put forth many definitions of groups, with some even claiming there is no such thing as a group; that groups exist only in the minds of people (Johnson & Johnson, 2006). Some claimed in the 1960s and 1970s, as the study of group behavior was exploding in the areas of business and psychology, that participants must interact face to face to be considered a group. Today, technologies such as the Internet and satellite communications have called that requirement into question. Some have suggested that groups must be interdependent and share common goals, while others insist that they must define themselves and be defined by others as a group (Johnson & Johnson, 2006).

Although all of these aspects provide food for thought, we find this simple definition to be the most useful for social work classes: two or more persons interacting in ways that they each influence one another (Shaw, 1981). Even this definition may cause us to argue about what it means to "influence" someone; however, its breadth and simplicity is appealing and useful as a starting point. This definition takes into account dyads, triads, all the way up to a large crowd. In this chapter, we will focus on what social workers call "small groups," which range from 3 to about 12 people.

Composition and Purpose.   Imagine yourself as a social worker on a committee to address the issue of homelessness in your community. This committee is classified as a task group, different from a treatment group, which is designed for a therapeutic purpose. Some may be classified as growth groups, which are designed to help members in their personal development; an example of a growth group would be the support group for caregivers of Alzheimer's patients described in the poem "The Caregivers" presented later in this unit. Others may be classified as therapeutic groups, a category broader than the name implies. For example, group work gurus Corey and Corey (2006) apply the term not only to treatment groups addressing emotional or behavior concerns, but any group engaged in therapy, consciousness-raising, self-help, or personal growth.

In other words, groups are organized for different purposes. While this statement may seem obvious, the effects of a group's purpose on the group itself may not be so obvious. Purpose will affect various aspects of the group such as membership or composition as well as dynamics, or what is happening as groups move and change, never remaining static. Purpose and composition also affect the

---

Competency Connection

Groups in Practice: Social Workers Can Use Diversity to Avoid the Phenomenon of "Groupthink"

Janis and Mann's study (as cited in Ephross & Vassil, 1988, pp. 128–129) explains how the phenomenon groupthink, occurs when the decision-making and problem-solving processes become undemocratic; when discussions are inhibited and closed off to some members; when silence among nonparticipating members implies their consent; and when members functioning as "mind-guards" work to preserve complacency and subjectivity. By incorporating group members who are diverse according to race, ethnicity, gender, age, and spiritual/religion preference, social workers allow more open, enlightening discussions, where participation by all members is encouraged and valued. Shared information stems from an individual's cultural perspective, background, and personal experiences. Diversity will spark thought-provoking discussions, as ideas will be explored and analyzed from multiple perspectives. Members will be attentive to hearing feedback from one another, knowing that all ideas, activities, and decisions consist of fragments encompassing many different customs, traditions, beliefs, and points of view.

Ephross, P.H. & Vassil, T.V. (1988). *Groups that work: Structure and process.* New York: Columbia University Press.

Janis, L., & Mann, L. (1977). *Decision making.* New York: Free Press.

---

dynamics of group norms, power and leadership. However, social workers are careful to consider groups within their environmental context.

Groups in Environmental Context

Field Theory.   As theories about groups were emerging in the middle of the 20th century, social workers began to draw on the work of German social psychologists like Kurt Lewin in addition to our traditions of social group work. According to Lewin's (1951) field theory, "any event is a resultant of a multitude of factors" (p. 44). Furthermore, "any behavior or any other change in a psychological field depends only upon the psychological field at that time" (p. 45). A "psychological field" can be understood as a person's environment. Field theory does not imply that the past is not important, but rather, in a group setting, the focus is on whatever is having an impact on the present and whatever influences in the environment are interacting with group members. Dynamics of the group, individual differences, and individual experiences that relate to the here and now all have an impact on the "present psychological field" (p. 45).

If in your study of social work you have become accustomed to thinking in terms of "person in environment," then field theory may seem a rather obvious concept to you. However, at the time it was emerging in the 1950s, field theory challenged group workers to consider the group as an environment or field while also considering the field in which the group was situated. The theory also encouraged workers to move their focus from past events (which had been the focus of Freudian psychoanalytic theories) to observe present occurrences within the group. This requires careful observation and analysis of human behavior. Shifting their focus, and acquiring a different set of practice skills required social workers to tune in to the group's environment in new ways.

Field theory would suggest that outcomes and performance of a group are directly dependent on all that the individual and group are experiencing at that time. Pertinent experiences, intergroup relationships, moods, and external stresses that each individual is currently experiencing are all dynamic influences on the outcome and performance of this group. When evaluating the group context and planning for change, the social worker must take into account the total situation, the group and its environment, in a holistic way. Think about your own experiences in groups, perhaps for a class assignment. Have you noticed how moods, external stresses, maybe even physical conditions such as not having enough sleep may affect the behavior of each individual and the group as a whole? Unfortunately, groups can neglect to address their environmental factors and intergroup relationships, missing important opportunities to consider how context affects behavior. Field theory reminds us how important the environment is to a group's processes.

Group Composition and Structure

Thinking back to the example above, for your task group to address the issues of people who are homeless in your community, it would be important to recognize the composition and structure of the group. Because the problem of homelessness has many influences and causes, and as the homeless population itself is diverse, it is imperative that the group be heterogeneous, including diverse members. This involves diversity in areas such as gender, race, ethnicity, and professional or personal background, and you may decide you need to think about other types of diversity particular to the context of the mission. Group members could be made up of professionals from different fields and from different agencies around town who could offer valuable input for the group. This would include not only social workers and professionals from pertinent organizations, but also other professionals such as city officials, lawyers, business owners, and other leaders. Social workers typically seek participation of the client group and may invite several homeless individuals to be a part of the group. Because of this diversity, it will be important to establish a group structure. This can be done by appointing leaders to the group such as a president, vice president, treasurer, and secretary. The task group could also assign subcommittees to address specific goals and areas of work for the group.

Elements of group structure such as size, norms, roles, and diversity will affect a group's processes. Group size may vary based on the purpose and task of the group. Some group work experts argue for ideal sizes of groups, while others leave more latitude to accommodate for the group's purposes. A group of five to seven participants promotes a high level of participation and allows members to feel more confident about sharing thoughts and feelings. As groups increase in number, dominant members may arise and other group participants may feel less satisfied and may interact less. Having an odd number of participants prevents a deadlock, which is an important aspect to consider in making decisions. As groups increase in size, subgroups based on commonalities often arise. Coalitions, a type of subgroup, arise from the group in order to achieve a goal that individuals could not attain on their own (Queralt, 1996).

Norms are rules that govern the work of the group. Norms evolve over time and signal members about their behavior; how to behave or how not to behave within the group (Johnson & Johnson, 2006). Norms may be prescriptive or proscriptive; prescriptive norms are those that describe the kinds of behaviors expected; proscriptive norms describe behaviors that are forbidden. Explicit norms are those that are clearly identified and discussed; implicit norms are rules that are assumed and unspoken (Queralt, 1996). Think about groups of which you are a member; do your social groups have norms that are informal and implicit? Are you also involved in group with more formalized and explicit norms, such as absence policies, confidentiality agreements, or norms about listening behaviors? As you work in groups within your classrooms, see if you can identify norms that are implicit or explicit, proscriptive or prescriptive.

In addition to norms, roles within the group will affect processes. Borrowed from the theatre, the concept of role is often used by social scientists to explain a set of expectations that define behavior. When applied to groups, roles describe the differentiation of group members and may emerge over time. Like norms, roles may be formalized (such as when a group leader has been appointed) or less formal (when a member falls into a role based on interest or skill). Once members are placed in roles, the group comes to rely on them to perform that role (Johnson & Johnson, 2006). An example of a role that can be assumed informally is that of "mediator" or "peacemaker"—someone who habitually works to resolve conflicts that arise within the group.

Take a look at the following chart, which outlines a variety of group roles and functions proposed by Benne and Sheats. Although this list was compiled in 1948, it is still relevant for human behavior today. As you look at the list, which is divided into task roles and socioemotional roles, see if you recognize those that come most naturally to you. Do you find that in different types of groups you gravitate toward different roles?

Members often bring into the group their roles from other settings. For example, a peacemaker in the family may be a peacemaker in the group. However, sometimes people in groups take on very different roles than they are used to performing because they are attempting to balance or complement another group member.

Different kinds of conflicts may arise as a result of these roles. Interrole conflict occurs when the behaviors associated with one role are incompatible with another role that must be performed. For example, it would be difficult to serve as both an evaluator and an encourager, as one is a task role and the other is a socioemotional role. Another conflict that can arise is that of intrarole conflict, in which the group member faces opposing demands from a single role. This may occur when a group member has the role of gatekeeper and interprets this to mean "prevent 'ordinary' group members from talking too much so as to allow the more influential people in the group to dominate the discussion," whereas other members "may want the gatekeeper to act more democratically" (Queralt, 1996, p. 316).

In addition to role functions, status plays an important role in the group. Generally, each group member starts off on an equal level. However, as the

Role	Function
Task Roles	
Initiator contributor	Recommends novel ideas about the problem at hand, new ways to approach the problem, or possible solutions not yet considered
Information seeker	Emphasizes "getting the facts" by calling for background information from others
Opinion seeker	Asks for more qualitative types of data, such as attitudes, values, and feelings
Information giver	Provides facts and data for forming decisions
Opinion giver	Provides opinions, values, and feelings
Elaborator	Gives additional information—examples, rephrasing, implications—about points made by others
Coordinator	Shows the relevance of each idea and its relationship to the overall problem
Orienter	Refocuses discussion on the topic whenever necessary
Evaluator-critic	Appraises the quality of the group's effort in terms of logic, practicality, or method
Energizer	Stimulates the group to continue working when discussion flags
Procedural technician	Provides operational details such as rules of order, materials, and so on
Recorder	Provides a secretarial function
Socioemotional Roles	
Encourager	Rewards others through agreement, warmth, and praise
Harmonizer	Mediates conflicts among group members
Compromiser	Shifts his or her position on a issue in order to reduce conflict in the group
Gatekeeper and expediter	Smooths communication by setting up procedures and ensuring equal participation from members
Standard setter	Expresses, or calls for discussion of, standards for evaluating the quality of the group process
Observer and commentator	Informally points out the positive and negative aspects of the group's dynamics and calls for change if necessary
Follower	Accepts the ideas offered by others and serves as an audience for the group

From "Functional Roles of Group Members" by K.D. Benne and P. Sheats, *Journal of Social Issues, 42*(2). Copyright ©1948 by the Society for the Psychological Study of Social Issues. Reprinted by permission.

group sessions progress, a few members may be seen as more important or as having more status, and therefore more power, influence, and control. This can occur because the group member demonstrates personal characteristics, such as wisdom or expertise, that are valued by the group. Status can also be achieved by contributions such as volunteering to take on responsibilities.

Members differentiate themselves by performing various roles or by acquiring different levels of status. But another type of member differentiation results from diversity among group members. The differences that individuals bring in terms of race, ethnicity, gender, or other characteristics (such as socioeconomic class, life experience, traits, abilities, and values) have the potential to enhance group process and provide a rich texture of ideas and practices to the group.

Unfortunately, differences often are not appreciated in productive ways. For example, a group may be working on a class project to advocate for a particular special cause, such as organizing a conference to increase awareness of GLBT populations. A particular group member may choose not to participate because his or her values present a conflict. This group member's resistance to the project could be seen as frustrating.

CULTURAL COMPETENCE: BUILDING COHESION IN DIVERSE GROUPS

It may take longer to develop group cohesion for very diverse groups, but in the end, a heterogeneous group may be more productive than a group in which everyone is alike (Gazda, Ginter, & Horne, 2001). The wise social worker will search for some commonalities and similarities with which to begin building cohesion. Or, another way to think of it: groups can be at the same time both homogeneous and heterogeneous. While we may appear to be very different at first glance, we can try to find commonalities that draw us together. Sometimes this will be in terms of our common experiences or our common purposes, the reasons that draw us to the group in the first place. Group leaders can use concrete subjects to draw attention to commonalities. While increased diversity may cause increased conflict, this can be very healthy when members learn and practice appropriate ways of responding and we will suggest practical ways of dealing with conflict in a later section (Fluhr, 2004; Yalom & Leszcz, 2005).

Diversity of Sex and Gender

In virtually every group work context, gender must be regarded as a relevant factor (Cohen & Mullender, 2003). Researchers studying the sex composition of groups note several trends that call for social workers to seek out equal representation of males and females whenever possible. This allows each member to be viewed as individuals, it reduces sex stereotyping, enhances the influence of female members (who have been undervalued historically), and overall develops a more effective problem-solving group (Schiller, 1995; Shaw, 1981). On the other hand, when groups are not balanced, female members may hold back because of greater aggressiveness by male group members. A female member may be evaluated negatively when she is the solo or "token" member; this may lead her to conform to the male majority (assimilation). Also, group members may make overgeneralizations made about the women in the group (Shaw, 1981; Walker, Ilardi, McMahon, & Fennell, 1996).

Group interventions based on feminist theory seek to prevent any inequality or unfair balances of power that lead to oppression or domination. Feminist theory does not address gender only, but also recognizes the roles that race, class, age, and other factors have in inequality. Social workers must be attuned to power differences of all kinds and seek to move the group toward balance.

Group members often stereotype one another based on gender and sex; the wise worker presses the group to confront their own stereotyping behavior and respond to each group member as a unique individual.

One of the most compelling group interviews I (Laine) ever conducted was with a group of gay, lesbian and transsexual persons involved in an organization called HUGS (Hearing and Understanding God's Scriptures). This group of people living in Kentucky identified as Christians wishing to deepen their spiritual experiences and connections by reading Christian scriptures together, but as sexual minorities they felt oppressed in the churches they had attended. As they came together for spiritual exploration, bible study and discussion, if any group member was tempted to stereotype other group members according to traditional gender roles, the members themselves asserted their unique qualities. In this group, gender and sex as it relates to power, status, and communication patterns within the group were an accepted subject of discussion because members spent years considering their own sexual minority status. This group reminded me of the value of speaking explicitly about issues of gender and sex as it relates to power and status within groups so that these issues do not remain as "the elephant in the room" that everyone sees but no one acknowledges. Groups with healthy communication patterns openly recognize differences and address any power differentials as part of their relationship-building.

Diversity of Race and Ethnicity

When considering racial and ethnic diversity, groups may be structured with at least two members of each ethnic group represented, in order to minimize tokenism, marginalization, or scapegoating. Tokenism occurs when extra attention is given to individuals who are different: the tokens. Being a token can cause pressure to perform according to expectations, lead to feelings of being used to meet diversity requirements, and lead to polarization of differences among group members (Brown & Mistry, 2005). Members are marginalized when they are pushed away to the margins rather than being a central part of the group, based on race or ethnicity. Scapegoating occurs when group members are blamed for situations or shortcomings because they are different from the majority of the group (Johnson & Johnson, 2006). While ensuring that at least two members from each ethnic group are present may be ideal, in our experience, social workers assembling task groups around particular issues, or creating treatment groups in rural areas or other areas where populations may be more homogeneous, do not have opportunities to choose the ideal.

Social workers must be prepared to lead members toward valuing one another's contributions to the whole task while strengthening each individual's sense that he or she has something unique to contribute. Brook, Gordon & Meadow (1998) suggest creating and maintaining an open and honest group atmosphere, being clear about expectations in early phases of the group, and staying attuned to power relations and dominance in groups. Groups should focus on topics that are more universal and recognize when a topic or area may not be experienced universally. Group leaders should recognize how oppression

Competency Connection

Groups in Research: Planning for Diversity of Gender, Race, and Ethnicity within a Research Team

It is important for social workers to consider the socio-cultural factors of ethnicity, culture, and gender when building effective research teams. Social workers representing various ethnic and cultural backgrounds offer personal knowledge and experience about heritage, religion, tradition, language, communication styles, as well as family roles and norms. Such diversity is needed before gathering and collecting data within ethnic communities. Likewise, incorporating gender-mixed team members includes both male and female points of views. Deborah Tannen (2001) explains how women are more likely to engage in rapport talk, in

which their conversations include "establishing connections and negotiating relationships," whereas men engage in report talk, in which their conversations are designed to be informational. The weight of both types of gendered expressions are needed, as well as racial and ethnic diversity, when conducting research projects. Diversity of experiences and backgrounds is valuable when debating strategies about research topics, methods, and designs.

Tannen, D. (2001). *You just don't understand: Women and men in conversation.* New York: HarperCollins.

has functioned in our nation's history and be sensitive to how that history affects the group. Be sure to focus on group topics or things that are universal and recognize what areas may not be universal (Brook et al., 1998).

One of the most compelling portraits of racial and ethnic diversity as it relates to group processes has been the film *The Color of Fear* by Lee Mun Wah (1995). This powerful film documents a group of eight men of diverse racial and ethnic backgrounds as they recount how they have been affected by race. Using the principle described above, the discussion group includes two men each from four ethnicities (African American, Asian, Latino, and Caucasian). Mun Wah, the group facilitator, allowed each man to describe his hurt, pain, and anger as it related to his experiences and required others in the group to respect and validate one another's descriptions. At dramatic points of conflict, Mun Wah gently encouraged each person to speak honestly with each other about their differences and the "baggage" that each brought to the group. By talking though their differences of experience, rather than ignoring or glossing over them, the men were able to deepen their understanding of the issues related to race and ethnicity.

Leaders also must acknowledge their own struggles with stereotypes and be realistic with the group about how difficult, but important it is for members to speak openly about diversity issues. Mun Wah, models well this type of leadership and underscores the power of talking openly about race and ethnicity and the fears (often unrecognized) that we all face as we encounter those who are different from us.

LEADERSHIP IN GROUPS

Small-Group Leaders and Co-leaders

Social workers are often in the role of leaders and co-leaders of task groups or treatment groups. Group therapists Corey and Corey (2006) outline several characteristics of effective group leaders that apply to group leaders. As you read the

Personal Characteristics	Professional Characteristics
Courage	Active listening
Willingness to model	Reflecting
Emotional presence	Clarifying
Goodwill and caring	Summarizing
Belief in group process	Facilitating
Openness	Empathizing
Nondefensiveness in coping with attacks (or coping with criticism)	Interpreting
Personal power (confidence in self and charisma)	Questioning
Stamina	Linking (relating concerns of one to the whole group)
Willingness to seek new experiences	Confronting
Self-awareness	Supporting
Sense of humor	Blocking (prohibiting certain activities from the group)
Inventiveness	Assessing
	Modeling
	Suggesting
	Initiating
	Evaluating
	Terminating

Adapted from Corey and Corey (2006, pp. 28–40).

list above, think about which of these characteristics are among your strengths and assets. Which of these characteristics do you need to cultivate as you move toward professional practice?

In your practice curriculum you will learn skills that will serve you well in group leadership, whether you are leading task groups, treatment groups, or both. Practicing social work skills will facilitate your striving for many of the characteristics listed above. While some trait theories of leadership have emphasized that leaders are born, and not made, we believe that social workers can develop skills in group leadership. We also believe that all group members have the potential for demonstrating leadership qualities in alignment with their own identities and at particular moments in the group's process. For example, a particular group member may have a knack for summarizing the group's progress and urging the group along toward its goals. At that moment, that group member is displaying leadership behaviors. This sharing of leadership roles among the group members is known as distributive leadership (Ephross & Vassil, 2005).

Co-leadership

Corey and Corey (2006) often practice co-leadership in therapeutic groups and note that there are several advantages to working with another leader. On the practical side, if one leader is ill, the session does not have to be canceled. Also, one co-leader can work with group members through highly emotional sessions while another leader scans the group for reactions. In addition, the co-leaders can discuss with each other their own emotional reactions to the group at a later time, and threat of burnout is reduced when the work is shared. For maximum effectiveness, co-leaders must meet regularly before and after each session to prepare, debrief, and evaluate. Co-leaders should trust and respect one another, communicate openly, and refrain from competing with one another or criticizing one another in front of the group (Corey & Corey, 2006). In our experience, many of these same practices are important for task group co-leaders to observe as well.

Mutual-Aid Tradition and Leadership

Steinberg (2004) has reminded social workers of the importance of the mutual-aid tradition in social group work. While the term *mutual aid* was coined by William Schwartz in the 1960s, this practice tradition has been in use since the early days of social work at the turn of the 20th century (Steinberg, 2004). It requires the worker to serve as a catalyst for group members helping one another. With the social worker's leadership, group members come to see one another as having something to give to the group as well as something to gain from it. Social workers lead the group to draw upon the strengths and assets of each member and of the group as a whole (Steinberg, 2004). Social workers in this practice mode focus on creating what Steinberg calls a democratic-humanistic culture, similar to Ephross and Vassil's (2005) democratic microcosm. This is different from an "individual-work-in-a-group" model, in which members take turns relating to a powerful therapist-leader as others look on. In true mutual aid, the individual members are clients and the group as a system is a client; the social worker keeps one eye on each while serving as a catalyst for members to help one another (Steinberg 2004).

In the mutual-aid tradition, the role of the worker is to empower the group to be actively involved in shaping its own processes. As Steinberg (2004) argues, the group will never be able to exercise the strengths and assets of its members if the worker is dominating and making all the decisions. The wise worker does not go to the extreme of giving up legitimate authority, rather he or she learns to share authority as appropriate. This allows group members to experience self-determination and active participation in the helping process. The leader must allow the group to "have a real say," as Steinberg phrases it.

DEVELOPMENT OF GROUPS OVER TIME

When you think about the groups in which you have been a member you can probably trace how the group changed over time. For example, have you noticed how in a newly forming committee or work group people are often

Tuckman (1965)	Garland, Jones, Kolodny (1978)	Schiller (1995) (Women's Group)
Forming	Preaffiliation	Preaffiliation
Storming	Power and control	Establishment of a relational base
Norming	Intimacy	Mutuality and interpersonal empathy
Performing	Differentiation	Challenge and change
(Adjourning)	Separation	Separation

very kind and accommodating, with everyone on their best behavior? Then as the group becomes more familiar with one another, differences of opinion, and even conflict may develop. Ideas about how groups develop make up a very important part of the literature on group behavior. In the early days of group study stage theories described how groups transitioned through linear, predictable stages leading toward the desired outcome of performing their tasks or achieving treatment goals.

As the group processes literature was emerging, Tuckman (1965) proposed a stage model that is still widely used today. He created an outline still taught in classrooms today, due in part to its easy-to-memorize structure of "forming, norming, storming, and performing," with the later addition of the word "adjourning" to address termination issues. Once you have read the article by Tuckman that follows this chapter, think back to the stages you have observed in the groups of which you are a member. Have you encountered group conflicts that propelled the group on to its greatest achievements?

While Tuckman's structure provides one of the most popular stage theories in group work, in our experience with groups, the stages are not so neatly defined as some of the theorists describe. In fact, we find a "messiness" about group work that presents invigorating challenges to group members and leaders alike. Rather than climbing all together from one neat platform to another, as suggested by stage theorists, groups may spiral around several processes and experiences, defying the stages predicted by the literature. The savvy social worker is able to recognize and promote behaviors and processes that will enhance the group's work, at whatever time in the group's life they may occur. We have developed the following chart so that you may compare several of the stage theories. What they have in common is a stair-stepped view of how groups progress, though each theorist uses different terms.

Expanding beyond the Stages

Although it is very valuable for a social worker to identify stages of group development, as we explained above, groups are sometimes messy and unpredictable. So how can a social worker build on this knowledge and apply it to the realities of groups that don't follow the neat patterns laid out by theorists? The key is for workers to observe and recognize behaviors of individuals and of the group in order to make good decisions.

CONFLICT IN GROUPS

We return now to the idea of conflict, or "storming," as this may be one of the most important processes for social workers to understand about a group's development over time. An inexperienced worker may fear that the group is falling apart or that all is going wrong if any conflict arises. On the contrary, conflict is a natural part of any group, and the wise social worker will view it as a welcomed and important part of development while leading the group through its conflict processes. While texts and teachers that deal with social work practice will help you to develop skills for dealing with this aspect of groups, we will highlight some observations about human behavior in the context of group conflict.

What do you experience when a group you are a part of encounters conflict? The conflict could be between two or more members, or it could be between one or more members and the leader. Do some members, in an attempt to avoid the conflict, tend to return to the politeness of the "forming" stage? Or does the group gang up on one member (scapegoating), with one person bearing the negative emotions of the entire group? Monitoring and understanding your own response to conflict is an important part of the social worker's self-understanding.

In this unit, we present a decision case, *Larry Steele's Group*, which illustrates some of the dilemmas social workers may face in group conflict. In this case, the social worker is charged with addressing one member's habit of being argumentative, and generally creating conflict in the group. This psychoeducational group is comprised of male perpetrators of domestic violence, which indicates that the clients are attempting to address their own anger, violence, and inability to handle conflict. As you read the case, imagine what you might do if you were in the social worker's position.

Too often social workers attempt to avoid conflict, but Ephross and Vassil (2005) remind us that conflict within groups is an inevitable part of a group's processes. In fact, the absence of conflict may imply the absence of growth and development in a group (Yalom & Leszcz, 2005). The wise social worker will be prepared for conflict and facilitate the group as it works through it into the next stage or cycle in the group's development. Sweeping conflict under the rug may damage a group's processes, while the healthy working through of conflict situations ultimately will strengthen the group (Wall & Nolan, 1987).

In order to think critically about conflict, let's categorize several different types of conflict in groups.

1. **Value conflict**—Members have opposing interests, values, or commitments.
2. **Induced conflict**—A leader or member may create conflict to help the group consider a variety of views and reach its goals.
3. **Misattributed conflict**—Discord arises due to an "honest mistake" about what actually happened.
4. **Data conflict**—Someone has the incorrect information or insufficient information to make a good decision.

5. **Structural conflict**—These emerge from differences in power, time, or some other boundary.

6. **Illusionary conflict**—These are rooted in misperceptions of or lack of knowledge about another group member.

7. **Displaced conflict**—Discord is not directed at the true source of the conflict, but at another source that is not really responsible.

8. **Expressive conflict**—Members are "blowing off steam" and may explode when they are too passive or ignore their own feelings for an extended period (Bisno,1988; Moore, 1986).

CONNECTING THEORY TO PRACTICE

How might a social worker use these foundational concepts about group behavior in practice? Social workers learn by doing, of course, and you will have opportunities to observe and be a part of groups during your field experience and continue to learn as you practice professionally. We hope you will think critically and analytically about what you are observing as you practice and recall the basic concepts of groups, from a definition of a group, to kinds of groups, group dynamics, and personal and professional characteristics of group members. We have drawn from literature from the traditions of group processes as well as social group work to point out various ways individuals behave within a group as well as how the group as a whole behaves and how these are affected by environments.

Why is this information so important to a social worker? First, everyone is a member of a group, whether through a family, a committee, a job, or classes. Not only are our clients members of group, we as social workers are also connected to groups. We bring with us to practice our own backgrounds and connections to groups of our families, co-workers, and professional organizations. Additionally, social workers are often asked to serve on committees, agency subcommittees, or task groups. You will want to continue to strengthen your own ability to think analytically about group behavior and sharpen the various tools you can use as a member or a leader in each of these types of groups.

It is important to understand the purpose of a group so you will be better able to understand its goals. The desired outcomes for a task group and treatment group are different. In planning group work, special attention should be devoted to the group's purpose. The role of the social worker and the group members varies depending on the purpose of a group. For example, a social worker may have the role of information giver in an educational group and the role of orienter in leading a support group. Understanding the different roles and being able to shape your role according to the context and the task at hand is an important skill for working with groups.

Not only is it important for you to understand the different purposes of a group and the roles group members may have, it is also important to evaluate how your unique strengths influence your ability to work with groups. We have shared with you some of the personal and professional characteristics of leaders, and we hope you have been able to identify which characteristics seem to best describe you as well as some characteristics you can continue to develop. These characteristics, along with our personalities and preferred leadership styles impact the way we work with others.

This chapter also introduced some concepts widely used by social workers about how groups develop over time; you can explore these ideas further as you read Tuckman's classic article on the stages of group development. Having a conceptual framework for thinking about the stages that groups may encounter can help you prepare in advance to overcome possible barriers that arise.

Understanding theoretically how issues of diversity affect groups will help you continue to develop your cultural competence. Since the mutual-aid tradition is such an important part of social work's roots, competent practice must include a consideration of equality among group members. However, with diversity comes differences of opinion and potential conflict. Viewing conflict as a natural and important part of working in groups (think about the "storming stage") can help you be prepared to deal with it competently as it arises.

Competency Connection

Ethics in Social Work with Groups: Standards for Social Work Practice with Groups

Section 6 of the Standards for Social Work Practice with Groups, second edition (2005), created by the Association for the Advancement of Social Work with Groups, Inc. sets ethical standards for group work. The standards urge social workers to pay attention to codes of ethics relevant to their locations of practice (e.g., National Association of Social Workers; Canadian Association of Social Workers) noting that "each [code] needs to be considered in the context of work with groups and may call for some modifications or additions that reflect the unique situations of group work."

Elements of Ethical Practice in Social Group Work

1. Knowledge of and use of best practices that reflect the state of the art and knowledge and research evidence regarding social work with groups.
2. A basic discussion with prospective members of informed consent and an explanation of what group work offers and requires of the members individually and as a group.
3. Maximizing member choice and minimizing coercive processes by members or worker to the extent possible. Emphasizing member self-determination and empowerment of the group.

4. Discussion of the importance, limits, and implications of privacy and confidentiality with the members.
5. Helping the group maintain the purposes for which it was formed, allowing for changes as mutually agreed upon.
6. Each member is given the help s/he requires within the parameters of the group's purpose, including individual meetings when appropriate.
7. Clarifying the decision making process.
8. Clarifying how members may be chosen for or excluded from the group.
9. Maintaining group records and storing them in a secure location. (Quoted from Standards, 2005)

The standards also remind us that social workers must consider technological advances such as e-mail, cellular phones, and other newer technologies and assess their implications for groups. For example, keeping our commitments to confidentiality may take special efforts in the face of emerging technologies.

The Standards are available for downloading from the AASWG Web Site, www.aaswg.org.

Perhaps most important in your own development as a professional is that you continue to grow in your awareness of how your own beliefs, strengths, and personal characteristics help shape professional social work practice. As Lewin's classic Field Theory suggests, each one of us comes to group experience with myriad personal characteristics and backgrounds that shape the interaction. Being self-aware in terms of our strengths, weaknesses, beliefs, and goals is essential to being an effective practitioner.

Reading 2

Resistance and Hostility in Group Members

GISELA KONOPKA

In this essay, social worker Gisela Konopka used a knowledge base of psychology and sociology to explain resistance a group worker may encounter. After she and her husband Paul fought in the German underground movement against the Nazis and survived imprisonment in concentration camps, Konopka immigrated to the United States in 1941. Drawing from her deep passion for democratic ideals and her oppressive life experiences, she formulated a unique vantage point for social group work, which she taught at the University of Minnesota.

We chose this essay because it will give you examples of the practice issues group workers encountered. In addition, it demonstrates Konopka's integration of social group work traditions with the knowledge base of group dynamics and group processes; the "two streams" we introduced earlier in the unit. Notice how she used her own practice wisdom garnered from experience and integrated it with emerging theories of her day from psychology, education, and other disciplines.

Johnny was busily building a fire on the porch of the rickety old wooden building which housed the agency. He thoroughly enjoyed his work and called to two other boys to help him which they did with great satisfaction. I went to them and said that it was fun having a fire going, but it could not be done on the porch. How about moving over to the adjoining playground? No, this was much more fun. I explained patiently that they might burn down the building-their building where lots of things were going on and which they enjoyed using. No response. I said firmly that the fire had to be extinguished and I proceeded to do it. Johnny and one other boy jumped at me furiously screaming that they would not care if the whole "damn building" with all those "damn people" would burn down, that they did not like it anyhow and they would never, never return again! With that they left swinging their arms and continuing to tell me that I never let them have any fun, that they did not like me.

From Konopka, G., "Resistance and Hostility in Group Members," in H. Trecker, Ed., Group Work Foundations and Frontiers. Copyright © 1955 Whiteside, Inc., New York. Reprinted by permission.

These were the two boys with whom several of us had worked intensely in the agency, the only place where they received any love and acceptance. Johnny was the same boy who at a recent club meeting had said softly to me, "Wish you were my mother. Wish I never had to go home."

A few years ago Hazel Osborn directed our attention to the fact that resistance is a phenomenon which is not known to case work agencies only.[1] She helped to dispel the notion that people come to us full of happiness and positive feelings alone and showed the ambivalent nature of the emotions of our members as evidenced by broken windows and furniture, swearing, and, more subtly, by absence from meetings, sulking and even by sweet compliance to rules while withdrawing from any creative involvement in program.

This behavior must be understood with relation to the purpose of our work with people. This purpose exists in common for the settlement, the "Y," the Jewish Center and all the types of agencies through which group work is practiced. That purpose is to help people with their interpersonal relationships so that they can lead more happy, satisfying lives while being part of a mutually dependent society. We want to help people to grow so that they feel their own worth, and the worth of others.

This kind of pride does not grow by itself and it is much more threatened in the growing up process than encouraged. Most of us do not have this calm happy pride. Most of us carry many scars that have come from blows to this pride and the way we deal with those blows has determined whether our hostility or our acceptance of people becomes stronger. Every child feels alone and frightened, because he is dependent. If this feeling is not reassured, or is little reassured, fear, loneliness, resentment and guilt grow to a continuous circle ending as hostility directed toward self and others. Ann Porter's words in her book "The Day Before" have great significance:

"Hate needs no instruction, but waits only to be provoked. Love must
be learned and learned again, there is no end to it."

It is the special task of our profession to support this learning process. It has often been said that the case worker does this when the situation shows a ready breakdown, while the group worker deals with the normal person to prevent such breakdown. That is only partially true. The group worker has the continuous task of helping the individual to gain this capacity to respect himself and others and deals with many aspects of this problem where difficulties have already arisen, because this is part of our "normal" life.

When we want to understand anti-agency behavior with which we deal we use very often the terms "resistance" and "hostility." It is important to know how these concepts differ from each other. Resistance is part of the general psychological makeup of every human being. Our whole growing-up process is a constant adaption to change during which we always want this change and we

---

1. Hazel Osborn, "Some Factors of Resistance which Affect Group Participation," *The Group,* Jan., 1949, Vol. 11, No. 2.

resist it. The child really enjoys being weaned, but he resists giving up the comfort of the mother's breast. The adolescent wants to grow up, but he fears the responsibility of independence. We want to learn about new ideas, want to know new people and places, but we are afraid of them, we resist. Resistance is part of the basic ambivalence of our emotional make-up.

Hostility has a different root. It springs from the cycle described earlier. All of us want to be loved, to be somebody special. All of us have to give up being the *only* in the affection of parents and of others when we have to share. This desire makes for resentment, for following guilt feelings, and, if not resolved creatively and positively through *some* expression, *some* suppression and a great deal of sublimation, will turn into hostility.

In discussing the manifestations and causes of anti-agency behavior, it is necessary to separate the thinking about children and about adults, since the reasons they come to our agencies are *fundamentally* different. Eric Ericson has described that clearly, when he wrote:

> "What is infantile play, then? We say that it is not the equivalent of adult play, that it is not recreation. The playing adult steps sideward into another reality; the playing child advances forward to new stages of mastery."[2]

If we see the playing of the child as "advancing forward to new stages of mastery" and add our general knowledge that every learning experience involves enjoyment as well as resistance, then we begin to expect that necessarily in every "normal" youngster we will see signs of resistance, even in a setting that offers "play." The pre-school and early school-age child who comes to our agency is offered a great deal of gratification for his needs. He requires a place where he can move freely, where he can run and push and shout, where he can make simple things and gain the first feeling of real achievement, and where he can make friends, and drop them and pick them up again (the age of ever-changing friendships). He needs to find adults who are not his parents, but who are like good fathers and mothers, who are around for comfort when he gets hurt and for fun when he wants to jump on their backs or laugh with them or for teaching when he needs help in making something. Those are deep and important gratifications of the young child's needs and he enjoys them and shows it at this age by cuddling and kissing and wrestling and being happy. But there are other aspects of the same picture: If Jim wants to climb on the worker's lap or tussle happily with him, Joe and Dick want to do it too, nor will they leave, even if Jim pushes them. When the worker laughs and says they all three can tussle with him or says he can't take it, they had better come one after another, he just does not seem to love Jim enough, and Jim becomes angry at all the boys and the worker. Jim is struggling to meet one of the most difficult demands of LIFE, to share a person. It is hard enough to share toys and food, but sharing *people* is most painful. It started back home, when the new babies arrived, and

---

2. E. Ericson, *Childhood and Society,* 1950, p. 195.

it continues at a place where he just wanted to have fun. So Jim hits or kicks back or-starts the fire on the porch, and he thinks he "hates" them all.

Susan feels the same way, only she shows it differently by making almost every game impossible, by saying she does not like it and dissolving into tears as she complains that nobody does what she wants. She stands in the corner, finger in her mouth, not being moved. Susan is not only shy—as one would think looking at her superficially—but Susan is very, very angry and feels left out in the cold.

The constantly repeated demand that we share frustrates a basic need to be the unique and only one, and that frustration bears hostility.

Need the worker throw up his hands and accept as inevitable that we will have unhappy frustrated souls always? No, the point is only that we will always have frustration in life, that it was a stupid, superficial and harmful misunderstanding that led us to think that we must remove all frustration from a person's life. The basic principles in dealing with frustration are:

1. To avoid adding unnecessary frustration to that which is essential in the life situation; and

2. To try to keep the degree of frustration somewhat in relation to the capacity of the individual to cope with it.

When we, for example, make too many rules that can be broken, or ask eight- to ten-year-old youngsters to be quiet for too long a time, or expect teen-agers actually to sleep when they have a slumber party, we simply are asking too much. We have over-taxed the capacity to strengthen the ego through helping it to understand the necessity of the frustration. It does not make sense to tell Joe and Susan that as nice children they must learn to share, if that is all we do, because that is just what they don't want to do. It helps Joe and Susan to let them feel that they are loved, and to understand that sharing is hard, but is done anyway, and at points to let them also see where it is to *their* advantage. With such help, children begin to learn the basic art of human relationships, which has empathy as its fundamental factor. The small child can learn this, but better so when he is helped to learn this in a pleasurable moment, than when he is deprived. It helps more to say to a child who has eaten cake and ice cream and is very happy and full of good food, "You know that is the way the little boy in India would like to feel too, and therefore we are sending food," instead of telling him *before* he eats that he should feel guilty about having so much and must share his money with the deprived child.

The same feelings of hostility in relation to sharing are found in older children who have to interrupt their play in the gym, because the next group must come in, or the need to clean the room, because it will be used by another group, etc.

There are two other aspects of group work, which involve ambivalent feelings of satisfaction as well as resistance. They are the demands we make of group members to *participate* and to make *decisions*, both inherent in the democratic philosophy of life basic to group work. We believe that this type of participation is gratifying to human needs and therefore leads to the feeling of happiness in the individual. We have said, and rightly, that people prefer to participate in decision making, that only when they do will they really carry them out. Yet, we know that people also are afraid of such involvement. Schiller called it the "laziness of the heart" and he meant the resistance to make an effort that is in all of us. Dostoyevski, in his *Grand Inquisitor*, showed with the deepest of insight what "burden of freedom" means. It is therefore out of the strong ambivalence that is basic to human beings facing the demand of free decisions and participation that we find expression of resistance in our agencies.

A group of 12-year-olds, for instance, wants to prepare for a picnic. If the worker suggests an outing in the nearby park, he is turned down angrily, not so much because they don't like the place, but because they don't want to be told by an adult. So he settles back and suggests that they consider alternatives. The discussion gets hotter and hotter until at one point several boys begin to shout angrily. "This darn place never lets you do what you want to and the guy who is supposed to help us sits around doing nothing." The burden of decision was too heavy, and out of the anxiety regarding their ability to make the right choice grew anger and resentment.

How will the group worker help? No recipe can be given. He understands the youngsters' need for guidance not too strongly offered. He knows that their anger is not really directed at him or the agency but at themselves for feeling so fearful and insecure. He does not want to let them go with this unhappy feeling of being incompetent, so he may agree with them, that it is tough to find the best place, but what is it that they would like to *do*? This helps them toward a solution, lets them save face, and, hopefully, brings them one small step toward seeing decision making as something pleasant, not only a burden.

There are many other areas in which we encounter anti-agency behavior which relate directly to our specific program or situation in the community. Our agencies uphold a philosophy of the worth of all human beings and demand a basic respect for everybody. If this ideal is translated into reality in a community setting where tensions among minority groups are strong, we must count on hostility against the agency which does not conform to the mores of certain subgroups in the neighborhood. This resistance can take many different forms:

1. Membership stays away, boycotts the agency and spreads rumors about it.
2. The dissenting group comes to the agency, but insists on complete separation from any other group in the agency.
3. The dissenting group expresses their hostility through vandalism.

It is clear that we cannot discontinue our basic philosophy in the face of such resistance, yet we have to understand those who feel hostile toward our agency policy of accepting all people. Where does this hostility spring from? We go back again to the original ambivalence in the human being wanting to know something new and different, but also resisting it. If there is no protection in meeting the new adventure (if mother's hand is not there when we try the first step), the effort will be much greater. Many of the children who come to our agencies for the first time encounter other human beings strange or different in the way they look or in the way they act. It may be that some part of the usually comforting environment—their own family—shows the same fear and resistance to the new encounter. Are we surprised that they meet this new experience with fear and resistance or with outright hostility? Their fear is intensified by two other psychological factors:

1. The need to identify closely with the primary group, the family; and

2. The need to identify with the closest and most powerful individual who is in the child's life usually father or mother.

If both the general family pattern and the father or mother are against our policy, the child is thrown into a terrifying conflict that must engender guilt and hostility. This is not basically neurotic behavior, but the kind of reaction normal to everybody in a generally unhealthy community climate. Here is further evidence of how our better understanding of mental hygiene will lead us more strongly to the need for social action as well as intensive work with the individual. It is here that we in the informal agencies learn something that child guidance clinics have practiced a long time; that is, we cannot work successfully with children without also working with parents. Our work with the feelings of hostility must be related to parents and children at the same time.

In the life cycle of the comparatively normal individual ambivalence becomes stronger, more pronounced, more difficult to handle in adolescence.

The struggle around the acceptance of sharing, of participating, of making decisions relates to coming to terms with other people. Yet the hardest struggle we face all through life is *coming to terms with ourselves*, to find out who we really are as different from anyone else, as an unique person and yet as part of the whole human race. The adolescent's struggle is around this problem and is not only a struggle for independence. It is the difficult struggle to establish himself as a person. This is development and it is work.

In adolescence, this struggle can carry the aspect of sickness, if it is not realized that this is an age of exaggeration and what is "abnormal" in another age period is "normal" in the adolescent. This finding of oneself becomes conscious in adolescence. Because of the fact that the self never measures up completely to the often very strong ideals of adolescence there is a great deal of self-hate. Because of the great discomfort of such feelings, we find much projection on others. The teen-agers' contemporaries are so close and so obviously in the same boat that too much guilt would be engendered were this projection directed toward other adolescents. Therefore the adolescent will project his negative feelings toward himself on the adult as well as projecting his feelings of wish-fulfillment of the ideal, on him too. This is the reason why we find the strange and confusing mixture of hero worship and crushes combined with violent dislike, resistance and hostility.

Often the individual worker will be the symbol for what is beloved while the agency as a whole will stand for all the shortcomings and restrictions. We find most "anti-agency" behavior in the adolescent. We find every form of it, described earlier in its most intensive expression.

One of our agencies reported a group of sixteen-year-old boys, who had already once been barred from the agency because of some damage they had caused. They had been rough with some of the teen-age girls, and they had distributed a newspaper containing offensive references to the girls. In this instance, adolescent boys used their newspaper in expressing their hostility towards the agency. In so doing, they were also exploring their own status as young males. They were expressing a real wish to understand better their own sex drives and to learn how to behave with girls, but they could not do it in an acceptable way. It was clear that if this underlying wish could be seen, good programming to help them grasp this understanding was much more called for than restrictive measures.

On the other hand, it is also at this age that we find the most constructive cooperative behavior, long hours of work for the agency, great idealistic acceptance of agency ideals (often combined with a complete rejection of parent-culture). At this age the adolescent begins to handle differences of values and can stand up more easily against conflicting values coming from his primary group environment. But he can handle them mostly in terms of complete acceptance or complete rejection. In our youth serving agencies the adolescent will often identify with the highest humanitarian ideals and be very scornful of those, especially adults, who do not live completely up to them. Their great need is for a much more accepting understanding of this period of growth. Given a great deal of trusted and early security and the stamina that helps withstand frustration, the adolescent, supported by understanding parents and workers, will come quite well through this period. Lacking all this, the self-doubt and hate will either turn violently against himself and we have the adolescent suicide or mental breakdown or strong withdrawal from or hate of their adult environment and we have the really delinquent child with many varying symptoms, destroying property, stealing or flight into genuine sex delinquency. It seems to me that when adolescent behavior in its depth is understood, it becomes impossible for the group work agency to be satisfied with the provision of superficial activities to pass the time. In imaginative ways, it must provide outlets for hostile and accepting impulses. At this time it can be a stronghold of mental hygiene in our society.

In young adulthood we will find many similar manifestations carried over from earlier ages since we never completely lose our struggle to achieve maturity. In addition, there are new pressures which often make for hostility. The choice of a vocation or profession is much related to the finding of oneself and every remnant of feeling of being pushed around or feeling too dependent or having no clear conception of oneself or over- or under-estimating one's capacities leads to new frustrations. This frustration, not tempered by understanding and acceptance, breeds resentment.

It needs to be pointed out, however, that anti-agency behavior of adults often has a reality basis in the way we deal with them. Group work agencies have so long worked with children and adolescents that they often deal poorly with adults and provoke hostility. It is not easy for one who has left childhood a comparatively short time ago to continue in a place where everybody knew him when he was that "cute" or "crazy" kid and where there are too many of that same kind of kids underfoot. I think we have seriously to consider whether there should not be separate, though not segregated, centers for adults. At a later age individual adults might again want to have a place in the same center where children are.

There is all too little work done with young adults and where service is given we too often carryover the form of our work with younger groups. In most younger groups the presence of a group worker, though received with ambivalence, is quite essential. This must and should be different in an adult group, with the exception of the group whose focus is on treatment. While the adult group will want a consultant at times to help with resources, a teacher to help with specific content or a personal counselor who will relate to specific individuals in the group, the mature adult group should not have a worker continually with them. This prolongs the idea of their immaturity and I think the resistance that adult groups show by not coming to our agencies or constant bickering over policy matters might have something to do with our way of infantilizing them.

Our efforts to achieve understanding of the behavior of our group members would not be complete if we did not examine our own reaction as individuals to the situations we have discussed. We are the same kind of people with the same kind of needs, and often react exactly the same way. When members frustrate our efforts to help them and give them a satisfying experience, we, too, feel guilty, because we did not achieve. This makes us angry and we find many ways of expressing our anger. We rationalize punishing behavior by saying one has to be "firm," because we know we should not be punishing. We run away from it by being completely "permissive," avoiding conflict and again rationalizing beautifully by saying that they must have an "outlet." We withdraw by finding reasons why the group should not meet, or by having violent headaches and being unable to come to the meeting and by finding it is the "best for the group" to dissolve entirely. Our anti-agency behavior is really not so different, though it usually takes somewhat different forms. We are human, yet if we let ourselves go this way, we are not fulfilling the purpose we accepted at the beginning of this article.

So—what can we do? The solution—never fully realized—lies in what we mean when we talk about professional knowledge and skill and a professional attitude. It has *nothing* whatsoever to do with coldness. On the contrary, it means, as Bertha Reynolds said: "The sensitivity of the layman raised to the nth degree." This sensitivity is raised by a great deal of knowledge of what makes people tick. The more we know about them, the easier we understand and the less frustrated we feel about their actions. This is the help which comes from professional *knowledge*. The *skill* comes by meeting those problems over and over again and meeting them for quite a while with some protection.

That is the secret of professional supervision. This protection gives us support and refuge while it puts demands squarely before us, helping us to apply theoretical knowledge and testing its validity over and over again.

The professional attitude means a conscious use of self. We begin to understand our own self, we learn about our own "frustration threshold" and by learning about it, we begin raising it, more and more. We not only can "take" more and more, but we begin to appreciate the human suffering and the human capacity behind the behavior with which we work.

"Here we must qualify, at least in its simplified interpretation the statement . . . namely, that frustration leads to aggression. Man, in the service of faith, can stand meaningful frustration."[3]

We can add to this deep concern for others, that can help us stand frustration in the same way that we hope to help the people with whom we work, that they may not have always to fight the world and themselves. We have to achieve in ourselves a sense of creativity, freedom, and enjoyment of the other fellow with all of his obnoxiousness and all of his lovability. Ours is a profession based on science, but carrying it out is art. We can do it only if we are carried by a deep enjoyment of people.

"Red Wine first, Jessie, to the passion and the power and the pain of life; and then a drink of White Wine to the melody that is in them."

Sean O'Casey
The Silver Tassie

---

3. *Op. cit.*, p. 373.

Reading 3

The Caregivers

In this poem, caregivers of persons living with Alzheimer's disease come together for mutual support. Located in a rural community, the group used a church building for its meetings. The sacred setting prompted reflection on the spiritual and emotional needs of these caregivers, both givers and receivers in the mutual-aid tradition.

The Caregivers
Reprinted by permission of Jane Childress.

The Alzheimers Support Group sits in a circle,
their lives gathered like fabric on the rod of this disease,
their chairs gathered around the communion table
now covered in burlap as if set just for them,
the Lenten people. On the last redbud
before this late Easter, tiny purple petals
defy the black branch. A fat candle
shaped like a tear squats there, and will not fall.
And always there is that overturned goblet on the table.
Oh, can't we set that cup upright?
Haven't we poured out enough?
Haven't we had enough of burlap?

Outside a storm gathers,
the wind rises, and they talk on.
When the lights go out in this church with no windows,
it is as if no one notices. What is the lights going out
to them? What is thunder, lightning, or wind?
What is sitting in darkness? They talk on,
shaggy beasts on a tundra who know their tough hides
and thick coats alone will not save them,
their warm breath in the midst of their circle
defying the cold, defying the darkness so black
they can't even see the person sitting beside them.
They talk on, faithful as the elephant
standing implacable beside her dead calf
who would stand there forever
until she turned to stone, or bone
if not for the others who nudge her away.

They talk on in the darkness
working out their salvation.
They are beyond fear and trembling.

Childress, J. (2000). The caregivers. Nacogdoches, Texas.

Reading 4

Taking Theory to Practice

The following decision case has been included in this unit to give you practice applying the concepts presented. The case is based on an actual practice situation; the information was gathered by interviewing a social worker at the MSW level. When exploring the case, try formulating the problems, analyzing the information you have, and deciding on potential courses of action. This exploration can be done on your own or in study groups, discussing parts or the entirety of the case, according to how your instructor may guide you. The point is to help you learn to apply theory to practice and to develop important problem-solving and critical-thinking skills. Although this case is located within the unit on groups, it may intersect with other areas of practice as well, such as organizations, communities, social movements, individuals, or families.

LARRY STEELE'S GROUP

MELISSA C. REITMEIER & TERRY A. WOLFER

As a contract therapist at the Domestic Abuse Institute for two years, Jacquelyn Ferrante had grown comfortable facilitating psychoeducational groups for men who had perpetrated domestic abuse. On a Tuesday evening in August 2001, preparing for another session, Jacquelyn quickly found her usual parking space at the church and was looking forward to getting to group early as usual to unwind and set up. She had just gotten out of her car and was gathering her things when a large black man she'd never met approached her rapidly. He was somewhat overdressed and wearing a large, shiny gold cross on a gold chain around his neck. It swayed as he made his way to Jacquelyn's car. Immediately,

Jacquelyn wondered, *Who is this running toward me?* Jacquelyn felt her pulse quicken.

THE DOMESTIC ABUSE INSTITUTE

The Domestic Abuse Institute (DAI) was a private, not-for-profit corporation, founded in Richmond, Virginia, in 1982. Its purpose was to provide counseling for perpetrators of domestic abuse and violence seeking attitudinal and behavioral change. DAI started small, serving only two counties, but gradually received funds to expand its services to more areas throughout the state. It accepted court referrals of individuals who could either fulfill a mandated commitment to the program or serve prison time for their crimes related to domestic abuse.

All therapists held master's degrees and were trained in group therapy methods and domestic violence issues. DAI used a manual-based, cognitive behavioral approach to group treatment: group members were provided workbooks that outlined the concepts and skills taught in each session. Some contract therapists followed the workbook to the letter, but Jacquelyn did not. To her mind, certain parts of the workbook simply did not apply to some members of the group. Furthermore, some group participants lacked the literacy skills necessary for using the workbook. Contact between DAI and the contract therapists occurred on an "as needed" basis. There was no formal team consultation process in place, yet Jacquelyn had always felt comfortable contacting her supervisor with questions or concerns.

Group counseling sessions were conducted on various nights and in various locations in counties throughout central Virginia. At intake, all participants attended two sessions in which staff provided psychological testing and information on group dynamics and expectations. Then group counseling was offered on a weekly basis in a small group setting, twelve 90-minute psychoeducational sessions for concepts and skills acquisition and then another twelve 90-minute process-oriented sessions for applying skills learned the previous twelve weeks. The psychoeducational approach differed from traditional therapy in that it emphasized teaching specific skills and focused on applying these skills in the here and now. Little time was spent on exploring the reasons for past behaviors.

Group members were required to finish 24 weeks of therapy to complete the mandated program. When clients completed the program, DAI provided a written report concerning their participation to the referring judge or agency for review and final determination. Members who did not complete the program successfully went back to court to have the judge decide how their cases should be handled.

Groups were flexibly structured. The groups were open-ended; new members could join at any time and continue until they completed the two 12-week modules. Reading levels, ethnicity, age, and socioeconomic status varied within groups. New intakes could pick which group to attend based on group time and location. There was a wide range of choices, with groups meeting every weeknight except Friday and several times on Saturday morning.

Group members' violations ranged from yelling at spouses or others in the home to serious physical assaults. Often, the general public referred to members of these groups as "batterers." However, Jacquelyn avoided this description. She preferred that people refer to these individuals as perpetrators of domestic violence.

JACQUELYN FERRANTE

Prior to earning an M.S.W. degree at Virginia Commonwealth University, Jacquelyn Ferrante, a 56-year-old Southern, Caucasian woman, had had a very successful 16-year career as an editor and writer. For several years before that she'd been a stay-at-home mom. Because she wanted a deeper understanding of the social implications of some of her work, she decided to pursue her master's degree in social work. Jacquelyn had grown up with a lot of men around, so it was not surprising that she would take an interest in serious social issues affecting men. After considering volunteering for a women's abuse group and having that fall through, Jacquelyn thought, *Hey, it would be interesting to see what the other side of the equation is.* She soon began volunteering at DAI, as a student in training, to get some experience in working with men who perpetrated domestic abuse. Jacquelyn knew right away she had found her niche and was excited about working with this population. As soon as she got her social work state license several months after graduation, she asked to run psychoeducational groups for DAI. Doug Brady, DAI's executive director, remembered Jacquelyn and was pleased to employ her as a contract therapist. Jacquelyn ran one group per week for DAI. Although Jacquelyn wanted to continue her work with men, she also worked a fulltime job at a research and training center.

Although Jacquelyn was only five feet tall and weighed 95 pounds, she had a powerful presence. She had always encouraged and demanded respect for group members and the group process. Her clients often told her that when they first saw her, they thought, "Here's another woman to screw me over." Jacquelyn handled such comments with aplomb, typically responding, "It makes sense why you might feel that way." She often encouraged members to explore their feelings behind the thoughts, "What emotions are you experiencing, right now? Let's discuss it." As a result, the men in her group had little problem conveying what they really thought.

Jacquelyn's group counseling sessions

Jacquelyn held her group at St. Peter's, an old Catholic church, in a small town about 30 miles from Richmond. Two other counseling groups met there at the same time: another men's group and a group for women perpetrators of domestic abuse. Maroon carpeting and dimly lit sconces filled the church corridors, and homemade signs guided group members to the group rooms. Because St. Peter's hosted several community activities simultaneously, Jacquelyn's group met in the church's nursery. To create a space conducive for group process, she simply arranged adult-size folding chairs in a circle where members could gather, learn skills, and share stories.

Jacquelyn's group typically included up to twelve men, aged 18-50, nearly all Caucasian. Jacquelyn never knew who or how many might be coming to group. Sometimes men from other groups would visit her group to make up for a class they couldn't attend for some reason or would stay in her group beyond the initial twelve weeks of psychoeducational skills if the nearest therapy groups were too full for them to join for the remaining twelve weeks.

Jacquelyn was never quite sure of an individual's medical or mental health history because DAI rarely sent her the completed intake evaluations before clients began the mandated course of treatment. Furthermore, the contract therapists were not involved in the two days of intake and orientation and had little knowledge about their clients' mental or medical health unless information was offered or disclosed during group sessions by the clients themselves. Initially Jacquelyn had made more of an effort to get the intake evaluations ahead of time, but she had finally concluded that they weren't all that significant. They rarely, if ever, resulted in anyone's exclusion from group. For example, once she'd gotten an evaluation with "Red Alert" written at the top, several weeks after a group member had been a part of group. When she inquired what this meant, Doug Brady had said, "This guy has a high propensity for anger and violence." Sure enough, the client was very angry; but he had been doing quite well in Jacquelyn's group.

Although Doug advised the therapists that he was available if they had concerns or questions, he typically took a "hands off" approach to supervision. Jacquelyn never knew how to read his behaviors when she sought supervision.

A New Member

Jacquelyn had been running a group for two years when an unfamiliar African American man approached her in the parking lot before a group session. As he approached, Jacquelyn wondered, *is this guy attending my group? He doesn't look like the other group members: besides, they never approach me. But if not, then who is he? My, he's so shiny.*

Taken aback by his approach, Jacquelyn asked, "Are you in my group?"

"Why, yes, I am, if you're Mrs. Fairing. My name is Larry, Larry Steele." Forging ahead, Larry volunteered bits of his personal history in a sequence that seemed disconnected to Jacquelyn. A bit overwhelmed by all this information, she made her way to the front of the church to go in and set up for group. As she walked, she turned to Larry and said, "You can come through the church with me, but after tonight you need to go through the back door."

Once they got inside the large outer doors, she led him through a hallway to open the back door to the nursery, where the group members usually entered. Larry followed, chattering the whole way. When Jacquelyn proceeded to set up the chairs and arrange the room, Larry volunteered to help. Because he was present and talking nonstop, she missed the usual opportunity to unwind and focus on the upcoming group session.

At the beginning of group, Jacquelyn started with a "check-in." Every member got an opportunity to say how their week had gone, and new members introduced themselves and shared their stories. During check-in, Larry repeated to the group essentially what he had said to Jacquelyn earlier.

"I'm well known in my community. Believe me, people would recognize me if I went to a group there. So I came out here instead. I've had a lot of things happen to me in my life—lost both my parents early, and my grandmother took all us children in. I've lost some of my siblings and a lot of friends, been in and out of mental institutions—I was diagnosed schizophrenic when I was 18. Some bad things have happened to me, and what happened with my wife was another one. But I'll get through this. . . . "

As he rambled on, Jacquelyn thought, *He's sharing too much, talking too much. And he wants to look great to the other group members. I wonder if he's going to be able to open himself up to this experience enough to get anything from it. Worse, will he keep others from doing their personal work? But poor guy. . . . He hasn't had a lot of chances in his life.*

At check-in the next week, Larry began, "Say, did you know that women are the cause of all the evils and problems in the world?" He was smiling, and his eyes moved to take in the whole circle as he spoke. "It goes back to the Garden of Eden, when Eve tempted Adam with the apple. And ever since then. . . . "

The others looked at Jacquelyn to see how she'd respond. Trying to keep the annoyance from showing on her face, Jacquelyn was thinking, *How do I deal with this? From the point of view of respect for women? He's not going to go for the story-as-metaphor approach, for sure. That gold cross he was wearing last week is something more than jewelry to this flaming fundamentalist.* Some of the men were snickering by this point, but a few were sitting straighter in their chairs, facial muscles tightened and lips in a straight line. For a moment, Jacquelyn wondered, *Does this kind of behavior justify his removal?* Then she told herself, *It's probably not severe enough. I'll just ignore it for now. Maybe he will "get it" after another week.*

By the third week, Jacquelyn began to wonder seriously what she should do about Larry. Out of the blue, Larry said, "If my son ever told me he was a homosexual, I would beat the hell out of him." He followed this up with some quotes from the Bible.

Jacquelyn responded by saying, "There will be respect in this room and respect for others' way of life." She kept thinking to herself, *He's had such a hard life; I don't want to add to his pain by recommending that he be taken out of the group. I hope he'll get it. Everything will be okay, if I just wait. Besides, by the fourth week most people have settled down enough to relax and give others a chance to talk.*

Thoughts of Larry's behaviors and her responses kept replaying in Jacquelyn's head as she drove home that evening. Jacquelyn tried to sort out why this man provoked such a strong reaction in her. She thought, *I hate this guy.* And her immediate next thought was, *What does this say about me as a therapist? How can I help this man?* She was shocked at how unprofessional she felt. Jacquelyn told herself, *Perhaps I should talk to Larry before the next meeting and ask him how we can address his behaviors.*

Before group session on the fifth week, two planes crashed into the twin towers in New York City. Thousands of people were thought dead and the nation was in shock. Due to the circumstances, Jacquelyn decided she would use group time to allow members the opportunity to talk about what had happened that day and how the group members were feeling about it. At the same time, she realized there might be some who didn't feel like talking or would rather be with their families or friends elsewhere. People responded differently to tragedy, so she offered, "If any of you want to be somewhere else for any reason, you can leave and still be counted present for the week."

When Larry wanted to lead the group in prayer, Jacquelyn responded, "This is not a religious group."

Larry glowered at her. "We're meeting in a church!" he countered, "And besides, it's the *right* thing to do."

After asking the other group members whether they had any objections, Jacquelyn gave Larry permission to lead the group in prayer.

Speaking firmly, Larry instructed the others to stand, clasp hands in the circle, and close their eyes. He offered a prayer and, without inviting others to pray, said, "Amen."

After asking Jacquelyn if she really meant they could leave, Larry left immediately.

The only other person who left was a young man whose father had been scheduled for a 9:00 a.m. meeting at the World Trade Center. The young man had not heard from his father. He left only after Jacquelyn urged him to go and be with his mother in case they got some news.

The Bruce Cyclone

At Larry's sixth group meeting, a newer member diverted Jacquelyn's attention. A Caucasian man in his 30s, Bruce Stone had come to group two weeks earlier, bringing a lot of resentment with him. To Jacquelyn, his intense blue eyes seemed almost sinister. He often sat rigid in his chair, with arms folded, glaring at the group. At check-in, he usually started by declaring, "This group sucks."

This particular week, the group had a good rhythm going at check-in when Bruce sauntered in fourteen minutes late, one minute short of the grace period to be counted present for the week. When Bruce entered the room, the group members sat up and took notice—even Larry. Jacquelyn thought, *Bruce is trying to be the leader of the pack, to undermine the men's loyalty to group.* Several group members checked their watches and glanced at Jacquelyn for her response. Bruce announced, "I got something I want to share."

Surprised that he would interrupt the process, Jacquelyn replied, "Well, take a seat, Bruce, and you can share when it's your turn."

Bruce picked a chair two seats away from Jacquelyn and pushed it back, out of the circle. He positioned his body so that Jacquelyn could not see his face.

When Bruce's turn came, Jacqueline asked him, "What would you like to share?"

"This group sucks, and I think you're all losers." Bruce burst out, looking directly at Larry.

Calmly, Jacquelyn probed, "Well, why do you feel this way?"

Looking through Jacquelyn with those bright blue eyes, Bruce continued, "Cause you're a loser and this group sucks!" Then looking at Larry, he announced, "You piss me off, you and your sweety-sweet comments to the others and always saying how well you're doing and how you've changed and you've gotten a grip on your anger and. . . . "

As the torrent of words flowed, Larry rose to address Bruce, "Don't tell me I'm a loser! You don't know me. You don't know what it's been like for me. I have tried real hard to get my life together. At least I am willing. I put forth an effort to learn in group. You don't do jack shit!"

Bruce rose to respond, his muscular 6-foot frame towering over Larry, and retorted, "You don't know what I do or what I try." Bruce scanned each group member's face, searching, and then he emphasized, "None of you have got a fucking clue!"

Another man rose to join the verbal fray, and words started flying between the three standing group members.

Jacquelyn watched as the tension grew in the group: faces twisting, bodies tensing and clients squirming in their seats. Respect was the keynote of Jacquelyn's group; she was sure all the men knew this. The third man's hands had become fists. With even more concern she looked back to Bruce and Larry. She thought, *There could be a fight here, and how in the world am I going to stop it? But somehow I have to.*

Jacquelyn rose out of her chair and said firmly, "Stop it! Just stop it. There will not be disrespect in this group, so everybody sit down. We're going to continue with what we were doing before this all started." Pausing momentarily, "Bruce, I want you to keep quiet during the rest of the meeting. Later we'll talk about what this means for you in group. I'll have to think about that and discuss with DAI what's happened and what we need to do about it."

The next day Jacquelyn called Doug and told him of the disruption in group. Doug shared Jacquelyn's concern and decided to remove Bruce from the group.

Decision Time

There was no specific policy at DAI for removing members. It was up to the therapists and the Executive Director to determine what behaviors warranted removal and reappearance before the court. During the two years Jacquelyn had run groups for DAI, she had only recommended removal of three clients, including Bruce. Those instances each seemed more serious than the current situation with Larry. However, Jacquelyn thought that Larry dominated the group and disturbed the other group members. She wondered whether she should recommend that Larry leave the group, too. Jacquelyn thought to herself, *He is open and sincere, and even seems motivated to learn. But he is consistently judgmental of other group members. He waits for me before group sessions, wants control of group itself, and wants to talk to me after group—he knows the answers to everything. He just won't let up.*

A week after the Bruce incident, Larry mentioned that his daughter had asked to go to a certain upcoming concert and said that he'd told her no, that he didn't approve. Danny, a teenager in the group, said, "That concert would be OK—the singer's a decent guy, not into profanity or putting down women or authority figures. Besides," the teen said, "if you just automatically tell your daughter she can't do certain things, no discussion, it will only be a matter of time before she does them behind your back."

Larry lit into the young man. "You don't have kids! What do you know? You've gotten into it with your own father." Then, with contempt, "Don't tell me how to raise my kids!"

Jacquelyn intervened immediately. "Do you remember what we've said about respect? Do you remember what happened just last week? Danny has listened to your opinion on many things, and he has a right to express his opinion and be heard."

That evening on the way home, Jacquelyn wondered, *Should I have recommended removing Larry from group a long time ago? It almost seems unjust to do it at this point, but still, there are other group members to consider. Things don't seem to be getting any better.*

SUMMARY

In this unit, we have described various structural components and reviewed how groups may develop over time. We have presented Tuckman's classic model as a way to think about group development and invited you to explore alternative ways of thinking about recurring cycles in groups. We have suggested various characteristics of groups leaders and invited you to think about your own strengths and challenges in relation to group leadership. Finally, we have elaborated on the "storming" or conflict phase of a group's development and the social worker's role in understanding conflict behaviors. By building a strong foundation of knowledge about group behavior, you may enhance your practice skills as you draw on that knowledge, In turn, your practice will increase your knowledge about behavior as you learn experientially about how people behave in groups.

REFERENCES

Andrews, J. (2001). Group work's place in social work: A historical analysis. *Journal of Sociology and Social Welfare, 28*(4), 45–64.

Association for the Advancement of Social Work with Groups (2005). *Social work practice with groups* (2nd ed.). New York: Author.

Benne, K.D., & Sheats, P. (1948). Functional roles of group members. *Journal of Social Issues, 42*(2).

Bisno, H. (1988). *Managing conflict.* Newbury Park, CA: Sage.

Brook, D.W., Gordon, C., Meadow, H. (1998). Ethnicity, culture, and group psychotherapy. *Group, 22*(2), 53–80.

Brown, A., & Mistry, T. (2005). Group work with mixed membership groups: Issues of race and gender. In: A. Malekoff and R. Curland (Eds.), *A quarter century of classics (1978–2004).* New York: Haworth Press, pp. 133–148.

Childress, J. (2000). *The caregivers.* Unpublished poem. Nacogdoches, Texas.

Cohen, M.B., & Mullender, A. (Eds.). (2003). *Gender and groupwork*. London: Routledge.

Corey, M.S., & Corey, G. (2006). *Groups: Process and practice* (7th ed.). Belmont, CA: Brooks/Cole.

Ephross, P.H. & Vassil, T.V. (1988). *Groups that work: Structure and process*. New York: Columbia University Press.

Ephross, P., & Vassil, T. (2005). *Groups that work: Structure and process*. New York: Columbia University Press.

Fluh, T. (2004). Transcending differences: Using concrete subject mater in heterogeneous groups. *Social Work with Groups*, *27*(2/3), 53–54.

Garland, J.A., Jones, H.E., & Kolodney, R.L. (1978). A model for stages of development in social work groups. In: S. Bernstein (Ed.), *Explorations in group work*. Hebron, CT: Practitioners Press, pp. 17–71.

Gazda, G.M., Ginter, E.J, & Horne, A.M. (2001). *Group counseling and group psychotherapy: Theory and application*. Needham Heights, MA: Allyn & Bacon.

Janis, L., & Mann, L. (1977). *Decision making*. New York: Free Press.

Johnson, D.W., & Johnson, F.P. (2006). *Joining together: Group theory and group skills* (9th ed.). Boston: Allyn & Bacon.

Lewin, K. (1951). *Field theory in social science: Selected theoretical papers*. New York: Harper.

Konopka, G. (1955). Resistance and hostility in group members. In: H. Trecker (Ed.), *Group work foundations and frontiers*. New York: Whiteside, pp. 130–142.

Mun Wah, L. (1995). *The color of fear*. San Francisco: Stir Fry.

Moore, C.W. (1986). *The meditation process: Practical strategies for resolving conflict*. San Francisco: Jossey-Bass.

Queralt, M. (1996). *The social environment and human behavior: A diversity perspective*. Boston: Allyn & Bacon.

Reitmeier, M.C., & Wolfer, T.A. (2005) Larry Steele's group. In: T.A. Wolfer and T.L. Scales (Eds.), *Decision cases for advanced practice: thinking like a social worker*. Monterey, CA: Brooks/Cole, pp. 35–42.

Schiller, L.Y. (1995). Stages of developing women's groups: A relational group model. In: R. Kurland & R. Salmon (Eds.), *Group work practice in a troubled society: Problems and opportunities*. New York: Haworth Press, pp. 17–38.

Shaw, M. (1981). *Group dynamics: the psychology of small group behavior* (3rd ed.). New York: McGraw-Hill.

Steinberg, D.M. (2004). *The mutual aid approach to working with groups* (2nd ed.). New York: Haworth Press.

Tannen, D. (2001). *You just don't understand: Women and men in conversation*. New York: HarperCollins.

Tuckman, B.W. (1965). Developmental sequence in small groups. *Psychological Bulletin*, *63*(6), 384–399.

Wall, V.D., & Nolan, L.L. (1987). Small group conflict: A look at equity, satisfaction, and styles of conflict management. *Small Group Behavior*, *18*(2), 188–211.

Walker, H.A., Ilardi, B., McMahon, A.M., Fennell, M.L.C. (1996). Gender, interaction, and leadership. *Social Psychology Quarterly*. *59*(3) 255–272.

Yalom, I., & Leszcz, M. (2005) *The theory and practice of group psychotherapy* (5th ed.). New York: Perseus.

Human Behavior in Organizations

LEARNING OBJECTIVE

To expose students to the basic concepts needed for a foundational understanding of types, management, leadership, cultures, and diversity of organizations so that they may apply theories and concepts about organizations and connect knowledge about human behavior in organizations to other social work courses.

INTRODUCTION

The purpose of this unit is to assist you in developing an understanding of organizations and their role in the social environment. The unit begins with an overview of key aspects of organizations, including definitions, types of organizations, management, leadership, structure, employee motivation, communication, decision making, organizational culture, and diversity. The chapter concludes with a discussion to help you make the connection between the content and social work practice.

We have also included several additional readings to supplement the material provided. First, to help you understand how social workers and others have viewed organizations historically, we include an article by Frederick Taylor, "The Principles of Scientific Management" (1916). This classic essay laid the groundwork for modern organizational theory and emerged at a time when sociologists and the new social work profession were building their perceptions of organizations. Although social workers have learned a great deal about organizations since that time, these principles continue to influence many organizations where social workers practice. The unit ends with a piece of music celebrating the hope offered by a nonprofit organization on its 10th anniversary. This song provides an alternative medium for portraying human service organizations and the challenges and opportunities they face. A decision case, "Carla Fights the System," will give you practice applying the theories and concepts you are learning about organizations as you try to analyze an actual case a social worker faced within her organization. Throughout the unit, the *Curriculum Connections* commentaries will assist you in understanding how the topic of organizations relates to other pieces of your social work education.

We hope that this unit will provide you with a solid understanding of human behavior as it relates to organizations. A strong theoretical foundation is essential for you to begin building your practice knowledge and skills for working with organizations. While many of you will not practice directly with organizations, this foundation is important to helping your client systems interact with organizations that impact their lives.

Reading 1

Human Behavior in Organizations:
An Overview

As social workers, why is it important for us to understand organizations? For one thing, we can hardly avoid them! As Hall (1996) writes, "We are born in them and usually die in them" (p. 1). He goes on to note, "Organizations have outcomes. They are not benign objects. They can spread hate, but also save lives and maybe souls. They can wage war, but also bring peace" (p. 2). In other words, organizations are a part of our everyday lives. Organizations influence other systems (individuals, families, groups, organizations, and communities) and are influenced by other systems. Thus, we need to understand organizations because of their role in the environment. More importantly, we need to understand them because we will work for them and with them in the course of helping our clients improve their quality of life.

Upon graduation, many of you will start your social work career working for a human services organization that primarily serves individuals and/or families. However, even if your primary focus is on micro systems, you still need a basic understanding of organizations. At the very least, this knowledge will help you understand your role as an employee and how to navigate the opportunities and challenges you will encounter while working for a human services organization.

Imagine the following scenario: You are a case manager in a community-based children's outpatient mental health clinic. Your primary responsibilities include initial assessments, treatment planning, evaluation, coordination of services provided by the clinic (social skills training, therapy, family support, and psychiatric services) and coordination of services provided by other service providers (juvenile probation, child protective services, schools, etc.). One of your clients, John Smith, is a 6th-grade student who has a history of academic and behavioral problems, which have resulted in various disciplinary actions, including contacts with law enforcement and juvenile probation workers. Currently, he is experiencing a significant amount of difficulty functioning in a regular education classroom and is in danger of being expelled. Although John appears to be eligible for special education services, John's parents report that the school district is unwilling to act on their request to formally assess his educational needs. Furthermore, John's parents are unaware of his educational rights and are reluctant to challenge the school district.

How would you handle the above situation? Based on the information provided, the primary concern is John's ability to function at school. Your intervention may involve educating John's parents about his educational rights and the school district's responsibilities. In addition, his parents may need your assistance in addressing their concerns with the school district, which is likely to involve changing the organization's approach to the situation. In order to formulate a strategy for organizational change, you will need a basic understanding of the various aspects of organizations, including management, leadership, structure, communication, decision making, culture, employee motivation, and diversity. This chapter will address each of these issues, as well as the relationship between theory and practice. However, before we move on to these topics, we need to talk about what constitutes an organization.

WHAT IS AN ORGANIZATION?

Throughout history, humans have organized themselves to accomplish their goals. Early organizations were responsible for constructing the Egyptian pyramids and ancient Chinese irrigation systems, as well as for the development of the Catholic Church (Etzioni, 1964). Examples of more recent organizations include governments, military forces, hospitals, schools, banks, and corporations. Take a moment to think about these examples. What are some common characteristics?

The examples mentioned involve two or more people working together to achieve an outcome. The following definition of organization is consistent with this line of thought: "regular and ongoing set of structured activities involving a defined group of individuals" (Austin, 2002, p. 15). Specifically, Austin recognizes that when people work together in the context of an organization, their work activities are "structured" or dictated by rules, guidelines, policies, and/or procedures. Typically these work activities serve to create goods, services, or social change (Austin, 2002). In other words, an organization is two or more people who come together to engage in structured activities for the purpose of achieving a desired outcome. In general, the desired outcome is either the creation of a product, the provision of a service, and/or social change. It is important to note that as a social worker you will interact with a variety of organizations, which will most likely vary, especially in terms of type, purpose, processes, structure, and degree of formality. However, most of them, including human services organizations, will be consistent with the definition provided above.

Regardless of your area of practice, every social worker is sure to work in or with human services organizations. In general terms, the purpose of human services is to improve our quality of life by addressing issues related to welfare and well-being (Hasenfeld, 1992). Over the course of history, human services have been provided by a variety of entities, including families, informal groups, and organizations (Austin, 1988). In terms of organizations, traditionally human services have been provided by organizations in the public and voluntary sectors.

Competency Connection

Organizations in Social Welfare History

The Freedmen's Bureau, Established 1865

The first social services agency to receive federal funding, and to specifically target African Americans was the Freedmen's Bureau. Established in 1865, the bureau helped African Americans make the transition from slavery to freedom by helping with food, clothing, and shelter. The organization also helped with, settling land disputes between freed slaves and white persons and addressing issues with unpaid work wages. The Freedmen's Bureau also established juvenile centers, asylums, and orphanages (Weaver, 1992). The organization's perception that poor, able-bodied men and women were paupers and beggars led them to promote temporary relief and to strongly advocate for self-sufficiency. The Freedmen's Bureau believed that education was the key to empowerment, and it is credited with having created some of the first African-American public schools and universities. In 1869, the Freedmen's Bureau completely withdrew from servicing the asylums and orphanages (Weaver, 1992) and when it closed its doors for good in 1872, control of its' educational programs were relinquished into the hands of the states.

Weaver, H. (1992) African-Americans and social work: An overview of the Ante-Bellum through progressive eras. *Journal of Multicultural Social Work*, 2(4), 91–102.

However, over the past 30 years or so, the privatization of human services has brought a noticeable increase in the number of private sector or for-profit human services organizations. Common examples of modern human services organizations include schools, mental health clinics, child protective services, public health clinics, hospice, hospitals, and community-based corrections.

Before moving on to theoretical approaches to organizations, let us take a moment to discuss the public, voluntary, and private sectors. The public sector consists of organizations that are operated by or for the local, state or federal government. These organizations are typically funded by the public via taxes and/or fees. The voluntary sector is comprised of nongovernmental not-for-profit, or nonprofit, organizations. Although not-for-profit organizations are allowed to earn a profit or surplus, it cannot be distributed among individuals or shareholders. Rather, the surplus must be put back into the agency budget and used to support operations. This is the opposite of private-sector or for-profit organizations, which can earn a profit and redistribute it to shareholders or owners. However, it is important to note that such earnings are taxable.

THEORETICAL APPROACHES TO ORGANIZATIONS

As the importance of organizations to society increased in the 20th century, scholars and administrators attempted to understand organizations more completely. This resulted in the development of various theories and explanations of how organizations operate and how humans behave within them. We have selected several theories to share with you that made a significant contribution to the knowledge base for organizations and human services organizations. Our discussion begins with the early approaches to organizations and moves through, in chronological order, the social and economic factors of the time that influenced the development of these ideas.

Early Approaches to Organizations

Many of the popular organizational theories were not developed in the context of human services or nonprofit organizations. Rather, they were developed with industrial organizations in mind, since the most prominent organizations during the 19th and early 20th centuries were industrial in nature. Early organizational theories tended to focus on internal aspects of the organization, with an underlying goal of increasing efficiency and productivity. These theories and concepts are commonly referred to as "classical theories" and include bureaucracy, scientific management, and universalistic management.

Before we move on, it is important to address the questions that may have come to mind. "If these theories focus on industrial organizations, why do I need to learn about them? As a social worker, shouldn't I be more concerned with theories directly related to human services organizations?" There are several reasons that a historical perspective is important. The first is that it will help you develop an understanding of the evolution of thought about organizations. In other words, when we look at current theories, you will understand how theorists came to their conclusions. In addition, these theories serve to teach us important lessons about organizations, each of which is relevant to human services organizations.

Bureaucracy.   Around the time that the industrial revolution was in full swing, people began to think about the best way to organize or structure an organization. One of the most common models was offered by Max Weber (pronounced vā′-bər), a German sociologist and political economist. In terms of organizations, Weber's focus was on the development of a model organizational structure, which he referred to as "bureaucracy." Weber viewed his model as an ideal type or a tool for comparing, describing, and understanding organizational structures and differences, not something that organizations should try to replicate (Crainer, 1998; Netting, Kettner & McMurtry, 2004; Sofer, 1972).

Weber's bureaucratic model was primarily concerned with organizational efficiency, precision, and reliability (March & Simon, 1993; Merton, 1952; Sofer, 1972). This emphasis helped organizations, especially large ones, increase their production and service delivery capacity (Netting et al., 2004; Sofer, 1972). Additional benefits of Weber's model include a focus on accountability, emphasis on job descriptions, and stressing the importance of hierarchy and of hiring competent staff (Kettner, 2002). While the bureaucratic model has some positive benefits, it is not without its critics.

One of the methods for achieving efficiency, precision, and reliability is uniformity in decision making. Uniformity is maintained via policies and procedures, to which employees are expected to strictly adhere and apply in the same manner to each situation, case, or client. Employees are also expected to maintain an impersonal relationship when interacting with clients. Whereas this approach tends to work well in organizations in which situations remain static or unchanging, such as assembly or manufacturing, it can be troublesome in human services organizations. Specifically, our clients experience similar issues, but individual characteristics make each case unique or personal. Thus, we must have some degree of flexibility in order to personalize or individualize our interventions. It is also important to note that clients who challenge decisions they perceive as impersonal are often met with a defensive response from the organization, citing adherence to policy as a justification for its decisions and actions (March & Simon, 1993). Clients could quite possibly interpret this situation as resulting from discrimination (March & Simon, 1993).

In addition to inefficiency, Merton (1952) identifies two more consequences of bureaucracy, bureaucratic personality and trained incapacity. As employees are oriented or trained to follow policies and procedures and subsequently reinforced for doing so, their focus shifts from assisting the client to complying with organizational expectations (Merton, 1952; Netting et al., 2004). The emphasis on compliance with policies and procedures, rather than helping clients is the bureaucratic personality. Merton (1952) also proposed that as employees are oriented to following policies and procedures without question, they lose their ability to think critically about issues and to assist clients. He refers to this as "trained incapacity." It is important to note that bureaucratic personality and trained incapacity can negatively affect an organization's efficiency and its client relationships (Merton, 1952). These criticisms and others seem to support the common descriptors for bureaucracies, including rule-bound, mired in red tape (needless or excessive procedures), inefficient, thoughtless, conforming blindly, impersonal, cumbersome, and detached. Can you think of specific examples to support each viewpoint? Why does this dichotomy exist?

Scientific Management.   Another interest during the early years of organizational thought was on increasing productivity. Frederick Taylor was one of the first to focus on this aspect of organizations. Taylor was employed at Midvale Steel Company, where he held a variety of managerial positions. There, he began studying ways to increase productivity by "breaking work into detailed, easily supervised tasks, cataloging them, establishing expected rates for finishing jobs, and structuring incentive schemes to boost output" (Licht, 1995, p. 131). Taylor's "time and motion" studies informed the development of his book *The Principles of Scientific Management* (1911). We have included the introduction and first chapter of this work later in this unit so that you can review it firsthand.

Scientific management is based on the belief that the primary responsibility of management is "to secure the maximum prosperity for the employer, coupled with the maximum prosperity for each employee" (Taylor, 1911, p. 9). In other words, the goal of management should be to maximize both profits and wages. The context in which Taylor uses "prosperity" is important to understanding his theory. In terms of the organization, it includes profits and development, with a goal of long-term sustainability (Taylor, 1911). As for employees, it involves increasing wages, as well as the worker's ability to perform his tasks with the highest degree of efficiency and least amount of physical effort (Taylor, 1911).

Under this model, management is responsible for planning and controlling work activities, which includes supervising, rewarding, and punishing employees (Crainer, 1998). These activities are guided by "science" or the "rules, laws, and formulae" that guide the daily activities of workers (Taylor, 1911). It is also important to note that Taylor believed that the smaller the time unit for wages, the more likely workers would be to perform at their physical limits (Etzioni, 1964). From this point of view, salaries would be the least desirable time unit and the most desirable is payment based on the actual work completed, or piecework (Etzioni, 1964).

Taylor's studies and ideas were important to industry, especially those that focused on mass production. For example, it served as a basis for Henry Ford's mass production techniques (Scott, 1998). Despite its importance to industry, resistance from managers and workers stifled its acceptance as an approach to management (Scott, 1998). Some potential reasons for the rejection of scientific management are its lack of regard for the individual characteristics (what is efficient for one may not be for another) and its potential for exploitation of workers because of the focus on output (Netting et al., 2004). Also, its placement of decision-making responsibilities with management overlooked the capacity of workers for innovation and decision making, a phenomenon that continues in modern times and can threaten an organization's ability to survive (Crainer, 1998).

On the other hand, Kettner (2002) notes that Taylor's work has proven beneficial to human services because of its recognition of a need for: (1) specialized knowledge and skills related to management, (2) education and training to prepare individuals for management, including continuing education, (3) the use of technology to increase efficiency in service delivery, and (4) the need for practice-based research to evaluate the effectiveness of interventions. As you think about this approach, what other elements are conducive to social work practice? What elements are not conducive to social work practice?

Universalistic Management.   During the same period when Taylor was developing scientific management, European scholars were also studying management. One such individual was Henri Fayol, a French engineer and manager who created an approach to management commonly referred to as "universalistic management." Fayol's approach was different from Taylor's in that Taylor focused on changing the organization by modifying the procedures used by line staff (Scott, 1998). In contrast, Fayol focused on the role of administration in organizational change (Scott, 1998). Specifically, he sought to identify the components of organizational structure that should be implemented by managers in order to achieve organizational stability, predictability, and productivity (Netting et al., 2004). His work resulted in the identification of 14 management principles, which he discussed in his 1916 publication *General and Industrial Management* (Crainer, 1998).

According to Scott (1998), universalistic management theorists focus specifically on two activities, coordination and specialization. Coordination of organizational activities is based on the following principles (Scott, 1998):

- **Scalar principle**—The organization should have a hierarchical structure with a pyramid-shaped chain of command and communication (responsibility for command lies at the top of the organization and most communication travels vertically rather than horizontally).

- **Unity of command principle**—Each employee should have no more than one immediate supervisor.

- **Span of control principle**—A supervisor should not be assigned more subordinates than he/she can reasonably oversee.

- **Exception principle**—Subordinates are responsible for routine activities or ones that do not require exceptions to policy and procedures. Supervisors are responsible for activities that require exceptions to policy and procedures.

Specialization focuses on how best to organize activities and departments within the organization. The principles associated with specialization include (Scott, 1998):

- **Departmentalization principle**—Similar activities should be grouped by unit or department, which may be based on purpose (goals or outcomes), process (activities or procedures), clientele (services provided to the same client group), and place (services provided in a common geographical area).

- **Line-staff principle**—Line activities are those that are instrumental to accomplishing organizational outcomes. Staff activities consist of service and support. Staff functions are not included in the organizational hierarchy, rather they are attached to the department/unit they support and answer directly to that department/unit.

As demonstrated by the above description, universalistic management theorists attempted to identify the common elements of organizational structure. While they offered a fairly broad and concrete description, they made the mistake of trying to generalize the elements to all organizations, regardless of type, purpose, or situation (Scott, 1998). It is important to note that as with Taylor, Fayol was accused of overlooking the individuality of workers and supporting organizational structures that could lead to exploitation of workers (Netting et al., 2004). What instances can you think of in which the above principles would produce the desired results of stability, predictability, and productivity in a human services organization? What about instances in which they would not produce the desired results in a human services organization?

Human Relations and Similar Approaches to Organizations

Several scholars on the topics of management and organizations took issue with the classical approach's basic premises that economic rewards and reducing physical effort are the keys to productivity. A direct result was the creation of new approaches that focused on participation, communication, and leadership (Etzioni, 1964). These approaches include Human Relations, Theory X and Theory Y, and Management by Objectives.

Human Relations School. Elton Mayo, an Australian psychologist, was also interested in factors that affected production. However, he did not agree with the basic principles of scientific management, especially that the key to increasing productivity was reducing physical effort. His views were supported by several studies conducted at Western Electric's Hawthorne Plant in Chicago, IL (Mayo, 1960).

Prior to Mayo's involvement, administrators at the Hawthorne Plant examined the effect of workplace illumination on productivity (Roethlisberger, Dickson & Wright, 1950). Specifically, they compared the productivity of groups working under higher illumination with that of those working under lesser illumination. They expected to find higher productivity with higher levels of illumination, but instead found that productivity increased for both groups. In fact, productivity did not decrease for the low illumination group until there wasn't enough light to see their work. The investigators concluded that production continued to increase, regardless of illumination, because the workers knew they were being observed. Perhaps you discussed this phenomenon in your introduction to psychology course; it is commonly referred to as the "Hawthorne effect," which is the tendency of people to change their behavior when they know they are being observed.

The illumination study prompted Mayo's research group to conduct additional studies to examine the impact on production of work conditions and social relationships in the workplace. The results of the Hawthorne studies led Mayo to conclude that productivity was impacted by social factors within and outside of the organization. Specifically, he said:

> The industrial inquiry nevertheless makes clear that the problems of human equilibrium and effort are not completely contained within the area controlled by the factory organization and executive policy. Certain of the sources of personal disequilibrium, and especially the low resistance to adverse happenings in the ordinary workroom must be attributed to the developing social disorganization and consequent *anomie* which is in these days typical of living conditions in or near any great industrial center (Mayo, 1960, p. 165).

Mayo went on to say that administrators needed to attend to these problems just as they would internal issues. This represents an important departure from the predominant approach of focusing on internal organizational factors (closed systems perspective). We will discuss open and closed systems approaches later in the chapter.

The Hawthorne studies also informed basic principles of the Human Relations School, such as that production levels are set by social norms, non-economic issues shape worker behavior, workers react as members of groups, and leadership sets group norms (Etzioni, 1964). The Human Relations School also emphasizes the role of the informal organization and the need to consider it in the course of organizational decision making, as well as the importance of balancing workers' needs and organizational goals (Etzioni, 1964). On the other hand, it is important to remember that while Mayo studied social relationships, his primary focus was increasing production, not improving relationships with workers (Netting et al., 2004). Critics have expressed a variety of concerns about human relations. For example, were the Hawthorne experiments methodologically sound? Did they overemphasize the effects of social factors on organizations?

Theory X and Theory Y.   Douglas McGregor, an American social psychologist, was also a key figure in the Human Relations School (Crainer, 1998). Specifically, he was concerned that many of the theories were relevant neither to modern organizations, their managers, nor the issues of modern society (McGregor, 1960). McGregor believed that they were based on false assumptions regarding human behavior. In response, he set out to develop a theory that would assist managers with predicting and controlling human behavior, which he believed was a key element of successful management.

First he proposed Theory X, his representation of a then-current approach to management and human behavior. Theory X is driven by the scalar principle (see "Universalistic Management" above) and is based on the assumptions that most people have an inherent dislike of work, try to avoid work and responsibility, and must be coerced or controlled in order to put forth the effort required for achieving organizational objectives (McGregor, 1960). On the other hand, McGregor believed that human beings are motivated by their needs, especially social and egoistic needs, such as belonging, acceptance, friendship, love, self-esteem, and reputation (McGregor, 1960). From his point of view, the traditional approach to management was inappropriate for individuals who were motivated by these kinds of needs.

Theory Y represents McGregor's attempt to address the issues he identified with Theory X. It is centered on the integration principle, which McGregor defines as the need for an organization to create conditions in which employees are able to meet their needs through the course of meeting organizational needs (McGregor, 1960). Theory Y is based on assumptions such as that physical and mental effort is as natural as play or rest, control and punishment are not the only way to reach organizational objectives, and staff will work independently to reach objectives they value. Also, people learn not only to accept but to seek responsibility, they value a high degree of imagination, ingenuity, and creativity in solving organizational problems and they have intellectual potential that is too often unrecognized (McGregor, 1960).

Theory Y offered a departure from traditional management because it recognized the needs of individuals and their ability to change (McGregor, 1960). It also places responsibility for organizational performance on management instead of the employees. "If employees are lazy, indifferent, unwilling to take responsibility, intransigent, uncreative, uncooperative, Theory Y implies that the causes lie in management's methods of organization and control" (McGregor, 1960, p. 48). In contrast, Theory X offers management the easy rationalization that ineffective organizations are due to the natures of their staff (McGregor, 1960). Theory X and Theory Y also differ in terms of locus of control. Theory X clearly takes an external approach; employee behavior must be controlled by an external force, that is, management (McGregor, 1966). Whereas Theory Y relies on an internal locus of control, employee behavior is controlled via self-direction and self-control (McGregor, 1966). Based on the above information, which approach do you think is the most appropriate for human services organizations? Why? What similarities do you see when comparing Theory Y and its assumptions to Abraham Maslow's Hierarchy of Needs?

Management by Objectives

Management by Objectives (MBO) was created by Peter Drucker, who has made numerous contributions in the area of nonprofit management (Crainer, 1998). Traditional approaches to management focused on managers' developing organizational structure and processes for following identified goals and objectives. Drucker suggests that the chosen structure and processes may not be the best or most efficient for achieving the goals and objectives. One of Drucker's key contributions, offered in *The Practice of Management* (1954), is that identifying goals and objectives should occur through a collaborative process that involves management and employees (Drucker, 1954). This leads to the development of appropriate structures and processes for accomplishing the goals and objectives. In addition to being able to manage by objectives, Drucker (1954) believed that the manager of the future would have to be prepared to engage in "new tasks," including: team building, effective and efficient communication, motivation of employees and co-workers; decision making that considers internal and external factors; and understanding the organization as a whole and how he/she fits within it.

One of the most important contributions of MBO is its emphasis on staff working together in the development of clear goals and objectives (Kettner, 2002; Netting et al., 2004). Employees who are involved in the process have a better understanding of how their particular job and responsibilities support the pursuit and achievement of organizational goals. Another important aspect of MBO is its emphasis on evaluating objectives. The organization is expected to collect evaluation data on a regular basis and make it available to managers in a timely manner. Managers are then expected to use the data in making decisions. The emphasis on evaluation is of particular importance to human services organizations and social workers. Other contributions of MBO with particular relevance to human services organizations include encouraging planning for the future and assisting with the evaluation of employee performance (Kettner, 2002).

Although MBO was innovative, the decision-making process was too dependent upon information to respond to changes in a timely manner (Crainer, 1998). Another criticism is that the process requires attention to both the "big picture" and details, but tends to focus more on the details (Netting et al., 2004). It also requires managers to possess skills related to planning and implementation (Crainer, 1998). Finally, organizational goals are not static, meaning that they change in response to changes in the organization and its environment. Therefore, the strategic plan must be an ongoing process or one that allows for modifications in order to accommodate changes. All too often the process ends with a written plan that is placed on a shelf and forgotten until it is time to create a new one.

Organizational Decision Making

Another important approach to organizations arose from theories and studies about how individuals make decisions. Herbert Simon was one of the first scholars to study the process of individual decision making in the context of organizations. The basis of his approach was a belief that understanding how organizational decisions are made was just as important as understanding the process of implementing them (Simon, 1976). He noted that the majority of administrative theories had focused solely on the latter (Simon, 1976). It is important to note that some scholars, such as Drucker (1954, 1959), addressed the process of making decisions in later works.

Simon's focus was on rational decisions in the context of organizations, which he defined as decisions that are consistent with organizational goals. It is important to note that organizationally rational decisions differ from those that are personally rational, ones that are consistent with personal goals. Even if it is the intent of the individual to engage in rational decision making, the process can be limited or "bounded" by personal and organizational characteristics. The personal characteristics included "skills, habits, and reflexes," which included one's mental abilities (Simon, 1976, p. 40). Simon also noted that individual decisions could be influenced by loyalty to the organization, to specific units or departments, or to one's self. Regardless of the case, individuals tend to make decisions that are favorable to those to whom they are loyal. Finally, he noted that decisions are made based on knowledge and available information. The lack of knowledge and accurate information can lead to decisions that are inappropriate for the given situation.

In terms of organizational barriers to decision making, Simon (1976) notes that the individual must be free to take the chosen course of action, have a clear understanding of the organization's goals and their relationship with the chosen course of action, and possess adequate information and knowledge about the conditions under which the decision is being made. Finally, he suggested that the challenges to rational decision making may encourage administrators to choose the path of least resistance. Simon refers to this as "satisficing" or seeking out and selecting an adequate solution rather than the best one.

Simon's work and the subsequent works of others on organizational decision making are of benefit to human services organizations. For example, a focus on the importance of quality information helps decision makers realize their need for up-to-date, relevant, and accurate information to assist in decision making (Netting et al., 2004). If information is incorrect or out of date, for instance, it can lead one to an inappropriate solution, and one that may harm clients. Given social work's current focus on evidence-based practice, in which practitioners make practice decisions based on the best research evidence available, this is of particular importance. It is also important not to confuse quality of information with quantity of information.

Whereas decision-making theory has been beneficial, it has also been criticized. For example, Pfeffer (1992) believes that the process of making a decision is overemphasized. He suggests that the time would be better spent teaching people how to implement decisions and address their consequences. Another example is the lack of attention to external factors that impact organizational decisions. The importance of considering such factors was identified by open systems theory, which will be discussed in the following section.

Open Systems Approach to Organizations

To this point, all of the approaches discussed have focused primarily, if not solely, on the internal aspects of the organization. In other words, little attention has been given to the impact of external factors on the organization. This changed in the late 1950s with the application of general systems theory to organizations, which led to the creation of the systems perspective of organizations and contingency theory. Its influence can be seen in many of the subsequent and more recent approaches to organizations and interorganizational relationships, such as power and politics, total quality management, and managing diversity.

Systems Perspective of Organizations (Open Systems Theory). The systems perspective of organizations emerged in the late 1950s as a result of the merging of concepts from structural-functionalism and general systems theory (Hassard, 1993). Structural-functionalism is a sociological theory based on the idea that social structures are similar to biological structures in that both possess the needs of survival and adaptation (Hassard, 1993). In terms of organizations, these needs are fulfilled via organizational interdependence or interrelationships. On the other hand, general systems theory evolved out of biological systems theory and seeks to understand systems through examination of their relationships, both among components or subsystems and with the environment (Burrell & Morgan, 1979; von Bertalanffy, 1968). Systems theory is based on the concept of holism, which proposes that in order to understand a system, the entire system must be the subject of inquiry, not its individual components (Whitchurch & Constantine, 1993). In the context of organizations, general systems theory focuses on the processes stemming from the interrelationships and how such processes influence the subsystems (Hassard, 1993). Blending structural-functionalism and general systems theory results in the systems perspective of organizations, which views organizations as:

> [a] group of phenomena that is inter-dependent in such a way that it strives to accomplish a common goal. Advanced systems contain subsystems which operate in an independent way but again tend to be inter-dependent and oriented toward the overall goal of the wider system. In fulfilling this goal, a system interacts with and exists within a specific environment. The nature of this interaction means that a system

can both influence, and be influenced by, its environment. This quality of interaction allows us to discuss the exchange of inputs and outputs, which in turn enables us to determine the system boundary. On recognizing the different forms of system boundary, we are able to talk of organizations displaying closed, partially open or open systems behaviour (Hassard, 1993, p. 310).

Additional characteristics of systems theory include recognition of the interdependent nature of relationships, the importance of meeting system needs, and the presence of interdependent subsystems (Raak & Paulus, 2001).

As stated above, the systems perspective categorizes organizations as closed, partially open, or open. A closed system is one that is isolated from its environment and views itself as independent or self-sufficient. Closed systems are primarily concerned with increasing internal efficiency, which explains their focus on internal structures, tasks, processes, and formal relationships (Hassard, 1993). Given that closed systems do not emphasize the importance of environment, they do not collect data on environmental changes (Katz & Kahn, 1966). Partially open systems are similar to closed systems in that their primary focus is on internal factors. The difference is that partially open systems acknowledge the impact of the environment on organizational functioning (Hassard, 1993). However, the attention given to external factors tends to be limited to being offered as potential explanations for the results of an organizational analysis (Hassard, 1993).

An open system differs from closed and partially open systems in that an open system actively engages with its environment. Specifically, open systems engage in dynamic exchanges or relationships that are characterized by a cyclical flow of energy or resources from the environment, into the organization, and back into the environment (Burrell & Morgan, 1979; Hassard, 1993; Katz & Kahn, 1966; Whitchurch & Constantine, 1993). During this process, the organization modifies it processes and structure to adapt to changes in the environment, allowing it to maintain its exchanges with the environment. This is often referred to as "the steady state" or "dynamic equilibrium" (Hassard, 1993; Katz & Kahn, 1966). An organization's survival is directly related to its ability to maintain its relationships with the environment, as well as to adjust to changes within the system and its environment. In other words, organizations that are unable to adapt to changes in the environment are at greater risk of extinction.

Contingency Theory.   As noted earlier, McGregor believed that many of the basic theoretical principles of the classical organizational theories were no longer relevant to organizations and society. During the 1960s, another theory emerged that took a similar stance in that it questioned whether a single theory could be appropriate for all organizations. Specifically, supporters proposed that every organization is impacted by a unique combination of external factors and survival is dependent on its ability to adapt to these factors (Scott, 1998). Since the factors are unique for each organization, the approach to organizing should as well. Hence, the question of whether one theory can fit all organizations. This line of thought led to contingency theory, which proposed that the best way to organize and manage an organization is "contingent" upon internal and external factors. Contingency theory is based on three underlying assumptions, the first two of which are: "there is no one best way to organize" and "any way of organizing is not equally effective" (Galbraith, 1973, p. 2 as cited in Scott, 1998). The third assumption is that the best way to organize depends on the nature of the organization's environment (Scott, 1998).

One of the greatest strengths of contingency theory is that it recognizes the importance of an organization's ability to be flexible in adapting to changes in the environment. This is especially true for human services organizations, which are constantly faced with changes in client needs, funding streams, policies, and expectations. Contingency theory is also important in that it has encouraged new directions in organizational thought (Netting et al., 2004).

Recent Approaches to Organizations

In looking back at the theories we have discussed to this point, we can see a clear evolution from closed system approaches to open systems approaches. We can also see a shift from a narrow focus on productivity to a broader one that considers factors that influence organizational functioning. Although recent approaches to organizations continue to take an open systems perspective and to examine factors that affect functioning, they also address factors that have not been previously discussed. For example, some of the more recent theories attend to power, organizational culture, quality, leadership and diversity.

Power and Politics.   Jeffery Pfeffer (1981, 1992) proposed that in order to understand an organization, you must understand its power and politics. Pfeffer (1992) defines power as the "potential ability to influence behavior, to change the course of events, to overcome resistance, and to get people to do things that they would not otherwise do" (p. 30). He goes on to define politics as "the processes, the actions, the behaviors through which this potential power is utilized and realized" (p. 30). Pfeffer (1981) proposed that power is related to organizational position and is exercised in order to meet goals, which could be those of the organization or a subunit (department, group, individual, etc.). Furthermore, the emphasis is on obtaining the desired outcome, which may or may not be the rational choice. For example, pursuit of an individual goal even though doing so is not in the best interest of the organization as a whole. Thus, organizational politics consist of the exercise of power in pursuit of individual and organizational goals, which may not be congruent or rational.

A criticism of Pfeffer's early work is that his attention was focused on the internal power and politics of the organization. In other words, he did not address the impact of external factors on the organization. However, this aspect was later addressed by other scholars. For instance, Netting et al. (2004) note that in 1976 Wamsley and Zald proposed that one must examine internal and external politics when seeking to understand an organization. This viewpoint was extended via the political economy model, which focused on the interaction between internal and external political (acquisition of power) and economical (acquisition of resources) activities (Netting et al., 2004). The interactions of these forces impact the organization as well as its environment, including relationships with other organizations.

Organizational Culture. Organizational culture is broadly defined as the behaviors, values, beliefs, traditions, perspectives, and expectations that are shared by members of an organization (Hardina, Middleton, Montana, & Simpson, 2007; Kettner, 2002). An organization's culture is shaped by its history and the shared experiences of its members. Its survival is dependent upon the process of orienting or socializing new members to the culture (values, behaviors, etc.), which is the responsibility of existing members, especially those with a long tenure. Socialization can be accomplished via formal and informal methods. Examples of formal methods include employee handbooks, manuals, and training (Queralt, 1996). Informal methods include the sharing of stories about the organization and mentoring by co-workers (Queralt, 1996). What other methods might be used to socialize members and encourage compliance?

One of the ways in which members may gain compliance is group or peer pressure. We can look back to Mayo's Hawthorne Experiments for an example. The Bank Wiring Room experiment was designed to study the influence of group norms on productivity. All of the employees in this room worked individually to assemble telephone switchboards. Furthermore, each worker was paid for each completed switchboard, meaning that the more he/she produced, the more he/she earned. Despite the individual nature of the work and pay, the study revealed the following: the group set a norm for the number of switchboards that could be assembled in a day, which was less than they were physically capable of producing; those who either exceeded or did not meet the norm were pressured by the group to comply with the norm; and during the study the average daily output for the group remained consistent with the group norm (Roethlisberger et al., 1950). What conclusions could you draw from these results?

Since organizational culture tends to permeate every aspect of the organization, it is often difficult to change, especially in organizations with stable membership. This resistance to change may make it difficult to introduce new ideas, thus impeding innovation and growth. For instance, new members may be reluctant to share innovative ideas in a culture that is openly resistant to change. Leaders who are new to an organization may also encounter such barriers. It may also make it difficult for the organization to respond to changes in its environment. On the other hand, the organizational culture may give the organization a competitive edge. Specifically, it can serve to bond people and encourage them to remain committed to a common goal (Scott, 1998). More importantly, it can instill a desire to commit, rather than doing so out of obligation (Scott, 1998). How might an unstable membership impact the process of socialization?

Quality. After World War II, Japan began the process of rebuilding its society, which included its industries. Much of their success with this endeavor is

---

Competency Connection

Organizations and Research

Using Research about Personality Types to Improve Organizational Dynamics

Using research, social workers can enhance and improve organizations. For example, by considering what research has shown about the 16 personality types from the Myers-Briggs Type Indicator, organizations can identify the personality type of their employees and use that information to strengthen the organization and enhance team-building strategies. Through type watching, organizations will discover who their employees are and what makes each of them tick.

According to typological theory, each of us is born with a predisposition for certain personality traits. In the book, *Type Talk at Work: How the 16 Personality Types Determine Your Success on the Job,* Kroeger, Theusen, and Rutledge (2002), identify four pairs of preference alternatives. Everyone possesses one trait from each of the pairs. The preference alternatives are

as follows: Extraverted (E) or Introverted (I); Sensing (S) or iNtuitive (N); Thinking (T) or Feeling (F); and Judging (J) or Perceiving (P) (p. 11). Each preference has specific qualities or traits that determine an employee's communication patterns, leadership qualities, organizational and problem-solving skills, and thought processes.

With type watching, organizations will be able to set up teams in a manner that allows employees of every personality type to be able to provide input and express themselves in their own unique ways. For more about the Myers-Briggs personality type questionnaire, see http://www.teamtechnology.co.uk.

Adapted from Kroeger, O., Theusen, J.M., & Rutledge, H. (2002). *Type talk at work: How the 16 personality types determine your success on the job* (rev. ed.). New York: Dell, and Berens, L.V., Cooper, S.A., Ernst, L.K., et al. (2001). *Quick guide to the 16 personality types in organizations: Understanding personality differences in the workplace.* Huntington Beach, CA: Telos.

---

attributed to W. Edwards Deming, who introduced the idea of quality management (Martin, 1993; Kettner, 2002). He proposed moving away from a profit focus to one that emphasized product quality, innovation, and ongoing research and development (Walton, 1986). By the 1970s, Japanese products, especially electronics and automobiles, had earned a solid international reputation for quality, giving them a competitive edge in the global marketplace (Kettner, 2002). Needless to say, this caught the attention of American industry, which had a reputation for poor product quality. As a result, Americans began to study Japanese approaches to management in hopes of improving the quality of products and services (Kettner, 2002). Two of the approaches that emerged from these studies were Total Quality Management and Theory Z.

Total Quality Management (TQM).   TQM is primarily based on Deming's work and was designed specifically for American organizations (Kettner, 2002; Martin, 1993). According to Martin (1993), TQM blends elements of scientific management (efficiency and research) and human relations (importance of culture and social relationships). The basic elements of TQM focus on implementing ongoing processes that ensure the production of quality products and services (Walton, 1986). It is important to note that consumers define quality and inform decision making via feedback related to customer satisfaction (Netting et al., 2004). TQM also emphasizes employee training, leadership via empowerment, creating a positive culture, teamwork, cooperation, and pride in one's work (Walton, 1986). The success of TQM is dependent upon the creation and maintenance of an organizational culture based "on product quality, consumer satisfaction, standardization of production, and employee empowerment" (Hardina et al., 2007, p. 39). An important part of creating this culture are quality circles or teams that focus on improving the processes used to create products and services (Hardina et al., 2007). Some of the barriers to implementing TQM include a focus on profits instead of quality and productivity, lack of organizational vision and purpose, instability in management, and an absence of long-range planning (Walton, 1986). What other organizational or cultural barriers might make it difficult to shift to TQM?

Theory Z. Another quality-centered approach is Theory Z. Theory Z and TQM share a focus on quality; however, Theory Z differs in that its assumptions about human behavior and organizations are based on a Japanese cultural perspective (Kettner, 2002; Schriver, 1998). Theory Z emphasizes the following: retaining employees until they are eligible for retirement (lifetime employment), gradually evaluating and promoting employees, providing employees with a variety of experiences (generalized rather than specialized career paths), making decisions based on consensus, actively involving employees in decision making, instilling a collective sense of responsibility, and approaching employee well-being holistically (Ouchi, 1981). Of particular importance is the use of teams or quality circles to make and implement collective decisions. It is also important to note that decisions are made in the best interest of the group, rather than out of self-interest (Kettner, 2002). Another important element is a belief in reciprocity; employee loyalty is fostered and maintained through the organization's loyalty to its employees. While Theory Z has some obvious strengths, cultural barriers make it difficult to implement in American organizations. What might these barriers be? Thinking back to the classical approaches, such as Weber's bureaucracy, how does Theory Z differ from more traditional approaches?

In thinking about the elements of TQM and Theory Z, how could these approaches be important to human services organizations? A significant issue for human services organizations is service quality, which is directly related to building and maintaining the trust of consumers and the general public (Martin, 1993). In other words, focusing on the delivery of quality services may help improve relationships with consumers. For example, TQM's emphasis on customer satisfaction also provides decision makers with up–to-date information about clients' needs, which helps ensure that services are relevant. TQM and Theory Z are also consistent with social work values, such as empowerment and self-determination. Can you make the connections between these approaches and social work values?

Leadership vs. Management. While the study of leadership dates back to the time of Aristotle, management is a fairly new concept that appeared with industrialization (Kotter, 1990; Northouse, 2004). Leadership can be defined as the process of directing and mobilizing both people and their ideas in order to achieve a goal or set of goals (Kotter, 1990). This process involves three specific functions: establishing direction (developing vision and strategies), aligning people in support of the chosen direction, and motivating and empowering people to fulfill the vision (Kotter, 1990, 1999; Northouse, 2004). In contrast, the purpose of management is to create order and consistency, as well as to increase effectiveness and efficiency. This is accomplished via the following activities: planning, budgeting, staffing, organizing, controlling, and problem solving (Kotter, 1990). Whereas leadership and management are distinctly different, they are complementary. It might help to think of it in this manner, leadership is primarily concerned with bringing about change and management focuses on maintaining the change (Kotter, 1990). Another perspective is that leadership is driven by purpose and management is driven by objectives (Antonakis, Cianciolo, & Sternberg, 2004). It is also important to note that in recent years the expectation that managers also engage in leadership activities has become more common (Kotter, 1999).

Please take a moment to think back through the theories we have discussed thus far and answer the following questions: Which theories focus on management? Which theories focus on leadership? In your opinion, what changes in thoughts and theories are related to the shift in focus on management to leadership? For example, what theory(ies) introduced the idea of including employees in decision making and planning?

Now that we have a clear understanding of the difference between management and leadership, let's talk about leadership in more detail. As we noted earlier, leadership is not a new concept. Some of the "classic" approaches to leadership include the following:

- The **great man theory** proposed that the characteristics necessary for leadership are innate. In other words, leaders are born with them rather than acquiring them over time.

- **Autocratic, or authoritarian, leadership** places all of the authority for decision making on the leader. He/she tends to use the power associated with his/her position to gain compliance with his/her expectations.

- **Democratic or participative leadership** allows employees to be involved in the decision-making process, but the final decision lies with the leader.

- **Laissez-faire leadership** is characterized by a "hands-off" approach or one in which the leader does not take an active role in leading the organization. In the absence of leadership, employees are left to make their own decisions.

Just as the approaches to organizations have evolved, so have approaches to leadership. The more recent approaches tend to focus on responsibility, accountability, employee motivation, and employee development. Examples of these newer approaches include the following:

- **Transactional leadership** focuses on the relationship between leaders and their constituents, which is based on exchanges. Leaders provide benefits or rewards to constituents in return for their loyalty and compliance.

- **Servant leadership** focuses on the motivation behind the choice to lead. Servant-leaders are motivated by a desire to serve others rather than themselves (Greenleaf, 1997, 2003). In doing so, they put the best interest of the group first.

- **Stewardship** is centered on the belief that a leader should place service to others before his/her own interests and be willing to be held accountable by his/her constituents for doing so (Block, 1996).

- **Transformational leadership** is primarily concerned with assisting constituents in reaching their full potential by addressing their higher-order needs (Northouse, 2004). Transformational leaders are also able to motivate others to act in the best interest of the group rather than in their own self-interest (Northouse, 2004).

As you read through the more recent approaches, did you notice any similarities between them and the organizational theories we have discussed? For example, which organizational theory is consistent with transformational leadership? (*Hint:* McGregor).

Leadership and Gender. Another interesting aspect of leadership that has received a fair amount of attention is whether there are differences in the leadership styles of men and women. Interest in the glass ceiling phenomenon, which we will discuss later, is a catalyst for many of these studies. While this topic has been discussed in the context of management, more recently the focus has been on leadership. So, what do you think? Would you expect men and women to approach leadership and management differently?

The literature suggests that men in leadership positions tend to use styles that are more directive, authoritative, and autocratic (Smith, 1997; Eagly & Carli, 2004). They are also more likely to view leadership in the context of vertical hierarchy (Smith, 1997). In other words, leaders are responsible for making decisions and issuing directives, which are followed by subordinates. This approach is accompanied by a belief that leaders hold power over or control subordinates, which is exercised in decision making, as well as via sharing of information and knowledge (Smith, 1997). Men tend to place a greater emphasis on employees' shortcomings and are less likely to engage in proactive problem solving (Eagly & Carli, 2004). Finally, it has been suggested that men tend to view conflict as negative and that it should be avoided or controlled.

Conversely, women tend to use leadership styles that are participative and democratic in nature, such as transformational leadership (Eagly & Carli, 2004; Northouse, 2004; Smith, 1997). A key element of this approach is the emphasis on partnerships and positive relationships among organizational participants, including employees and clients (Hardina et al., 2007; Hyde, 2003). For example, Hyde notes that "women are more likely than men to endorse those values, goals, and activities that enhanced participation by staff and clients in agency life" (2003, p. 55). The approach to decision making is consistent with this in that the process is inclusive, collaborative, and based on consensus (Hardina et al., 2007). Along these lines, power is shared with others and viewed as being based on cooperation and interdependence (Hardina et al, 2007; Smith, 1997). Women also appear to be more likely to use rewards to encourage desired behavior and to motivate employees through positive interpersonal relationships (Eagly & Carli, 2004; Hardina et al., 2007). Conflicts are viewed as opportunities for change and are addressed via collective problem solving and consensus building (Smith, 1997). Additional characteristics attributed to women in leadership positions include a belief in information sharing in order to promote employee development, emphasis on a supportive work environment characterized by mutual trust and support, and an understanding of the importance of diversity in the workplace (Smith, 1997).

Given the above information, how do the leadership styles differ between men and women? Are these differences consistent with the expectations you held prior to reading this section? Although it has been suggested that the aforementioned characteristics should contribute to the effectiveness and suitability of women for leadership (Eagly & Carli, 2004; Northouse, 2004), women continue to be underrepresented in leadership positions, especially those in the upper levels of organizations. Eagly & Carli (2004) suggest that this is due, at least in part, to the double bind created by the need to balance being communal and competent. In other words, women who are competent may be viewed by male counterparts as a threat, which is contrary to being perceived as communal. Oakley (2000) offers a similar observation of the double-bind, "they must be tough and authoritative (like men) to be taken seriously" (p. 324). However, such behavior places them at risk of being perceived negatively. What other factors would affect the ability of women to obtain upper-level leadership positions?

When considering the information presented here, as well as other sources on the topic, it is important for you to be mindful of concerns related to the research. First of all, women of color are underrepresented in the samples (Northouse, 2004). Also, little consideration is given to other factors that may contribute to differences, such as age, physical ability, and sexual orientation (Northouse, 2004). How might these limitations impact the results and their implications?

DIVERSITY AND CULTURAL COMPETENCE

Whereas our current workforce is diverse, this has not always been the case. In thinking about American history prior to World War I, what was the most dominant characteristic of workers? What about leaders? During this time, the workforce was dominated by men and leadership roles were dominated by Caucasian men. However, this was changed by World Wars I and II, when many men joined the armed forces, which took them away from their jobs. These positions, especially those in war-related industries, had to be filled. This need created opportunities for women and other nondominant groups to enter the workforce. (Many of you probably know about the World War II icon "Rosie the Riveter.") Women were also presented with opportunities to assume leadership positions. However, much of this was short-lived. For example, the end of World War II brought the return of the men to the workforce and an expectation that women would return to their "traditional" roles (Smith, 1997). What social movements and legislation helped reverse this and increase diversity in the workforce?

Although the Civil Rights Movement, Women's Movement, and Affirmative Action helped with workforce diversity by increasing access to entry-level positions, women, people of color, and people from other nondominant groups have continued to experience difficulties with advancement into positions with greater responsibilities (Elliot & Smith, 2004; Northouse, 2004; Thomas, 2001). Elliot & Smith (2004) found this to be particularly true for African-American women, who experience inequality as a direct result of discrimination and have an increasingly difficult time attaining jobs with power. In fact, their representation in leadership has remained static, while Caucasian women have experienced some increases (Northouse, 2004). Native-born, college-educated Asian-American men have also been found to experience difficulty with advancement. Specifically, they were found to supervise approximately 14 percent fewer employees than comparable nonwhite men (Takei & Sakamoto, 2008). Yamane (2002) found similar results when studying Filipino Americans. The study indicated that they face a substantial amount of discrimination within the labor market and are less likely to serve in a managerial role.

The difficulty women and people from other nondominant groups experience with advancement is commonly referred to as the "glass ceiling," which is described as "an invisible barrier to advancement opportunities" that in many cases prevents women and minorities from reaching positions above midlevel management (Smith, 1997, p. 215). Whereas the glass ceiling is a common concept in the literature, in recent times some scholars have taken issue with its limited focus. Specifically, it addresses only the barriers to obtaining high-level positions, when women face many more barriers than this one even before they reach higher levels (Eagly & Carli, 2007). In order to capture this concept, Eagly & Carli (2007) have suggested reframing the glass ceiling as a "labyrinth" consisting of a multitude of challenges and difficulties. Barriers include, but are not limited to, wage discrepancies, prejudices, discrimination, stereotyping, tokenism, societal resistance to female leadership, differences between male and female styles of leadership, and demands of family life (Eagly & Carli, 2004, 2007; Northouse, 2004; Oakley, 2000). It is important to note that maintaining diversity is dependent upon the organization's ability to overcome these barriers.

The culturally competent social worker must be able to recognize and address lack of diversity in organizations. Thomas (1991) proposed Managing Diversity, an approach to management that addresses the barriers women and other people from nondominant groups may face. Managing Diversity consists of three steps, the first of which is Affirmative Action. Thomas viewed Affirmative Action as the necessary first step, the purpose being to create opportunities for women and others from nondominant groups to enter the workforce. The second step, valuing differences, involves the implementation of organizational activities designed to minimize the presence of -*isms* (racism, sexism, ageism, etc.) by increasing employees' understanding of and tolerance for differences (Thomas, 1991). It is through such tolerance that the organization will move on to the third step, managing diversity. The final step involves changing the organization's culture and environment to one that empowers all employees to reach their full potential (Thomas, 1991). This method is significantly different from more traditional ones because it targets diversity at an individual, interpersonal, and organizational level rather than at simply the individual and interpersonal levels (Thomas, 1991). The end result is the organization's realization of the importance of diversity and voluntary engagement in activities to recruit, maintain, and use a diverse workforce.

Why is diversity an important aspect to consider when discussing organizations, especially human services organizations? Kettner (2002) reminds us that the ability of a social services organization to serve its clients is dependent upon its diversity. Specifically, he says that "it is critical that the voices that help shape organizational and programmatic approaches to problem solving be representative of diverse community perspectives" (p. 46). This is important because enlisting diverse individuals in decision-making roles helps an agency maintain relevance over time and continue to be in touch with the needs of its clients (Kettner, 2002). However, doing so requires a significant degree of cultural competence or understanding of the different values, beliefs, traditions, and practices of other cultures represented by the organization's staff and clients (Kettner, 2002).

Competency Connection

Organizations and Policy Issues

Employment Policies and Affirmative Action

There are many arguments for and against Affirmative Action as a way to address organizational inequalities. Opponents argue for the discontinuation of the policy, citing that there is no longer resistance by organizations to hiring racial/ethnic minorities and women and that the policy perpetuates reverse discrimination against white males, who may be passed up for jobs so that women and minorities are slotted in positions to fulfill the requirements. Proponents say that not only do organizational inequalities and discrimination still persist, but that the policy is still needed to address modern-day inequities women and minorities may face once they are actually hired. For example, women and minorities may be unable to access or may even be excluded from sources of social support, such as social networks, sponsors, and mentors (Soni, 1999). Another issue is the difference in wages between Caucasian and minority females, which has steadily increased over the past 30 years. In 1979, young Caucasian females typically earned 5% more than young African-American females. The difference between the two groups exceeded 15% in 1990 and since then has ranged between 12% and 15% (Pettit & Ewert, 2009). Given that women and minorities continue to face barriers and differences once they are hired, hopefully the future of Affirmative Action will be geared toward revamping, rather than dismantling the policy. Affirmative Action can be used as a social justice vehicle that ensures women and minorities are treated equally in the hiring process, and that once hired, they are truly accepted into the organization, and have the support needed in order to function properly in their positions.

Pettit, B., & Ewert, S. (2009). Employment gains and wage declines: The erosion of Black women's relative wages since 1980. *Demography, 46*(3), 469–492.

Soni, V. (1999). Morality vs. mandate: Affirmative action in employment. *Public Personnel Management, 28*(4), 577–594.

CONNECTING THEORY AND PRACTICE

To this point we have talked about what constitutes an organization and provided you with a broad overview of organizational theories. Our discussion has addressed a variety of aspects, including management, leadership, structure, employee motivation, communication, decision making, organizational culture, and diversity. While we attended to the connection between these theories and human services organizations, in this section we want to assist you in making the connection between the theories and practice with organizations, especially human services organizations. In order to accomplish this, we will revisit the scenario presented in the chapter introduction.

Just as you did earlier, take a moment to imagine that you are a case manager in a community-based children's outpatient mental health clinic. One of your clients, John Smith, is struggling to function in a regular education classroom and is in danger of being expelled. The school district has ignored John's parent's request to assess him for special education services and they are reluctant to challenge the district. As we previously discussed, your intervention may include helping his parents understand their rights and the district's responsibilities, as well as assisting them in addressing their concerns with the district. These tasks will most likely include changes in the district's approach to John and, quite possibly, special education services in general. In order to resolve this situation, what might you need to know about the school district?

A good place to start is learning more about the school district's structure, especially in terms of hierarchy, decision making, and communication. Why would this be important? Knowing where in the hierarchy or chain of command to begin seeking resolution is imperative. First of all, it saves you time. Passing over people can also create animosity that will most likely affect your ability to resolve the issue. Another important piece of information is how communication occurs within the organization. Violating this protocol may also create animosity and difficulties. Perhaps this question would be best answered using our scenario.

First of all, we need to lay out the relevant organizational structures. John is on a campus that serves regular and special education students in the 6th, 7th, and 8th grades. The campus has the traditional school structure of teachers, assistant principal, and a principal. The campus also has a school counselor and diagnostician, both of whom are responsible for screening students for special education services. The school counselor and diagnostician report to the principal and the director of special education services. The principal reports to the district superintendant. Let us assume that the initial referral for special education would come from John's teacher; therefore it is reasonable to start with him/her. In this case, what might happen if you started with the district superintendent? How might this affect your future interactions with John's teacher, counselor, diagnostician, and principal? How might that affect John's relationships with them? How might it affect his parents' relationships with them?

Assume that you are employed by the school district as a school social worker and John is your client. Your responsibility is to represent his best interest, which may be in conflict with what the school district's position. How would this affect your approach to the situation?

Competency Connection

Organizations and Social Work Practice

Organizations Serving Children—the National Indian Child Welfare Association

Nonprofit human services agencies such as the National Indian Child Welfare Association (NICWA) often employ social workers to practice with individuals, families, and communities. NICWA was founded in 1987 by an social worker with a master of social work degree, and it seeks to provide culturally sensitive child welfare services for Native American children and their families. The association's vision is to ensure that Native American children are protected from abuse, neglect, and sexual exploitation. NICWA makes certain that child welfare agencies are in compliance with the 1978 Indian Child Welfare Act by ensuring that Native American children are placed with either Native American families or in environments that respect Indian culture, customs, traditions, and heritage. The organization's mission is accomplished through educating and training Native American child welfare workers, conducting research, maintaining current literature on Indian child welfare issues, and through work on public policy. Human services organizations like this one employ social workers and other professionals to serve, advocate for and protect children.

SOURCE: National Indian Child Welfare Association. http://www.nicwa .org; Retrieved March 9, 2010.

Reading 2

Principles of Scientific Management

FREDERICK WINSLOW TAYLOR (1911)

This work laid the groundwork for modern organization and decision theory. It describes a system of clearly defined laws and rules. Leaders are trained within the system, rather than recruited from outside the company. The author was an engineer, but his work was used widely by those working with organizations. Its use in sociology connected it to the emerging profession of social work. The fundamental principles of scientific management apply to all kinds of human activities. Consider the historical context of this article; what was happening in our nation at this time. Does the author seem to possess the "cultural competence" we expect of our generation(s)?

INTRODUCTION

President Roosevelt, in his address to the Governors at the White House, prophetically remarked that "The conservation of our national resources is only preliminary to the larger question of national efficiency."

The whole country at once recognized the importance of conserving our material resources and a large movement has been started which will be effective in accomplishing this object. As yet, however, we have but vaguely appreciated the importance of "the larger question of increasing our national efficiency."

We can see our forests vanishing, our water-powers going to waste, our soil being carried by floods into the sea; and the end of our coal and our iron is in sight. But our larger wastes of human effort, which go on every day through such of our acts as are blundering, ill-directed; or inefficient, and which Mr. Roosevelt refers to as a lack of "national efficiency," are less visible, less tangible, and are but vaguely appreciated.

We can see and feel the waste of material things. Awkward, inefficient, or ill-directed movements of men, however, leave nothing visible or tangible behind them. Their appreciation calls for an act of memory, an effort of the imagination. And for this reason, even though our daily loss from this source is

Excerpted from Taylor, F.W. (1916, December) *The principles of scientific management.* Bulletin of the Taylor Society.

Stop Watch with Decimal Parts

greater than from our waste of material things, the one has stirred us deeply, while the other has moved us but little.

As yet there has been no public agitation for "greater national efficiency," no meetings have been called to consider how this is to be brought about. And still there are signs that the need for greater efficiency is widely felt.

The search for better, for more competent men, from the presidents of our great companies down to our household servants, was never more vigorous than it is now. And more than ever before is the demand for competent men in excess of the supply.

What we are all looking for, however, is the readymade, competent man; the man whom some one else has trained. It is only when we fully realize that our duty, as well as our opportunity, lies in systematically cooperating to train and to make this competent man, instead of in hunting for a man whom some one else has trained, that we shall be on the road to national efficiency.

In the past the prevailing idea has been well expressed in the saying that "Captains of industry are born, not made"; and the theory has been that if one could get the right man, methods could be safely left to him. In the future it will be appreciated that our leaders must be trained right as well as born right, and that no great man can (with the old system of personal management) hope to compete with a number of ordinary men who have been properly organized so as efficiently to cooperate.

In the past the man has been first; in the future the system must be first. This in no sense, however, implies that great men are not needed. On the contrary, the first object of any good system must be that of developing first-class men; and under systematic management the best man rises to the top more certainly and more rapidly than ever before.

This paper has been written:

First. To point out, through a series of simple illustrations, the great loss which the whole country is suffering through inefficiency in almost all of our daily acts.

Second. To try to convince the reader that the remedy for this inefficiency lies in systematic management, rather than in searching for some unusual or extraordinary man.

Third. To prove that the best management is a true science, resting upon clearly defined laws, rules, and principles, as a foundation. And further to show that the fundamental principles of scientific management are applicable to all kinds of human activities, from our simplest individual acts to the work of our great corporations, which call for the most elaborate cooperation. And, briefly, through a series of illustrations, to convince the reader that whenever these principles are correctly applied, results must follow which are truly astounding.

This paper was originally prepared for presentation to The American Society of Mechanical Engineers. The illustrations chosen are such as, it is believed, will especially appeal to engineers and to managers of industrial and manufacturing establishments, and also quite as much to all of the men who are working in these establishments. It is hoped, however, that it will be clear to other readers that the same principles can be applied with equal force to all social activities: to the management of our homes; the management of our farms; the management of the business of our tradesmen, large and small; of our churches, our philanthropic institutions, our universities, and our governmental departments.

Principles of Scientific Management, Frederick Winslow Taylor (1911)

CHAPTER ONE: FUNDAMENTALS OF SCIENTIFIC MANAGEMENT

THE principal object of management should be to secure the maximum prosperity for the employer, coupled with the maximum prosperity for each employee.

The words "maximum prosperity" are used, in their broad sense, to mean not only large dividends for the company or owner, but the development of every branch of the business to its highest state of excellence, so that the prosperity may be permanent.

In the same way maximum prosperity for each employee means not only higher wages than are usually received by men of his class, but, of more importance still, it also means the development of each man to his state of maximum efficiency, so that he may be able to do, generally speaking, the highest grade of work for which his natural abilities fit him, and it further means giving him, when possible, this class of work to do.

It would seem to be so self-evident that maximum prosperity for the employer, coupled with maximum prosperity for the employee, ought to be the two leading objects of management, that even to state this fact should be unnecessary. And yet there is no question that, throughout the industrial world, a large part of the organization of employers, as well as employees, is for war rather than for peace, and that perhaps the majority on either side do not believe that it is possible so to arrange their mutual relations that their interests become identical.

The majority of these men believe that the fundamental interests of employees and employers are necessarily antagonistic. Scientific management, on the contrary, has for its very foundation the firm conviction that the true interests of the two are one and the same; that prosperity for the employer cannot exist through a long term of years unless it is accompanied by prosperity for the employee, and *vice versa*; and that it is possible to give the workman what he most wants—high wages—and the employer what he wants—a low labor cost—for his manufactures.

It is hoped that some at least of those who do not sympathize with each of these objects may be led to modify their views; that some employers, whose attitude toward their workmen has been that of trying to get the largest amount of work out of them for the smallest possible wages, may be led to see that a more liberal policy toward their men will pay them better; and that some of those workmen who begrudge a fair and even a large profit to their employers, and who feel that all of the fruits of their labor should belong to them, and that those for whom they work and the capital invested in the business are entitled to little or nothing, may be led to modify these views.

No one can be found who will deny that in the case of any single individual the greatest prosperity can exist only when that individual has reached his highest state of efficiency; that is, when he is turning out his largest daily output.

The truth of this fact is also perfectly clear in the case of two men working together. To illustrate: if you and your workman have become so skilful that you and he together are making two pairs of shoes in a day, while your competitor and his workman are making only one pair, it is clear that after selling your two pairs of shoes you can pay your workman much higher wages than your competitor who produces only one pair of shoes is able to pay his man, and that there will still be enough money left over for you to have a larger profit than your competitor.

In the case of a more complicated manufacturing establishment, it should also be perfectly clear that the greatest permanent prosperity for the workman, coupled with the greatest prosperity for the employer, can be brought about only when the work of the establishment is done with the smallest combined expenditure of human effort, plus nature's resources, plus the cost for the use of capital in the shape of machines, buildings, etc. Or, to state the same thing in a different way: that the greatest prosperity can exist only as the result of the greatest possible productivity of the men and machines of the establishment—that is, when each man and each machine are turning out the largest possible output; because unless your men and your machines are daily turning out more work than others around you, it is clear that competition will prevent your paying higher wages to your workmen than are paid to those of your competitor. And what is true as to the possibility of paying high wages in the case of two companies competing close beside one another is also true as to whole districts of the country and even as to nations which are in competition. In a word, that maximum prosperity can exist only as the result of maximum productivity. Later in this paper illustrations will be given of several companies which are earning large dividends and at the same time paying from 30 per cent. to 100 per cent.

higher wages to their men than are paid to similar men immediately around them, and with whose employers they are in competition. These illustrations will cover different types of work, from the most elementary to the most complicated.

If the above reasoning is correct, it follows that the most important object of both the workmen and the management should be the training and development of each individual in the establishment, so that he can do (at his fastest pace and with the maximum of efficiency) the highest class of work for which his natural abilities fit him.

These principles appear to be so self-evident that many men may think it almost childish to state them. Let us, however, turn to the facts, as they actually exist in this country and in England. The English and American peoples are the greatest sportsmen in the world. Whenever an American workman plays baseball, or an English workman plays cricket, it is safe to say that he strains every nerve to secure victory for his side. He does his very best to make the largest possible number of runs. The universal sentiment is so strong that any man who fails to give out all there is in him in sport is branded as a "quitter," and treated with contempt by those who are around him.

When the same workman returns to work on the following day, instead of using every effort to turn out the largest possible amount of work, in a majority of the cases this man deliberately plans to do as little as he safely can—to turn out far less work than he is well able to do—in many instances to do not more than one-third to one-half of a proper day's work. And in fact if he were to do his best to turn out his largest possible day's work, he would be abused by his fellow-workers for so doing, even more than if he had proved himself a "quitter" in sport. Underworking, that is, deliberately working slowly so as to avoid doing a full day's work, "soldiering," as it is called in this country, "hanging it out," as it is called in England, "ca canae," as it is called in Scotland, is almost universal in industrial establishments, and prevails also to a large extent in the building trades; and the writer asserts without fear of contradiction that this constitutes the greatest evil with which the working-people of both England and America are now afflicted.

It will be shown later in this paper that doing away with slow working and "soldiering" in all its forms and so arranging the relations between employer and employee that each workman will work to his very best advantage and at his best speed, accompanied by the intimate cooperation with the management and the help (which the workman should receive) from the management, would result on the average in nearly doubling the output of each man and each machine. What other reforms, among those which are being discussed by these two nations, could do as much toward promoting prosperity, toward the diminution of poverty, and the alleviation of suffering? America and England have been recently agitated over such subjects as the tariff, the control of the large corporations on the one hand, and of hereditary power on the other hand, and over various more or less socialistic proposals for taxation, etc. On these subjects both peoples have been profoundly stirred, and yet hardly a voice has been raised to call attention to this vastly greater and more important subject of "soldiering," which directly and powerfully affects the wages, the prosperity, and the life of almost every working-man, and also quite as much the prosperity of every industrial establishment in the nation.

The elimination of "soldiering" and of the several causes of slow working would so lower the cost of production that both our home and foreign markets would be greatly enlarged, and we could compete on more than even terms with our rivals. It would remove one of the fundamental causes for dull times, for lack of employment, and for poverty, and therefore would have a more permanent and far-reaching effect upon these misfortunes than any of the curative remedies that are now being used to soften their consequences. It would insure higher wages and make shorter working hours and better working and home conditions possible.

Why is it, then, in the face of the self-evident fact that maximum prosperity can exist only as the result of the determined effort of each workman to turn out each day his largest possible day's work, that the great majority of our men are deliberately doing just the opposite, and that even when the men have the best of intentions their work is in most cases far from efficient?

There are three causes for this condition, which may be briefly summarized as:

First. The fallacy, which has from time immemorial been almost universal among workmen, that a material increase in the output of each man or each machine in the trade would result in the end in throwing a large number of men out of work.

Second. The defective systems of management which are in common use, and which make it necessary for each workman to soldier, or work slowly, in order that he may protect his own best interests.

Third. The inefficient rule-of-thumb methods, which are still almost universal in all trades, and in practicing which our workmen waste a large part of their effort.

This paper will attempt to show the enormous gains which would result from the substitution by our workmen of scientific for rule-of-thumb methods.

To explain a little more fully these three causes:

First. The great majority of workmen still believe that if they were to work at their best speed they would be doing a great injustice to the whole trade by throwing a lot of men out of work, and yet the history of the development of each trade shows that each improvement, whether it be the invention of a new machine or the introduction of a better method, which results in increasing the productive capacity of the men in the trade and cheapening the costs, instead of throwing men out of work make in the end work for more men.

The cheapening of any article in common use almost immediately results in a largely increased demand for that article. Take the case of shoes, for instance. The introduction of machinery for doing every element of the work which was formerly done by hand has resulted in making shoes at a fraction of their former labor cost, and in selling them so cheap that now almost every man, woman, and child in the working-classes buys one or two pairs of shoes per year, and wears shoes all the time, whereas formerly each workman bought perhaps one pair of shoes every five years, and went barefoot most of the time, wearing shoes only as a luxury or as a matter of the sternest necessity. In spite of the enormously increased output of shoes per workman, which has come with shoe machinery, the demand for shoes has so increased that there are relatively more men working in the shoe industry now than ever before.

The workmen in almost every trade have before them an object lesson of this kind, and yet, because they are ignorant of the history of their own trade even, they still firmly believe, as their fathers did before them, that it is against their best interests for each man to turn out each day as much work as possible.

Under this fallacious idea a large proportion of the workmen of both countries each day deliberately work slowly so as to curtail the output. Almost every labor union has made, or is contemplating making, rules which have for their object curtailing the output of their members, and those men who have the greatest influence with the working-people, the labor leaders as well as many people with philanthropic feelings who are helping them, are daily spreading this fallacy and at the same time telling them that they are overworked.

A great deal has been and is being constantly said about "sweat-shop" work and conditions. The writer has great sympathy with those who are overworked, but on the whole a greater sympathy for those who are *under paid*. For every individual, however, who is overworked, there are a hundred who intentionally underwork—greatly underwork—every day of their lives, and who for this reason deliberately aid in establishing those conditions which in the end inevitably result in low wages. And yet hardly a single voice is being raised in an endeavor to correct this evil.

As engineers and managers, we are more intimately acquainted with these facts than any other class in the community, and are therefore best fitted to lead in a movement to combat this fallacious idea by educating not only the workmen but the whole of the country as to the true facts. And yet we are practically doing nothing in this direction, and are leaving this field entirely in the hands of the labor agitators (many of whom are misinformed and misguided), and of sentimentalists who are ignorant as to actual working conditions.

Second. As to the second cause for soldiering—the relations which exist between employers and employees under almost all of the systems of management which are in common use—it is impossible in a few words to make it clear to one not familiar with this problem why it is that the *ignorance of* employers as to the proper time in which work of various kinds should be done makes it for the interest of the workman to "soldier."

The writer therefore quotes herewith from a paper read before The American Society of Mechanical Engineers, in June, 1903, entitled "Shop Management," which it is hoped will explain fully this cause for soldiering:

"This loafing or soldiering proceeds from two causes. First, from the natural instinct and tendency of men to take it easy, which may be called natural soldiering. Second, from more intricate second thought and reasoning caused by their relations with other men, which may be called systematic soldiering.

"There is no question that the tendency of the average man (in all walks of life) is toward working at a slow, easy gait, and that it is only after a good deal of thought and observation on his part or as a result of example, conscience, or external pressure that he takes a more rapid pace.

"There are, of course, men of unusual energy, vitality, and ambition who naturally choose the fastest gait, who set up their own standards, and who work hard, even though it may be against their best interests. But these few uncommon men only serve by forming a contrast to emphasize the tendency of the average.

"This common tendency to 'take it easy' is greatly increased by bringing a number of men together on similar work and at a uniform standard rate of pay by the day.

"Under this plan the better men gradually but surely slow down their gait to that of the poorest and least efficient. When a naturally energetic man works for a few days beside a lazy one, the logic of the situation is unanswerable. 'Why should I work hard when that lazy fellow gets the same pay that I do and does only half as much work?'

"A careful time study of men working under these conditions will disclose facts which are ludicrous as well as pitiable.

"To illustrate: The writer has timed a naturally energetic workman who, while going and coming from work, would walk at a speed of from three to four miles per hour, and not infrequently trot home after a day's work. On arriving at his work he would immediately slow down to a speed of about one mile an hour. When, for example, wheeling a loaded wheelbarrow, he would go at a good fast pace even up hill in order to be as short a time as possible under load, and immediately on the return walk slow down to a mile an hour, improving every opportunity for delay short of actually sitting down. In order to be sure not to do more than his lazy neighbor, he would actually tire himself in his effort to go slow.

"These men were working under a foreman of good reputation and highly thought of by his employer, who, when his attention was called to this state of things, answered: 'Well, I can keep them from sitting down, but the devil can't make them get a move on while they are at work.'

"The natural laziness of men is serious, but by far the greatest evil from which both workmen and employers are suffering is the *systematic soldiering* which is almost universal under all of the ordinary schemes of management and which results from a careful study on the part of the workmen of what will promote their best interests.

"The writer was much interested recently in hearing one small but experienced golf caddy boy of twelve explaining to a green caddy, who had shown special energy and interest, the necessity of going slow and lagging behind his man when he came up to the ball, showing him that since they were paid by the hour, the faster they went the less money they got, and finally telling him that if he went too fast the other boys would give him a licking.

"This represents a type of *systematic soldiering* which is not, however, very serious, since it is done with the knowledge of the employer, who can quite easily break it up if he wishes.

"The greater part of the *systematic soldiering*, however, is done by the men with the deliberate object of keeping their employers ignorant of how fast work can be done.

"So universal is soldiering for this purpose that hardly a competent workman can be found in a large establishment, whether he works by the day or on piece work, contract work, or under any of the ordinary systems, who does not devote a considerable part of his time to studying just how slow he can work and still convince his employer that he is going at a good pace.

"The causes for this are, briefly, that practically all employers determine upon a maximum sum which they feel it is right for each of their classes of employees to earn per day, whether their men work by the day or piece.

"Each workman soon finds out about what this figure is for his particular case, and he also realizes that when his employer is convinced that a man is capable of doing more work than he has done, he will find sooner or later some way of compelling him to do it with little or no increase of pay.

"Employers derive their knowledge of how much of a given class of work can be done in a day from either their own experience, which has frequently grown hazy with age, from casual and unsystematic observation of their men, or at best from records which are kept, showing the quickest time in which each job has been done. In many cases the employer will feel almost certain that a given job can be done faster than it has been, but he rarely cares to take the drastic measures necessary to force men to do it in the quickest time, unless he has an actual record proving conclusively how fast the work can be done.

"It evidently becomes for each man's interest, then, to see that no job is done faster than it has been in the past. The younger and less experienced men are taught this by their elders, and all possible persuasion and social pressure is brought to bear upon the greedy and selfish men to keep them from making new records which result in temporarily increasing their wages, while all those who come after them are made to work harder for the same old pay.

"Under the best day work of the ordinary type, when accurate records are kept of the amount of work done by each man and of his efficiency, and when each man's wages are raised as he improves, and those who fail to rise to a certain standard are discharged and a fresh supply of carefully selected men are given work in their places, both the natural loafing and systematic soldiering can be largely broken up. This can only be done, however, when the men are thoroughly convinced that there is no intention of establishing piece work even in the remote future, and it is next to impossible to make men believe this when the work is of such a nature that they believe piece work to be practicable. In most cases their fear of making a record which will be used as a basis for piece work will cause them to soldier as much as they dare.

"It is, however, under piece work that the art of systematic soldiering is thoroughly developed; after a workman has had the price per piece of the work he is doing lowered two or three times as a result of his having worked harder and increased his output, he is likely entirely to lose sight of his employer's side of the case and become imbued with a grim determination to have no more cuts if soldiering can prevent it. Unfortunately for the character of the workman, soldiering involves a deliberate attempt to mislead and deceive his employer, and thus upright and straightforward workmen are compelled to become more or less hypocritical. The employer is soon looked upon as an antagonist, if not an enemy, and the mutual confidence which should exist between a leader and his men, the enthusiasm, the feeling that they are all working for the same end and will share in the results is entirely lacking.

"The feeling of antagonism under the ordinary piece-work system becomes in many cases so marked on the part of the men that any proposition made by their employers, however reasonable, is looked upon with suspicion, and soldiering becomes such a fixed habit that men will frequently take pains to restrict the product of machines which they are running when even a large increase in output would involve no more work on their part."

Third. As to the third cause for slow work, considerable space will later in this paper be devoted to illustrating the great gain, both to employers and employees, which results from the substitution of scientific for rule-of-thumb methods in even the smallest details of the work of every trade. The enormous saving of time and therefore increase in the output which it is possible to effect through eliminating unnecessary motions and substituting fast for slow and inefficient motions for the men working in any of our trades can be fully realized only after one has personally seen the improvement which results from a thorough motion and time study, made by a competent man.

To explain briefly: owing to the fact that the workmen in all of our trades have been taught the details of their work by observation of those immediately around them, there are many different ways in common use for doing the same thing, perhaps forty, fifty, or a hundred ways of doing each act in each trade, and for the same reason there is a great variety in the implements used for each class of work. Now, among the various methods and implements used in each element of each trade there is always one method and one implement which is quicker and better than any of the rest. And this one best method and best implement can only be discovered or developed through a scientific study and analysis of all of the methods and implements in use, together with accurate, minute, motion and time study. This involves the gradual substitution of science for rule of thumb throughout the mechanic arts.

This paper will show that the underlying philosophy of all of the old systems of management in common use makes it imperative that each workman shall be left with the final responsibility for doing his job practically as he thinks best, with comparatively little help and advice from the management. And it will also show that because of this isolation of workmen, it is in most cases impossible for the men working under these systems to do their work in accordance with the rules and laws of a science or art, even where one exists.

The writer asserts as a general principle (and he proposes to give illustrations tending to prove the fact later in this paper) that in almost all of the mechanic arts the science which underlies each act of each workman is so great and amounts to so much that the workman who is best suited to actually doing the work is incapable of fully understanding this science, without the guidance and help of those who are working with him or over him, either through lack of education or through insufficient mental capacity. In order that the work may be done in accordance with scientific laws, it is necessary that there shall be a far more equal division of the responsibility between the management and the workmen than exists under any of the ordinary types of management. Those in the management whose duty it is to develop this science should also guide and help the workman in working under it, and should assume a much larger share of the responsibility for results than under usual conditions is assumed by the management.

The body of this paper will make it clear that, to work according to scientific laws, the management must take over and perform much of the work which is now left to the men; almost every act of the workman should be preceded by one or more preparatory acts of the management which enable him to do his work better and quicker than he otherwise could. And each man should daily be taught by and receive the most friendly help from those who are over him, instead of being, at the one extreme, driven or coerced by his bosses, and at the other left to his own unaided devices.

This close, intimate, personal cooperation between the management and the men is of the essence of modern scientific or task management.

It will be shown by a series of practical illustrations that, through this friendly cooperation, namely, through sharing equally in every day's burden, all of the great obstacles (above described) to obtaining the maximum output for each man and each machine in the establishment are swept away. The 30 per cent. to 100 per cent. increase in wages which the workmen are able to earn beyond what they receive under the old type of management, coupled with the daily intimate shoulder to shoulder contact with the management, entirely removes all cause for soldiering. And in a few years, under this system, the workmen have before them the object lesson of seeing that a great increase in the output per man results in giving employment to more men, instead of throwing men out of work, thus completely eradicating the fallacy that a larger output for each man will throw other men out of work.

It is the writer's judgment, then, that while much can be done and should be done by writing and talking toward educating not only workmen, but all classes in the community, as to the importance of obtaining the maximum output of each man and each machine, it is only through the adoption of modern scientific management that this great problem can be finally solved. Probably most of the readers of this paper will say that all of this is mere theory. On the contrary, the theory, or philosophy, of scientific management is just beginning to be understood, whereas the management itself has been a gradual evolution, extending over a period of nearly thirty years. And during this time the employees of one company after another, including a large range and diversity of industries, have gradually changed from the ordinary to the scientific type of management. At least 50,000 workmen in the United States are now employed under this system; and they are receiving from 30 per cent. to 100 per cent. higher wages daily than are paid to men of similar caliber with whom they are surrounded, while the companies employing them are more prosperous than ever before. In these companies the output, per man and per machine, has on an average been doubled. During all these years there has never been a single strike among the men working under this system. In place of the suspicious watchfulness and the more or less open warfare which characterizes the ordinary types of management, there is universally friendly cooperation between the management and the men.

Several papers have been written, describing the expedients which have been adopted and the details which have been developed under scientific management and the steps to be taken in changing from the ordinary to the scientific type. But unfortunately most of the readers of these papers have mistaken the mechanism for the true essence. Scientific management fundamentally consists of certain broad general principles, a certain philosophy, which can be applied in many ways, and a description of what any one man or men may believe to be the best mechanism for applying these general principles should in no way be confused with the principles themselves.

It is not here claimed that any single panacea exists for all of the troubles of the working-people or of employers. As long as some people are born lazy or inefficient, and others are born greedy and brutal, as long as vice and crime are with us, just so long will a certain amount of poverty, misery, and unhappiness be with us also. No system of management, no single expedient within the control of any man or any set of men can insure continuous prosperity to either workmen or employers. Prosperity depends upon so many factors entirely beyond the control of any one set of men, any state, or even any one country, that certain periods will inevitably come when both sides must suffer, more or less. It is claimed, however, that under scientific management the intermediate periods will be far more prosperous, far happier, and more free from discord and dissension. And also, that the periods will be fewer, shorter and the suffering less. And this will be particularly true in any one town, any one section of the country, or any one state which first substitutes the principles of scientific management for the rule of thumb.

That these principles are certain to come into general use practically throughout the civilized world, sooner or later, the writer is profoundly convinced, and the sooner they come the better for all the people.

Reading 3

Compassion Song

The song "Compassion" was written and performed by a volunteer board member of a nonprofit organization serving families experiencing poverty, violence, homelessness, and other crises. The song expresses gratitude and hope for the organization on its 10-year anniversary, while at the same time acknowledging overwhelming social problems. How does an artistic expression such as a piece of music allow us to experience social issues at deeper levels, beyond words? How might a song "speak" to an audience of donors, board members, volunteers, community leaders, clients, or even social workers, in ways that a brochure, newspaper article, website or other written piece cannot? Students may have an opportunity to play or sing the song, an old Irish fiddle tune called "Joy of My Life" in which the music itself expresses hope that inner joy can be found in spite of hardship. We have printed this traditional tune in case you want to use your instruments or voices to try out the song.

Compassion

To the tune "Joy of My Life," Irish Traditional
Lyrics by Lauren Barron, M.D. Reprinted by permission.

There are houses on Austin you've seen them before
But one stands alone with a sign on the door
The sign says Compassion and you might be surprised
If you knew just a little of what happens inside
It's hard to believe it's been open ten years
That's a lot of hard stories and plenty of tears
But there's joy and there's comfort, there's help among friends
And there's rest 'til the rest of the journey begins

Chorus:
May this house of Compassion continue to be
A welcoming harbor for each refugee
A haven of healing with rooms full of grace
May each soul find the shelter they need in this place

There are women who're broken and kids who've grown old
Most need a bed or a hand they can hold
And some have a "history" but I guarantee
They're a lot more like you than you think they will be

(Chorus)

Whoever, whatever, wherever we've been
Is not as important as starting again
And I can tell you I've seen it—I know that it's real
That the people who live there are learning to heal

(Chorus)

The Joy of My Life
SOURCE: Francis O'Neill: *The Dance Music of Ireland* (1907) no. 79

Reading 4

Taking Theory to Practice

We include the following decision case to give you practice applying the concepts presented. The case is based on an actual practice situation gathered by interviewing a social worker with a Bachelor of Social Work degree. When exploring the case, try formulating the problems, analyzing the information you have, and deciding on potential courses of action. This exploration can be done on your own or in study groups, discussing parts or the entirety of the case, according to how your instructor guides you. The point is to help you learn to apply theory to practice and to develop important problem-solving and critical-thinking skills. Although this case is located within the unit on organizations it may intersect with other areas of practice as well, such as groups, communities, social movements, individuals, or families.

CARLA FIGHTS THE SYSTEM

MARY ANNE POE

It was September 15, 2002, and a sunny Friday afternoon beckoned. Yet Carla Hudson, a social worker with the Women's Resource Center, had one more meeting before the weekend began. One of her clients, Maria Velasquez, was simply not getting the extra help she needed from Head Start, so Carla was on the way to meet Maria's new case manager, Andrea Nichols. Though trying to assume the best, she still wondered whether Andrea would respond any better than the previous worker. *If not*, Carla thought, *their refusal looks like ethnic discrimination!*

WOMEN'S RESOURCE CENTER (WRC)

WRC began in 1975 as a volunteer organization serving women in violent domestic situations. By 2002, WRC had expanded to nine offices offering services in twelve counties in north Alabama. Sonya Vickers had been the executive director for eight years. She supervised a staff of 20, all baccalaureate level workers except for two LCSWs recently hired to do sexual assault therapy. Funding for the agency came from a variety of state and federal grants, United Way, and private donations. Services were offered free of charge. In 2001, WRC responded to about 10,000 crisis calls and provided services for some 4,000 women and their children. The agency staffed a 24-hour crisis line, operated three shelters, provided individual and group counseling, offered hospital and court assistance, and managed a speaker's bureau for community education.

About half of the staff at WRC were Black or biracial, including the executive director. About 70 percent of those served by the agency were White and middle-aged and close to 30 percent of the clients were Black. Very few clients of other racial or ethnic backgrounds called the crisis line or sought services.

The region served by WRC was largely rural. Jasper, the largest town, had a population of 85,000. The overall population in the area was about 65 percent White and 35 percent Black. Only 1–2 percent was Latino or other ethnicities. Just like many regions of the country, though, this area had a growing Latino population, primarily Mexican migrant workers. Schools, clinics, government agencies, and businesses were struggling to adapt to the changes brought by these newcomers. Most of the local Latino population was poor with only limited ability to speak English. Their housing, employment, health, and education needs created challenges for the social institutions and agencies in an area that still struggled to manage sometimes volatile Black/White relationships.

CARLA'S BACKGROUND

Carla Hudson grew up in Jasper, Alabama. She had worked in various social service jobs before finishing her bachelor's degree in social work in May 1999. One of only two Black students in her cohort at a small private college, Carla was well acquainted with the experience of being a minority group member. Furthermore, she was a 30-year-old, nontraditional student in a very traditional setting. She had excelled in the BSW program, though, and graduated with honors. The social work program recognized her skills and her passion for social work by naming her the "Social Work Graduate of the Year." The job at WRC opened for her immediately after graduation.

Carla began her BSW career as a crisis counselor. In more than three years on the job, she had grown and developed professionally. Carla's primary role was to respond to crisis calls and follow up with case management. She listened to the women and their stories and made referrals to various services the agency offered.

After just a short time at the agency, Carla realized that women affected by domestic violence in the surrounding rural area needed a support group. So she started a group on Monday nights. The group had thrived. Carla was an advocate for women affected by violence and her clients easily sensed her commitment to them and to justice. She operated from a strengths perspective that empowered them to regain control of their own lives. Her coworkers saw Carla as a role model—a strong, assertive woman who had overcome her own difficulties with poverty, abuse, and discrimination. They recognized her passion for her work and for making the world a more just place to live.

MARIA VELASQUEZ

As a 24-year-old Mexican immigrant, Maria Velasquez was one of the newcomers that the community of Jasper was struggling to accept. She had two children, ages 6 and 3. Maria moved with her family from just outside Chihuahua, Mexico, to a Mexican immigrant community in Stafford, Virginia, when she was in seventh grade. She and her family became U.S. citizens about three years later. She learned enough English to graduate from the local high school, but still had great difficulty reading and writing it.

Maria had a long history of sexual abuse by her stepfather. One time her mother actually caught the stepfather fondling her. Maria told Carla that her mother just cried and cried, begging her, "Forgive him, forgive him, please." Perhaps these experiences made a relationship with Rodney Johnson, a 21-year-old Black man who was enlisted in the U. S. Army, attractive to her when she was 16 years old. He became her ticket out of an unpleasant home environment. They married when she was 18 years old.

Soon after they were married, the U.S. Army moved Rodney and Maria to Spain for about a year. By this time, Rodney's abuse of Maria had already begun. When she refused sex, he raped her. He used other forms of sexual abuse against her as well as ridicule and threats. She once reported an assault to military authorities while in Spain, but subsequently dropped charges because of his threats. When Rodney completed his service with the Army in 1997, they moved to Jasper, his hometown. Their first child, Lartyania, was just two months old at that point.

MARIA'S FIRST CALL TO WRC

Maria first called WRC three years later, in July 2000. She had just given birth to her second child, a son they named Raul. Maria was napping on the sofa in their living room with the newborn and Lartyania just behind her. Rodney woke her by pouring hot water on her face and shouting at her, "Get your lazy butt up!" He grabbed her arm and slung her toward the front door, leaving the two children on the sofa. Maria scrambled to the door and ran to a neighbor's house and called Debra, the wife of Rodney's brother. She came to Maria and after more arguing and fighting with Rodney in the front yard of their house, she helped Maria get the children and leave. Debra gave Maria the number for WRC and said, "Call these people, they will help you."

Carla was the worker who received the initial call from Maria. She listened to Maria's story and offered various options: Maria could press charges, take out an order of protection, and/or be assessed for admission to one of WRC's shelters. When Maria chose to enter the shelter, Debra brought Maria and the children to the WRC office for the assessment. Carla gave Maria a folder with the policies about the shelter and an application, and encouraged Maria to take her time with them. Carla was at her desk straightening a bit while she gave Maria time to read over the material. After a short time, she noted that Maria had stared for a long time at the papers and shuffled them around. She seemed downcast, almost embarrassed. *I wonder if she's able to read these papers?* Carla mused. With that thought, she got up from her desk and joined Maria at the table.

"I think I am finished with those things now. Let's review this together," Carla said.

Carla carefully read it all to her, being sure that Maria understood the importance of confidentiality and secrecy about the location of the shelter. Maria had no driver's license, transportation, or money. Though Carla had no difficulty understanding Maria's spoken English, it seemed clear that Maria's literacy skills were limited.

Carla learned more about Maria's dire condition as she continued to assess her situation during those first weeks Maria was in the shelter. She talked with Maria almost every day, either at the shelter or by phone, in order to understand Maria's background better. Rodney had prevented her attendance at English classes. He had closely guarded the family's financial business. He was unemployed, but had income from the military that she had known nothing about. He secured loans, used credit cards in Maria's name, and manipulated all their financial matters, making her vulnerable.

Over the next few weeks, Carla assisted Maria with applications for government-sponsored assistance programs. She was eligible for vouchers from Women, Infants and Children's program (WIC), $375 per month in food stamps, and $185 per month from Temporary Assistance for Needy Families (TANF). Maria was Carla's first Spanish-speaking client and Carla had not realized how difficult it could be for clients with little English literacy to negotiate the application process. All the paperwork was overwhelming. Though Carla usually did not go with clients to the Department of Human Resources (DHR) office, she did accompany Maria on occasion because Maria told her that the workers would not explain what she needed to do and she could not read the instructions well. Maria told Carla repeatedly, "The workers act rude to me."

Carla assisted Maria by helping her read applications and complete them. Carla helped her get a job at a hotel and enroll Lartyania and Raul in Head Start. Carla and the other women in the shelter comforted Maria during those long weekends when Rodney had the children for visits. When other women in the shelter helped her learn to drive, she got her driver's license by taking a Spanish language version of the test. Soon, Carla began encouraging Maria to go to school where she could gain reading and writing skills in English.

After living about six months in the shelter, Maria had become stronger. One day she said to Carla, "I think I am ready to go home."

"You do? What do you think will be different now?" Carla responded. *Oh, no! I hope she doesn't decide to go through with this,* Carla thought.

"I think I can manage it now. I feel strong. This place is nice, but it's not home."

"We have group tonight. Why don't you bring it up there and see what the group thinks," Carla suggested.

That night Maria did bring up her plans to return to Rodney. Others in the group were adamant, "Don't go, Maria," they said almost in unison. But this was a decision that only Maria could make. Carla supported Maria's right to choose for herself.

"Each person has to live with her own decisions and needs to use her own judgment," Carla reminded the group when Maria defended her choice to return to Rodney. "We may not think this is the best thing for Maria to do, but she has to decide for herself."

When she was preparing to leave a few days later, Carla encouraged Maria one last time, "Keep your checking account a secret and deposit part of each paycheck without letting Rodney know. And please keep coming to group."

"I will," Maria assured her with a hug.

THREE MONTHS LATER

"I've made a big mistake," Maria sobbed, when Carla answered her call to the crisis line early in April, just three months after Maria had moved out of the shelter. "It's all started up again."

Maria wanted to move back into the shelter. Carla worked on those details after getting assurance that Maria and the children were safe. Carla learned that Maria had kept the promise to keep her money hidden from Rodney and by now had saved a total of $1,500.

In the next few months, Carla counseled with Maria individually and continued to lead the support group that Maria attended. Maria was glad to be back in the shelter. She had changed jobs and was working at Wal-Mart. Carla connected Maria with another local relief agency that helped her secure an apartment and a car. This agency introduced her to a local church group that paid her rent and utilities until she became eligible for Section 8 housing. Maria moved into her own apartment in September, but continued in WRC's support group and stayed in regular contact with Carla. Maria had help from legal services getting a divorce, but she still had to contend with Rodney's having visitation privileges with the children.

Despite the couple's divorce, Rodney's abuse continued and Maria's fears increased. Several times, Rodney followed her car as she left work. Once she had moved into her own apartment, he sometimes called her 20–25 times a day. Another time, he slit her tires and cut the brake lines on her car. He even towed her car from the Wal-Mart parking lot to his house one day. Carla helped Maria get a recording device installed on the phone. With Carla's encouragement, Maria eventually had Rodney arrested for stalking. She got an order of protection. At one point Rodney contacted the Department of Children's Services and reported that Maria was abusing her children. He made visitation times with the children stressful.

In spite of Rodney's harassment, Maria continued to gain confidence and power in her own life. With encouragement from Carla and the women's group, Maria returned to school in January at Jasper Community College (JCC) with the help of a Pell Grant. She started out in remedial classes. She struggled to keep up with her young children, a job, and her school work. After the first semester, Maria found herself on academic probation because of poor grades in her English classes. How could she get some help with her studies? Her teachers had suggested that she get a tutor. They had offered no other help. She could not afford private tutoring.

Maria turned to Carla and the women's support group again for help. Her failure at school was a great discouragement. Carla realized that Maria needed more support in her educational pursuits.

"Have you discussed your problems at JCC with your Head Start caseworker?" Carla asked one night after group. "I think they can provide support for a parent's education."

"They've never offered any help," Maria answered. "I'll ask."

HEAD START

Maria's daughter, Lartyania, had been in Head Start for almost three years. Raul, Maria's son, had also been admitted to the Head Start program. Each family in Head Start was assigned a caseworker who provided an array of social services including referrals, family needs assessments, and crisis intervention. In particular, Head Start provided educational assistance to parents of children in their program when the parent's education or lack of education affected their children.

"My caseworker told me to talk to my teachers at JCC," Maria reported to Carla the next week at group. "I told them I had already asked and that I had even checked on tutoring offered by the school."

"I'll call the caseworker," Carla said. "Maybe I can get some help."

The next day, Carla called the caseworker, Kristin Wilson, to inquire about the situation.

"Tell Maria to ask her teachers at JCC for some extra help," Kristin suggested to Carla. "Maria has a good job at Wal-Mart and doesn't need any more help from us."

"But she has already discussed her problems with her instructors. She can't use the tutoring services there because of her job schedule. Maria can do a lot better helping her kids if she has good language skills. Surely you see this," Carla responded.

THE DILEMMA

For the next several months, Carla's work with Maria focused on trying to help Maria get the education and especially the English reading and writing skills she needed. Kristin seemed continually unresponsive to the difficulties that Maria experienced, even after several conversations with Carla. Maria's teachers at JCC had not extended any extra help either, according to Maria. When she asked them for help, they always referred her to the tutoring services on campus. Carla called JCC to explore what support services were available to students. They had a tutoring program but the tutoring services were not available when Maria could use them. Over time, Carla became convinced that Head Start could be helping with tutoring. She did not understand Head Start's resistance to providing this help.

Finally, Carla decided to advocate more aggressively at Head Start and contacted the Head Start director to present Maria's case. In this conversation, the director assured Carla, "I will investigate and ensure that Maria will get the services she needs and deserves."

A few days later, Maria called Carla and sounded very upset. "Head Start is mad at me. My worker, Miss Kristin, called me today. She fussed at me. She said, 'You got me in trouble with my boss. I told my boss that Head Start had helped you with your rent and utilities and lots of other things. We've got lots of people to help. We have given you lots of help!'"

"I told Miss Kristin," Marie continued, "'But you haven't helped me with rent and utilities. Why would you tell her that?' Then Miss Kristin said to me, 'That doesn't matter right now. Don't discuss Head Start business with Carla any more. We'll handle Head Start business.'"

Carla responded that she would follow up on this for Maria. Curious whether Head Start had provided any help with rent, she asked Maria to bring in all her records about rent and utilities. Although Maria had not been able to read the monthly statements, she had carefully kept them together in a shoebox. When Carla reviewed the records she discovered that Kristin was wrong. According to Maria's records, Head Start had not provided any of this help to Maria. Carla wondered, *Why is Kristin lying? What is the problem over there?*

Carla decided to call Kristin again to plead for assistance with tutoring one last time but Kristin was not in charge of Maria's case any more. She had left Head Start just a few days before for another job. Carla learned that Maria's case had been transferred to Andrea Nichols, and made an appointment for a face-to-face visit the next day. *I'm going to get to the bottom of this,* Carla thought. *Maybe Andrea will be more helpful. I don't like getting in another agency's business, but I think this is discrimination. What other reason than discrimination could it be? Do all Spanish-speaking people in this town have so much difficulty getting services? Maria has had a hard time at almost all the agencies I have helped her with. Maybe I should contact that Latino legal advocacy group in Montgomery. I guess I'll see how this visit goes first,* Carla's problem-solving thoughts rambled on.

Andrea greeted Carla at the appointed time. Once they got settled in Andrea's office, she asked, "Now, tell me again about the problem with Maria. I have known Maria for a while even though she was not on my caseload."

"I am still concerned that Maria is not getting all the services she should be getting. She needs tutoring for her studies at JCC," Carla said.

"Uh, uh, uh, Maria," Andrea mumbled, twirling her long, blonde hair around her fingers as she talked. "Maria can read English when she wants to. She is just not trying. I guess she throws away any messages we send home with her children." Carla was surprised by this response. *How does Andrea know this? She must have talked with Kristin. Those two blondes have decided together not to help Maria.*

"I don't think you understand the difficulty she has. I have worked with her for several years now. She speaks English fairly well. She just can't read it. She can't pass her courses because of it," Carla replied. "Are you going to help her or not? Head Start is supposed to offer these services to parents." Carla was beginning to feel the heat in the room. *They just think we're troublemakers.*

"I don't know what else we can do for someone like Maria. She's just not trying," Andrea said.

"Is there some reason that this Mexican immigrant can't get the services that Head Start is supposed to offer?" Carla asked. "She should have help that she needs with tutoring. Her English reading and writing directly affects her children's welfare. That's what the Head Start parent services are for, right?"

Carla already felt that she was at a dead end with this worker, too. *I wonder what the director thinks about this situation. How can I force the system to give Maria the help she needs and that they are supposed to offer?*

"She wouldn't follow up on it. She just wants you to do everything for her. They're all like that. She just needs to study more," Andrea summed up her thoughts to Carla.

"So, that's it? That's what you think about it? Well, I guess I will be in touch. I know she needs this support but it doesn't seem like there is any help here," Carla said while getting up to leave. She could hardly see straight she was so angry. *Andrea is a new worker for Maria and she hasn't even given her a chance. This is not the end of the story for me,* Carla thought. *I am tired of hassling with this discrimination. What else could it be?* She did not know what to do next, but she had to take it to the next level. *Should I call the director again? Should I call the Latino legal advocates in Montgomery? Or should I just give up on Head Start and look elsewhere for help for Maria to pay for the tutoring she needs?*

SUMMARY

Our goal for this unit was to assist you in developing your understanding of organizations, especially the following aspects: types of organizations, structure, management, decision making, leadership, culture, and diversity. Drawing on the definition of an organization as two or more people who come together to engage in structured activities for the purpose of achieving a desired outcome, we reviewed several categories of organizational theory. While the early classical theories (such as Bureaucracy, Scientific Management, and Universalistic Management) tended to focus on internal aspects of the organization with an underlying goal of increasing efficiency and productivity, later human relations approaches focused on behaviors and motivations of people within organizations.

We also examined systems perspectives based on the concept of holism and emphasizing the interdependent nature of systems and the importance of considering total system needs. The idea of holism, and viewing individuals and organizations as systems form an important foundation for social work practice, not only with organizations, and other larger systems, but with individuals as well.

While recent approaches to organizations continue to take an open systems perspective and to examine factors that affect functioning, they also address factors such as power, organizational culture, quality, and leadership. Understanding the differences between management and leadership is crucial to a social worker, and we emphasized the importance of diversity and cultural competence in working with organizations.

For further exploration of the early classical theories of organization, in Reading 2 we introduced you to Frederick Taylor's article "The Principles of Scientific Management" (1916), along with Reading 3, a song called "Compassion," about opportunities and challenges faced by modern human services organizations. Analyzing "Carla Fights the System" provides you with an opportunity to practice applying organizational theories and concepts.

We hope that this unit has assisted you in developing your understanding of human behavior in organizations and the importance of such to social work practice. As we noted in the unit introduction, such an understanding is imperative for effective practice with organizations. Even if you do not engage in direct practice with organizations, it will help you function within your organization of employment. It will also serve you as you help clients negotiate the social services system.

REFERENCES

Antonakis, J., Cianciolo, A.T., & Sternberg, R.J. (2004). *The nature of leadership.* Thousand Oaks, CA: Sage.

Austin, D.M. (1988). *The political economy of human service programs.* Greenwich, CT: JAI Press.

Austin, D.M. (2002). *Human services management: Organizational leadership in social work practice.* New York: Columbia Press.

Barron, L. (2004). Compassion (musical recording), Waco, TX.

Berens, L.V., Cooper, S.A., Ernst, L.K., Martin, C.R., Myers, S., Nardi, X.X., et al. (2001). *Quick guide to the 16 personality types in organizations: Understanding personality differences in the workplace.* Huntington Beach, CA: Telos.

Block, P. (1996). *Stewardship: Choosing service over self-interest.* San Francisco, CA: Berrett-Koehler.

Burrell, G., & Morgan, G. (1979). *Sociological paradigms and organisational analysis: Elements of the sociology of corporate life.* London, England: Heinemann Educational Books.

Crainer, S. (1998). *Key management ideas* (3rd ed.). London: Financial Times Professional.

Drucker, P. F. (1954). *The practice of management.* New York: Harper & Row.

Drucker, P.F. (1959). Long-range planning: Challenge to management science. *Management Science, 5*(3), 238–249.

Eagly, A.H. & Carli, L.L. (2004). Women and men as leaders. In J. Antonakis, A.T. Cianciolo, and R.J. Sternberg (Eds.), *The nature of leadership.* Thousand Oaks, CA: Sage, pp. 279–301.

Eagly, A.H. & Carli, L.L. (2007). Women and the labyrinth of leadership. *Harvard Business Review, 85*(2), 62–71, 146.

Elliot, J. & Smith, R. (2004). Race, gender, and workplace power. *American Sociological Review, 69*(2), 365–386.

Etzioni, A. (1964). *Modern organizations.* Upper Saddle River, NJ: Prentice Hall.

Greenleaf, R.K. (1977). *Servant leadership: A journey into the nature of legitimate power and greatness.* New York: Paulist Press.

Greenleaf, R.K. (2003). *The servant-leader within: A transformative path.* New York: Paulist Press.

Hall, R.H. (1996). *Organizations: Structures, processes, and outcomes* (6th ed.). Englewood Cliffs, NJ: Prentice Hall.

Hardina, D., Middleton, J., Montana, S., & Simpson, R.A. (2007). *An empowering approach to managing social service organizations.* New York: Springer.

Hasenfeld, Y. (1992). The nature of human service organizations. In: Y. Hasenfeld (Ed.), *Human services as complex organizations.* Newbury Park, CA: Sage, pp. 3–23.

Hassard, J. (1993). *Sociology and organization theory.* New York: Cambridge University Press.

Hyde, C. (2003). Multicultural organizational development in nonprofit human service agencies: View from the field. *Journal of Community Practice 11*(1), 39–59.

Katz, D. & Kahn, R.L. (1966). *The social psychology of organizations.* Hoboken, NJ: Wiley.

Kettner, P. (2002). *Achieving excellence in the management of human service organizations.* Boston: Allyn & Bacon.

Kotter, J.P. (1990). *A force for change: How leadership differs from management.* New York: Free Press.

Kotter, J.P. (1999). *On what leaders really do.* Cambridge, MA: Harvard Business School Press.

Kroeger, O., Theusen, J.M., & Rutledge, H. (2002). *Type talk at work: How the 16 personality types determine your success on the job* (rev. ed.). New York: Dell.

Licht, W. (1995). *Industrializing America.* Baltimore: Johns Hopkins University Press.

March, J., & Simon, H. (1993). *Organizations* (2nd ed.). Cambridge, MA: Blackwell.

Martin, L.L. (1993). *Total Quality Management in human service organizations. Sage Human Services Guide 67*. Newbury Park, CA: Sage.

Mayo, E. (1960). The human relations of an industrial civilization. New York: Viking Press.

McGregor, D. (1960). The human side of enterprise. New York: McGraw-Hill.

McGregor, D. (1966). The human side of enterprise. In: W.G. Bennis & E.H. Schein (Eds.), *Leadership and motivation: Essays of Douglas McGregor*. MA: MIT Cambridge, Press.

Merton, R.K. (1952). Bureaucratic structure and personality. In: R.K. Merton, A.P. Gray, B. Hockey, and H.C. Selvin (Eds.), *Reader in bureaucracy*. New York: Free Press, pp 361–371.

Netting, F.E., Kettner, P.M., & McMurtry, S.L. (2004). *Social work macro practice* (3rd ed.). Boston: Pearson Education.

Northouse, P.G. (2004). *Leadership: Theory and practice* (3rd ed.). Thousand Oaks, CA: Sage.

Oakley, J.G. (2000). Gender-based barriers to senior management positions: Understanding the scarcity of female CEOs. *Journal of Business Ethics, 27*, 321–334.

Ouchi, W.G. (1981). *Theory Z: How American business can meet the Japanese challenge*. New York: Avon.

Pettit, B., & Ewert, S. (2009). Employment gains and wage declines: The erosion of Black women's relative wages since 1980. *Demography, 46*(3), 469–492.

Pfeffer, J. (1981). *Power in organizations*. Marshfield, MA: Pitman.

Pfeffer, J. (1992). *Managing with power*. Boston: Harvard Business School Press.

Poe, M.A. (2006). Carla fights the system. In: T.L. Scales and T.A. Wolfer (Eds.), *Decision cases for generalist practice: Thinking like a social worker*. Monterey, CA: Brooks/Cole, pp 67–74.

Queralt, M. (1996). *The social environment and human behavior: A diversity perspective*. Needham Heights, MA: Allyn & Bacon.

Raak, A.V., & Paulus, A. (2001). A sociological systems theory of interorganizational network development in health and social care. *Systems Research and Behavioral Health Science, 18*(3), 207–224.

Roethlisberger, F.J., Dickson, W.J., and Wright, H.A. (1950). *Management and the worker: An account of a research program conducted by the Western Electric Company, Hawthorne Works, Chicago*. Cambridge, MA: Harvard University Press.

Schriver, J.M. (1998). Human behavior and the social environment (2nd ed.). Boston: Allyn & Bacon.

Scott, W.R. (1998). *Organizations: Rational, natural, and open systems* (4th ed.). Upper Saddle River, NJ: Prentice Hall.

Simon, H.A. (1976). *Administrative behavior: A study of decision-making processes in administrative organization* (3rd ed.). New York: Free Press.

Smith, D. (1997). Women and leadership. In Northouse, P.G. (Ed.), *Leadership: Theory and practice*. Thousand Oaks, CA: Sage, pp 204–226.

Sofer, C. (1972). *Organizations in theory and practice*. New York: Basic Books.

Soni, V. (1999). Morality vs. mandate: Affirmative action in employment. *Public Personnel Management, 28*(4), 577–594.

Takei, I., & Sakamoto, A. (2008). Do college-educated, native-born Asian Americans face a glass ceiling in obtaining managerial authority. *Asian American Policy Review, 17*, 73–85.

Taylor, F.W. (1911). *The principles of scientific management*. New York: Norton.

Taylor, F.W. (1916, December). *The principles of scientific management. Bulletin of the Taylor Society.*

Thomas, R.R. (1991). *Beyond race and gender: Unleashing the power of your total work force by managing diversity*. New York: AMACOM.

Thomas, R.R. (2001). From Affirmative Action to affirming diversity. *In: Harvard Business Review on Managing Diversity*. Cambridge, MA: Harvard Business School Press, pp. 1–32.

von Bertalanffy, L. (1968). *General systems theory*. New York: Braziller.

Walton, M. (1986). *The Deming management method*. New York: Dodd, Mead.

Weaver, H. (1992) African-Americans and social work: An overview of the Ante-Bellum through progressive eras *Journal of Multicultural Social Work, 2*(4), 91–102.

Whitchurch, G.G. & Constantine, L.L. (1993). Systems theory. In: P.G. Boss, W.J. Doherty, R. LaRossa, W.R. Schumm, & S.K. Steinmetz (Eds.), *Sourcebook of family theories and methods: A contextual approach*. New York: Plenum Press, pp 135–163.

Yamane, L. (2002). Native-born Filipina/o Americans and labor market discrimination. *Feminist Economics, 8*, 125–144.

UNIT III

Communities

LEARNING OBJECTIVE

To expose students to the basic concepts needed for a foundational understanding of types, functions, elements, and strengths of communities so that they may apply theories and concepts about communities to a practice case, and connect knowledge about human behavior in communities to other social work courses.

INTRODUCTION

The focus of this unit is on communities and their role in the social environment. The unit begins with the basic concepts of community, including definitions, community types, community functions, population, social class, ethnicity, neighborhoods, economy, values, power structures, relationships, and strengths. A thorough understanding of each of these concepts is essential to developing the knowledge necessary for competent community practice. This unit also includes a section designed to help you connect the content to social work practice.

Unit 3 includes several supplemental readings to illustrate the main concepts presented. In the 1960s and 1970s, as community development became a concern of more and more social workers, Roland Warren was one of the foremost sociologists thinking about communities. Social workers of the 21st century need to be familiar with this period of social welfare history and this primary source article, "The Good Community—What Would It Be?" (1970), provides an interesting and thorough discussion of the issues of the time. Taking a creative look at communities globally, we have provided a photographic essay called "Thriving Communities in Northeastern Africa," created by social work student Amanda Cox. The essay depicts the strengths, resilience, and sense of community that exists in Africa despite the many challenges and social issues. See how many community themes you can identify in each photograph. We end the chapter with the decision case, "Jim's License to Drive," which will allow you to practice applying what you have learned about communities and use a practitioner's critical-thinking skills.

Our hope is that this unit will provide you with a solid understanding of communities that will assist you in building your knowledge and skills related to community practice. Whether or not your practice is defined specifically as "community practice," the knowledge and skills related to communities are essential for you to understand the community context of any client or client system.

Reading 1

Human Behavior in Communities

As we noted in the chapter on organizations, you may very likely begin your social work career as an employee of a human services organization that focuses on delivering services to individuals and families rather than macro systems (organizations and communities). So, as with organizations, you may wonder why it is important for all social workers to develop an understanding of communities. First of all, each of your clients will belong to at least one community, which constitutes an aspect of their social environment. Since we approach clients holistically, considering a community's impact on your client is just as important as examining any other aspect of the client's environment. In fact, a client's success may hinge on the social worker's ability to assist in changing various aspects of the community, such as structure, economy, and policies.

It is also likely that through the course of working with individuals or families, you will discover that your clients share common issues. Being a curious social worker, you would ask yourself "Is the commonality coincidental or due to environmental factors or issues?" If you find the latter to be true, then the appropriate action would include working with the clients individually to address their issues and the larger group to change the environment. For example, let us revisit the scenario presented in the previous unit on organizations.

You are a case manager in a community-based children's outpatient mental health clinic who is responsible for initial assessments, treatment planning, evaluation, and coordination of services provided by the clinic and other service providers. The majority of your clients are from low- to middle-income households. Historically, their parents have been able to provide for their basic needs, such as housing, food, clothing, and healthcare. However, over the past 3 months you have noticed that the percentage of your clients who do not have consistent access to basic necessities has risen from 10% to 60%. Recognizing that this situation is most likely due to more than coincidence, you decide to investigate. Your investigation reveals that the majority of the households consisted of at least one income earner who was employed at one of two local manufacturing companies. Both companies have been impacted by a steady decline in the regional economy and have responded by reducing their production and workforce. The regional workforce is currently unable to absorb all of the displaced employees and local sources of formal assistance are limited.

How would you handle the above situation? Based on the information provided, the primary concern is the inability of parents to meet the needs of their children. Therefore, your interventions should focus on meeting basic needs. This could be accomplished through formal and informal sources of mutual support, which we will discuss later in this chapter. But, what if the sources of mutual support are inadequate or nonexistent? In such a situation, you would work with your clients and other groups in the community to develop such resources. While this approach addresses your clients' immediate concerns, it does not address the underlying issues. How might you contribute to strengthening the economy or diversifying the workforce? Both of these endeavors would require interventions at the local and regional levels. Planning and implementing such interventions is complicated and requires a solid understanding of groups, organizations, interorganizational relationships and communities.

In addition to its importance in addressing the issues we identify through the course of practice with individuals and families, an understanding of communities and community practice is supported by social work values and ethics. Take a moment to contemplate your previous discussions about social work values and ethics. What values and ethical principles are related to practice with larger systems?

One of the most important connections is to social and economic justice, which is defined as equal access to social and economic resources. Think about a community you grew up in or lived in for at least 2 years. Did every member of the community have equal access to social and economic resources? Unfortunately, the answer is most likely no. Reversing such inequities is most often initiated through changes in organizations, communities, and policies. These changes may be brought about through community practice and social movements.

Our goal for this reading is to expose you to the basic concepts needed to help you develop a foundational understanding of communities. Such an understanding will provide a solid foundation for content related to practice with communities and other macro systems. Topics to be addressed include defining communities, types of communities, the various aspects of communities, and community strengths or assets.

WHAT IS A COMMUNITY?

Before reading further, take a moment to think about the concept of community and answer the following questions: How would you define community and what elements constitute a community? Please write out your answer, as we will ask you to refer it in the following discussions on defining community and types of communities.

Defining Community

As with any concept, there are many definitions for community, several of which are provided below. Consider the following definitions and think about how they relate to your definition.

- "A community exists when a group of people form a social unit based on location, interest, identification, or some combination of these characteristics" (Fellin, 2001, p. 1).

- "It is groups of people who sense a common identity, bond with one another, and become attached to or affiliated with through regular interaction" (Longres, 2008, p. 78).

- Community "includes individuals, groups, organizations, and families; shared interests; regular interaction to fulfill shared interests through informal and formally organized means; and some degree of mutual identification among members as belonging to the collective" (Schriver, 1998, p. 475).

- "A community may be defined as a locality in which people share common ties and engage in interrelated activities." (Queralt, 1996, p. 223).

- Community is "that combination of social units and systems that perform the major social functions having locality relevance" (Warren, 1978, p. 9).

- "People who live within a geographically defined area and who have social and psychological ties with each other and with the place where they live" (Mattessich & Monsey, 2001, p. 6).

Now, compare the above definitions with the definition you wrote. What are the similarities and differences?

Netting, Kettner, and McMurtry (2004) noted that despite the numerous definitions of community, common elements exist, including space, people, interaction, and shared identity.

Based on our experience with social work students, we would venture to say that most of you based your conceptualization of community on a city, town, or neighborhood of which you either are or were a member. Many people define and think about communities in the context of location. In fact, this chapter will focus on communities of location. However, nonplace communities can be formed around a common identity or interest. We will discuss the types of communities later in this section, but before doing so we will discuss the broader context of community.

Let us return to the example provided in the introduction for this chapter and approach it from a systems perspective. The community mentioned in the case study can be treated as a system that consists of various subsystems (individuals, families, groups, and organizations). The community can also be approached as a subsystem of a larger system, such as a county or parish. The counties or parishes serve as subsystems of the state. Following this logic, we can carry this example to the national and international levels. In the international or global context, the United States and other nations are subsystems that form a global community. Therefore, the community is a system that exists in an environment consisting of systems (local, county/parish, state, national, and international systems) which directly and/or indirectly impact its functioning. In other words, international, national, state, and county/parish issues can affect the local community's ability to function. Given this, when we examine a local community, we must consider the subsystems that constitute the community, as well as the larger systems that form its environment.

While keeping the above discussion and example in mind, answer the following question: What current state, national, and international factors might impact the local economy, workforce, and sources of formal assistance? In general, potential factors might include the economy, politics, social problems, as well as political, economic, and religious ideologies. Now, assume you are tasked with planning an intervention to address the local economy, workforce, and formal assistance. Why should you consider the external factors identified? In most cases, failure to address environmental factors will negatively impact the likelihood of successfully addressing the issue. Thus, we must consider the issue in the broader context when planning and implementing community interventions. Now that you have considered various definitions and perspectives of communities, we want to focus your attention on some specific types of communities.

Competency Connection

Communities in Social Work Practice: Common Techniques of Community Organizing from ACORN

The Association of Community Organizations for Reform Now (ACORN) is a national coalition of community organizations that "seek social justice for low-to-moderate income families" (ACORN, n.d.). ACORN works to improve housing conditions by rallying for programs that "offer grants to homeowners for repairs, and discount utility rates to the poor."

ACORN advocates for families to obtain fair and affordable mortgage rates, and works to strengthen communities by appealing to local banks to reinvest in community development projects within economically disadvantaged neighborhoods. ACORN also works to improve the quality of education of poor children by advocating for lower student-to-teacher ratios, increased funding for remodeling campuses, and better educational supplies and equipment.

ACORN is also a strong supporter of living wage campaigns, which involves putting pressure on "companies who receive public funded grants and contracts to incorporate living wage ordinances." Implementing living wage ordinances would allow employees to earn wages that exceed the national minimum wage. Increased incomes would provide workers with more money to pay their rent and utility bills and more money to provide clothing and food for their families. In order to bring living wage ordinances to fruition,

activists are seeking research reports and data to help them determine proposed living wage rates. These studies will show how living wages will impact communities and their workers. Detailed information will outline the costs and benefits on local and state levels. Data will show how living wages will impact workers who are living below the poverty line. For instance, studies will point out how proposed living wages would affect workers who are receiving housing subsidies, food stamps, and/or Temporary Assistance for Needy Families (TANF) by showing whether or not their benefits will be decreased or whether or not these workers will earn enough money to sufficiently live welfare-free. Likewise, evaluation research studies need to be conducted on cities and states that have already enacted living-wage ordinances. These reports will demonstrate how living wages are making economies stronger and how living wages have empowered workers to live a better quality of life. Check out ACORN's Living Wage Resource Center at http://livingwagecampaign.org to view current living wage research reports and for information and resources on how to initiate and develop new living wage campaigns.

SOURCE: ACORN.org (Association of Community Organizations for Reform Now) http://acorn.org.

Types of Communities

As previously discussed, community is commonly conceptualized as being tied to or bound by a specific geographical location. These communities are referred to as "communities of location." However, location is not a necessary element of community. Nonplace or nongeographical communities are tied by common identities or interests that may or may not be tied to a geographical area. Examples of nonplace communities include communities of identification, communities of interest, and virtual communities. These types of communities and personal communities will be discussed below.

Communities of Location.   A community of location is a "collective group of people living in a common place such as a neighborhood, town, city or metropolitan area" (Fellin, 2001, p. 49). Communities of location are also referred to as geographical, spatial, territorial, locality-based, and place communities (Fellin, 2001; Netting et al., 2004). The key element of a community of location is that it exists only in a specific space or geographical location. Examples of communities of location include neighborhoods, barrios, *colonias*, enclaves, slums and ghettos, boroughs, villages, towns, cities, and metropolitan areas. Membership in a community of location is determined by community boundaries, such as town or city limits and county lines. The boundaries are typically set and enforced by government entities. The boundaries are often imaginary lines identified by marker, such as a city limit sign. Geographical features may also serve as boundaries. For example, a river, the Rio Grande, serves as part of the United States–Mexico border.

Communities of Identification.   A community of identification is a nonplace community "based on common individual and group features such as ethnicity and culture, race, religion, lifestyle, ideology, sexual orientation, ability, or social class" (Fellin, 2001, p. 50). Members tend to be bound by a sense of common identity and view themselves as a member of the group (Fellin, 2001). In other words, members are self-identified, rather than being labeled a member by another. Communities of identification include communities based on social class, ethnicity, religion, gender, and sexual orientation (Fellin, 2001). It is important to note that communities of identification may be tied to a place or location, such as neighborhoods based on social class or ethnicity.

Communities of Interest.   A community of interest is a nonplace community "based on common interest and objectives, such as professional associations, occupational groups, and advocacy or social movement organizations" (Fellin, 2001, p. 57). Communities of interest are considered a subtype of communities of identification, the difference being that communities of interest have a narrower focus (Fellin, 2001).

Virtual Communities.   A relatively new type of nonplace community is the virtual community, which is a community based on relationships established and maintained via the Internet, e-mail, listservs, discussion boards, social networking websites, chat rooms, and other such methods of communication. As social workers, we should be concerned about the barriers to accessing and participating in such communities. Many people also lack the required knowledge and skills to participate in these communities. And, not everyone has access to a computer and Internet connection.

While the availability of public computers is steadily increasing in urban areas, many rural areas are far behind in technology. Public computers may be located too far away for residents to access them regularly. Many rural areas may not have access to high-speed Internet service, limiting them to dial-up service. Virtual communities offer many benefits, but we need to be mindful of the barriers and their potential impact on our clients. We also need to consider issues of confidentiality as it relates to technology.

Personal Community.   A personal community consists of all the communities to which a person belongs, including location, identification, interest, and virtual. Since the combination of memberships and the meaning assigned to them varies from one person to the next, each individual's personal community is unique (Netting et al., 2004). In the context of individual practice, it is important to understand your client's various communities, the expectations associated with membership and their impact on his or her life. When working with larger systems, personal communities will help you understand individual and group motivations. In both cases, personal communities may serve as either a strength or as a potential source of conflict.

UNDERSTANDING COMMUNITIES

Now that you have a better understanding of what constitutes a community, we want to focus our discussion on communities of location. We have chosen a few that we believe are of particular importance to you as a generalist social worker, such as the functions of a community, population, social class, ethnicity, neighborhoods, economy, values, and power structures. We will also discuss several concepts related to community relationships, including *gemeinschaft, gesellschaft,* civic responsibility, and social capital.

Community Functions

As with any social system, a community's health and survival is dependent on its ability to meet the needs of its subsystems. Warren (1978) proposed that an ideal community carries out functions through which it is able to meet the needs of all its members. He identified five specific functions: production, distribution, and consumption; socialization; social control; social participation; and mutual support.

Production, Distribution, and Consumption. This function involves the production of goods and services that are necessary for the survival of the community and its members. Goods and services may be produced by individuals, families, local businesses, and/or businesses located in other geographical regions. Although the majority of goods and services were once produced by families and local businesses, this changed around the turn of the 20th century. Today, we are mostly dependent on others to produce and distribute the goods and services we need, many of which are imported from outside the community. For instance, most of us buy produce (fruits and vegetables) at a local grocery store, where it is imported from outside the community, rather than a local farmers' market. As we purchase local goods and services, businesses acquire the financial resources they need to continue producing and distributing goods and services. This cyclical process is the basis of the local economy. Changes in the local economy that impact our ability to consume goods can upset this delicate balance, which can threaten the community's ability to provide for its members. We will discuss local economy later in the chapter.

Socialization. Socialization is "the process through which individuals, through learning, acquire the knowledge, values, behavior patterns of their society and learn behavior appropriate to the various social roles that their society provides" (Warren, 1978, p. 177). The primary systems for socializing children and adolescents are the family and school, but children are also influenced by their peers and the media. Socialization continues into adulthood and is carried out by various systems in the community. Religious organizations serve this purpose as well; for example, Hasidic Jewish children are socialized by the passing down of their traditions values, beliefs, and customs through the church, community, and family.

Social Control. Warren (1978) defines social control as "the process through which a group influences the behavior of its members toward conformity with its norms" (p. 181). The group ensures conformity by codifying the norms and consequences for violating them, which are implemented by institutions. For example, law enforcement agencies enforce laws dictating how vehicles are to be operated on public roadways. More subtle forms of social control are also present in the community. Many social services and assistance programs require recipients to comply with expectations in order to receive benefits. For example, single mothers seeking assistance via TANF are expected to identify the father(s) of their child(ren). This requirement is driven by the expectation that fathers should provide for or support their children. What other forms of social control can you identify?

Social Participation. Communities provide many opportunities for members to associate or interact with one another. Such opportunities can be classified as informal or formal. Informal social participation typically occurs via groups based on family (immediate and extended) or friendship. Opportunities for formal social participation are provided by a variety of formal groups that are based on various aspects of the community, such as economic issues, government, planning, housing, education, and recreation (Warren, 1978). Specific examples include service organizations, homeowners associations, team sports, and parent–teacher organizations. Social participation would also include community-wide social events, such as festivals, parades, etc. Think about the community in which you currently reside: what opportunities for informal and formal social participation exist? Are they equally accessible to all members of the community?

Mutual Support.   Mutual support refers to assistance provided to community members in times of stress or crisis. The source of such could be any number of things, including health issues, loss of income, and homelessness. Members may seek assistance from formal or informal sources of mutual support. Formal mutual support includes assistance provided by formal community organizations, the most common being social services agencies such as community mental health services, homeless shelters, food pantries, and community health clinics. When examining formal mutual support in a community, it is important to identify the available resources and those that are noticeably absent. We should also consider the accessibility of existing services and the community's overall attitude towards formal assistance.

Informal mutual support or assistance is provided via informal networks, such as those based on family or friendship, for example, a teenager who voluntarily mows the grass for his elderly neighbor. How might you use various types of formal and informal mutual support to address issues in your community?

Demographics

Demography is the scientific study of a population; it examines a variety of characteristics, including age, ethnicity, occupation, education, gender, and residence (Thio, 1992). Demographics can determine why people choose to live where they live in regard to location, physical appearance of the neighborhood, social and economic characteristics, and prevailing business practices (Fellin, 2001). Before discussing these and other relevant demographic categories, we want to talk briefly about the national census.

U.S. Census.   One of the most common sources of demographic data is the national census that is conducted every decade by the U.S. Census Bureau (USCB). During the first year of every decade (i.e., 1990, 2000, 2010, etc.), the USCB collects a wide variety of information about Americans and their households, including but not limited to age, race/ethnicity, education, income, and employment. The census data is then compiled and used to describe the characteristics of a geographical area. The geographical areas, from smallest to largest, are as follows: census block, block group, census track, place, county subdivision, county, state, division, region, and nation. In terms of local communities, we are particularly interested in the areas that will assist us in describing and understanding a community and its subparts.

- A census block is a geographic area "bounded on all sides by visible features, such as streets, roads, streams, and railroad tracks, and by invisible boundaries, such as city, town, township, and county limits, property lines, and short, imaginary extensions of streets and roads" (USCB, 2000). In urban areas census blocks tend to include a relatively small geographical area, such as a city block. Census blocks in areas of less population density, such as suburban or rural areas, tend to encompass a larger geographical area.

- A block group is a cluster or block of census groups.

- Census tracks are comprised of block groups and are typically comprised of between 1,500 and 8,000 residents (USCB, 2000). Census blocks tend to encompass a relatively small geographical area, but as with census blocks, the area may vary with population density.

- A place is a "concentration of population either legally bounded as an incorporated place or delineated for statistical purposes as a census designated place" (USCB, 2005). Incorporated places include communities that are identified by legal boundaries, such as villages, towns, and cities. Place also includes areas that have been identified by the USCB as a "census designated place" (CDP) or a geographic area that is treated as an equivalent of a place, but is not legally bound. An example of a CDP would be an unincorporated area of a county.

Examining census data from census blocks, block groups and census tracks allows us to make specific observations that would most likely go unnoticed if we considered only place-level data. For instance, looking at ethnicity by census blocks and census tracks allows us to see whether ethnic groups are concentrated in particular areas of the community. We could also look at socioeconomic data in conjunction with ethnicity, which might reveal a relationship between the two. For example, we may find that areas predominantly occupied by ethnic minorities also tend to be occupied by members of lower socioeconomic status. Or, we may find that ethnic minorities and families of lower socioeconomic status are dispersed across the community, indicating a fair amount of integration. While these situations could suggest the presence or absence of discrimination and oppression, it is important to gather additional information before making such a judgment.

Population Size and Density. In addition to describing a population's characteristics, the census data allows us to talk about the size and density of a community's population. Population size is simply the number of people residing within a community's boundaries. Population density is the number of people residing within a geographic area, typically a square mile. Why is it important to talk about density in conjunction with size? Suppose you are studying two communities, both with a population of 30,000 people. However, Community A covers an area of 32 square miles, giving it a population density of 937.5 people per square mile. Community B covers 12 square miles, giving it a population density of 2,500 people per square mile. How might the difference in population density impact the need for and distribution of social services? How might it affect the intensity and scope of social issues? (*Hint:* Think about discussions in earlier courses about the effects of urbanization, immigration, and industrialization on American society in the late 19th and early 20th centuries.)

Urban vs. Rural. Population size and density also play an important role in designating a community as urban or rural. All geographic areas that are located within an urbanized area or urban cluster are classified as urban. An urbanized area is a census block or group of census blocks with a minimum population density of 1,000 people per square mile (Daley & Avant, 2004; Olaveson, Conway, & Shaver, 2004; USCB, 2002). An urbanized cluster consists of census blocks with a minimum population density of 500 people per square mile that are adjacent to an urbanized area (Daley & Avant, 2004; Olaveson et al., 2004; USCB, 2002). Rural areas are defined as any area that is not included in an urbanized area or urbanized cluster.

Whereas the aforementioned definitions use population density to differentiate between urban and rural communities, this is just one of many aspects to consider. Daley & Avant (2004) suggest that we can also talk about the differences between rural and urban areas in the context of culture or lifestyle. For example, suppose an area that is rural in terms of culture and lifestyle is located in an urbanized cluster. In this case, by definition it would be identified as urban. However, if we assume it is urban, but its culture and lifestyle are rural, we may have an inaccurate understanding of the geographic area and its people. Another danger associated with the urban/rural dichotomy is the tendency to view these as monolithic concepts. In other words, you cannot assume that two communities classified as rural will be identical or experience issues in the same manner. The same holds true for urban areas.

Social Class and Ethnicity. Social class and ethnicity are demographic concepts that are of particular importance to understanding communities. Social class groups are communities of identification whose membership is determined by income, occupation, education, and lifestyle (Fellin, 2001). The social class categories include the upper class, middle class, working class, and lower class (Thio, 1992). The upper class, made up of only 1% to 3% of the population but possessing 25% of the nation's wealth, can be subdivided into the upper upper class, or the "old rich," and the lower upper class, or the "new rich" (Thio, 1992). The "old rich" are those who have transgenerational wealth, such as the Rockefeller and Vanderbilt families. "Old money" implies respect, family ties, and social influence. On the other hand, "new rich" include individuals or families who obtained money within their generation, such as Michael Jordan or Bill and Hillary Clinton. This newly acquired money often moves the person into a higher social class, but this new money is often seen by critics as flashy or showy or as lacking experience; they generally garner less respect than the "old rich." The middle class can be further divided into the upper middle class, consisting of professionals and business persons, and the lower middle class, made up of those holding lower-level white-collar jobs. In addition, the working class includes a division of working poor, those who possess little education and few skills and who are generally underpaid for their blue-collar jobs.

Why is this information important to understanding communities? Social class influences the ability of members to provide for their basic needs. It may also influence where one chooses to live, the type of home one lives in, and the community members with whom one associates. Examining these data for an individual provides insight into his or her ability to function. When we consider the information in an aggregate format for a community, we are able to identify differences in the distribution of social and economic resources. We will also develop a better understanding of the overall health and functioning of the community.

Demographic data related to social class may also provide us with some insight regarding social mobility or the degree to which a class system allows for movement between classes. In addition to vertical movement, our class system also allows for lateral or horizontal movement, which occurs when an individual moves from one to job to another within a status bracket. Intragenerational (an individual's movement within the class system) and intergenerational (movement that occurs across generations) also occur. For instance, we often see intergenerational movement when examining the first and subsequent generations of immigrant families.

Upward mobility, or one's ability to advance within the class system, is the basis of the American Dream. While many prefer to believe that every member of our society has an equal opportunity for advancement, this is not the case for many groups. For example, lower socioeconomic groups are often unable to amass the resources necessary to advance, even after several generations of striving. Unfortunately, this is often the case for members of ethnic minority groups, regardless of social class. In fact, Elliot and Smith (2004) found that "relative to white men, all groups encounter increasing inequality at higher levels of power" (p. 365). This is particularly true for African-American women, who experience inequality and have an increasingly difficult time attaining jobs with power as a direct result of discrimination (Elliot & Smith, 2004). Takei and Sakamoto (2008) studied native-born, college-educated members of the labor force and found that Asian-American men supervise approximately 14% fewer employees than comparable nonwhite men. This indicates that Asian-American men battle a glass ceiling with regard to managerial authority. Filipino Americans also face this glass ceiling, as they are less likely to have a managerial role (Yamane, 2002). In fact, Filipino Americans face a significant amount of discrimination within the labor market, based on factors such as gender, location, and educational level (Yamane, 2002). This type of discrimination may be caused by institutionalized racism.

Neighborhoods

Earlier in the chapter we asked you to write down your definition of a community. As you were formulating your definition, were you thinking of a neighborhood? Most of us have either lived in a neighborhood or, even if you come from a rural area, you have been exposed to this concept via television, movies, and literature. So, based on your experiences, what elements or features are present in neighborhoods?

A neighborhood is a community of location that constitutes a subsystem of a larger community, such as a town or city. While neighborhoods vary, common features include residential housing, primary and secondary schools, parks, churches, police stations, and fire stations. Residences are the most common feature of neighborhoods (Fellin, 2001), and their types can provide clues about the inhabitants. For instance, multiple-family dwellings (duplexes, apartments, condominiums, etc.), as well as neighborhoods with many single-family rental properties may indicate that residents prefer mobility because terminating a lease is easier than selling a house. On the other hand, rental properties may indicate that residents do not have the resources to purchase a home because of a variety of factors, including the ability to acquire assets, credit history, and discriminatory lending practices. What might a strong presence of homeownership in a neighborhood indicate?

We may also be able to draw conclusions about the cost of housing from the types of residences in a neighborhood. For instance, homes constructed with wood or composite siding tend to cost less to build/purchase than homes constructed with brick or stone. In many cases, older homes are less expensive than newer homes. Homes also tend to increase in value/cost with increases in square footage. Property value can also be impacted by the neighborhood's proximity to parks, schools, businesses, and industries. Other factors that impact housing costs include availability of utilities (electricity, gas, water, and sewage), sanitation services, roads, and emergency services.

How do residents choose a neighborhood? Individuals tend to choose neighborhoods that are consistent with their lifestyle as determined by occupation, education, and income (Fellin, 2001). Changes in lifestyle, an increased income, for example, may bring a change in a neighborhood resulting from a move from renting to home ownership or from a smaller home to a larger one. Of course, this type of mobility may also be downward, as income decreases. A choice to leave a neighborhood may also be driven by changes in the neighborhood, such as a change in the racial composition of the neighborhood that may prompt members to move. This process is commonly referred to as "succession," or "the replacement of one group by another, usually in terms of race, ethnicity, or religious affiliation" (Fellin, 2001, p. 160). An example of succession is white flight, a process that involves the movement of Caucasian residents from urban neighborhoods to suburban areas, motivated by both racial and nonracial factors, including prejudice, an influx of racial minorities, and issues arising from school desegregation (Fellin, 2001). Succession is of particular interest to us because it can lead to neighborhood segregation, especially when combined with the barriers to movement often faced by ethnic minorities, including finances, housing discrimination, restrictive ordinances or covenants, and zoning ordinances (Fellin, 2001). What other factors might drive the process of neighborhood succession? What social issues, other than neighborhood segregation, might arise from it?

Competency Connection

Communities and Policy Issues

Local zoning laws control neighborhoods and minimize diversity

With legalized racial segregation ending in the 1960s, it is hard to believe that many of today's American neighborhoods still lack racial multiplicity. This is largely due to the local zoning laws that are used to control neighborhoods, often in ways that minimize diversity, while also making a dividing line according to income and social class. Hilfiker (2004) calls this "segregation by class," whereby zoning laws are created to exclude the poor. A possible solution would be for every jurisdiction to mandate affordable housing. The benefit of "integration and social cohesiveness can be

strengths of traditional towns, because they consist of walkable neighborhoods that mix stores and workplaces with housing in every price range" (Hylton, 2003). All families would have access to adequate housing and better jobs, and children of all socioeconomic backgrounds would have equal access to a high-quality education, as more tax money would be invested in schools that typically receive scant funding because of the area being economically disadvantaged.

Hilfiker, D. (2004, May). Still separate, still unequal. *Sojourners Magazine*.

Hylton, T. (2003, January 19). Discourage sprawl: Segregation in Milwaukee. *Milwaukee Journal Sentinel*.

Colonias. Neighborhoods are often formed around a common ethnic identity, demonstrating the intersection of communities of location and identity. A *colonia* is a neighborhood or community located in close proximity to the United States–Mexico border that is characterized by high poverty rates and inadequate utilities and services (Richardson, 1999; Texas Department of Housing and Community Affairs, 2002; Texas Department of Human Services, 1998; U.S. Department of Housing and Urban Development, 2003; Ward, 1999). *Colonias* are present throughout the border region. More than 1450 *colonias* are in Texas, and are home to approximately 500,000 people, 98% of whom are Hispanic (May, Ramos, & Ramos, 2002; Texas Health and Human Services Commission, 2003). The large number of *colonias* in Texas may be due to a lack of comprehensive policy initiatives to address the factors most often attributed to the growth of *colonias*. Unfortunately the growth of *colonias* has not been accompanied by relief of the issues common to Texas *colonias*. These communities continue to suffer from lack of basic services and infrastructure (Ward, 1999); poverty, unemployment, and limited education (Texas Comptroller of Public Accounts, 1999); geographic, social, and economic isolation (Texas Health and Human Services Commission, 2003); environmental waste (May et al., 2002) and substandard self-constructed housing structures consisting of available and affordable materials (Cisneros, 2001; Texas Comptroller of Public Accounts, 1999; Ward, 1999). Why would anyone choose to live in a *colonia*? Simply put, *colonias* offer an obtainable housing option for those who are excluded from the traditional market.

Economy

As discussed earlier, one of the key functions of a community is the production, distribution, and consumption of goods and services. In review, this is a cyclical process that serves to ensure that products and services vital to the community's survival are available. The purchasing of goods and services provides the financial resources necessary for production. It is dependent on the exportation of local products to other regions and the importation of products from other regions. In terms of understanding communities, we are interested in identifying the degree of economic stability and the economy's ability to provide for the basic needs of the community's members.

When seeking to assess the stability of a local economy, one of the key elements is the degree of diversity, or lack thereof, in the economic base. In other words, what specific sector(s) constitute the majority of the local economy? The major industry categories used by the U.S. Bureau of Labor Statistics (http://www.bls.gov) include the following:

- **Goods-producing (excluding agriculture)**—This category includes mining, construction, and manufacturing.

- **Service-producing**—This category includes utilities, wholesale trade, retail trade, transportation and warehousing, information, financial activities, professional and business services, educational services, health care and social assistance, leisure and hospitality, federal government, state and local government, and other services.

- **Agriculture, forestry, fishing, and hunting**—This category includes crop production, animal production, and support activities related to agriculture and forestry.

This information for your community should be available from the Bureau of Labor Statistics, your state Workforce Commission, and your local government. You may also be able to acquire this information from your local Chamber of Commerce or Economic Development Corporation.

So, why is it desirable to have a diverse economy? The narrower or less diverse an economy is, the more susceptible it is to changes in the sectors that form its base. While this is true for all communities, it is easier to see in the smaller ones. So, let us think about a small rural community of approximately 10,000 people. Assume that more than 50% of the local economy is dependent on agriculture, with the majority of that being related to timber. Specifically, timber is grown, harvested, processed (paper and building materials) locally and then exported to other markets. Now, assume that the state and national economy has experienced a steady decline, bringing issues in the housing and lending markets. This has been accompanied by a decline in new-home construction, resulting in a lower demand for building materials. The local impact has been reductions in consumption of raw materials and production. In other words, growers, harvesters, and producers have been affected. As the local economy slows, community members begin to restrict their spending, which impacts the retail and service sectors of the economy. What would happen if it continued to worsen and a local production plant was forced to close? Would the local economy be able to absorb those who were suddenly unemployed? Could the local economy survive the loss of wages? Suppose that timber and related industries comprised only 20% of the local economy. What difference might that make?

In addition to considering the economic base of the community, we also need to examine the community's ability to meet the financial needs of its members. For example, are there ample opportunities for employment? Are community members able to earn a living wage rather than minimum wage? Minimum wage is the minimum hourly wage an employer can pay an employee. Minimum wage is set by federal and state governments and is currently $7.25 per hour (effective July 24, 2009). Of course, there are exceptions to this (for details, go to the U.S. Department of Labor's website at http://www.dol.gov/index. htm). A living wage is the minimum hourly wage an individual can earn and still be able to sustain himself or herself and his or her dependents in the local community. Living wages vary from one community to the next and are usually higher than the minimum wage.

Another important element is the ability of the community to assist those who are unable to meet their basic needs, which is accomplished via formal and informal mutual support. As previously discussed, formal mutual support services are those provided by community and government organizations and informal mutual support is provided by informal networks created by family and friends. In terms of the economy, we are interested in formal mutual support. Of particular interest is the availability and accessibility of services in the local community. We should also be concerned with the community's ability to support such services, especially those operated by nonprofit organizations. Typically, nonprofits are dependent on local donations, which tend to decrease with declines in the local economy. Therefore, their ability to serve the community may be hindered the most when the need is the greatest. Finally, we are interested in the community's attitudes toward giving and receiving assistance, because these attitudes are closely related to its values.

Values

Before talking about values in the context of communities, it is important to define the term. Values are "the customs, beliefs, standards of conduct, and principles considered desirable by a culture, a group of people, or an individual" (Barker, 1999, p. 507). Although we tend to think about and discuss values in the context of individuals, communities also have a central or core set of values to which all members are expected to adhere. The core values are determined and enforced by those who hold power in the community. Community associations and organizations also serve to uphold the community's core values (Netting et al., 2004). Often these core values are based on White Anglo Saxon Protestant values (Fellin, 2001); this singular perspective is referred to as a "monocultural perspective." Thinking about your study of cultural diversity in the social work curriculum, what are some examples of White Anglo Saxon Protestant values?

Whereas power systems in communities often claim a monocultural perspective, this is consistent with neither social work's value of diversity nor the multicultural nature of society. Obviously, there is likely to be more than one set of values in a community and each subsystem in a community will have a set of values that may or may not be consistent with the core values of the larger community.

Why is it important for us to be able to identify and understand community values? Our values affect our perception of our environment, including community issues (Mizrahi, 2002). To demonstrate this, let us return to the community example provided in the section on "Economy." Community groups oriented to the values of self-reliance and work may perceive the solution to unemployment as seeking another job, reducing spending, etc. Groups with this orientation would be less likely to support social programs and government intervention to resolve the issue. On the other hand, groups oriented to cooperation would be more likely to support these actions. Finally, it is important to note that oppression and conflict in the community often result from value conflicts.

Before moving on to community power structures, take a moment to think about a community with which you are familiar. What are the core values of the mainstream community? What subsets of values exist in the community? Are the subsets consistent or inconsistent with the mainstream values? What issues have arisen from differences in values?

Power Structures

Among its various functions, a community's power structure enforces norms and values and plays a role in decision making. Formal community decisions are made by the formal power structure, which consists primarily of the local political system. Local political systems (municipal and county/parish) serve a variety of functions, including service provider (recreation, infrastructure, public safety, and health and social welfare), financial manager, overseeing community decision making, social control, and conflict management (Fellin, 2001). The structure of these systems varies, but in general it includes an executive position (mayor, city manager, and/or county administrative judge) and a council or commission of elected representatives who are charged with overseeing the local government's operation. These members are either elected or appointed by our elected officials. Depending on the size of the community, the local government may also include a variety of departments or agencies that are responsible for fulfilling the various functions. Examples of such include parks and recreation, libraries, police, social services, and public works. The formal power structure might also include other systems, such as education, social services, and businesses.

How might we go about influencing the formal power structure of a community? One of the most important methods is to participate in local government and politics. Some related activities include public hearings, voting, and advocacy. We will talk more about this aspect of the community in the next section. We can also use a community's informal power structure, which consists of community members and organizations who are not a part of the formal power structure but who are able to influence the formal power structure (Fellin, 2001). On one hand, the informal power structure is helpful in that it provides access to the decision-making process. In fact, it may be the only way for a group to have its needs considered. On the other hand, the informal nature of the system may encourage covert activities intended to influence the formal power structure to act in the best interest of a few people rather than for the common good. It may also be used to exclude groups from the decision-making process.

How are these structures important to social workers? First of all, addressing macro-level issues will often require changes in the structures and processes of larger systems. More often than not, these decisions lie with the formal power structure, and social workers may need to participate in the formal process. This means we must have a good understanding of the formal power structure, its processes, and members. We may also find ourselves in practice situations in which participation in the formal process is not enough, so we must use the informal power structure to influence the formal structure. As Mizrahi (2002) explains, "we may utilize these strategies to bring pressure to bear on the structure of authority to convince them to make the needed changes, fund programs, reallocate resources, and so on" (p. 520).

Take a moment to think about a community with which you are familiar. How is the informal power structure used to influence the formal power structure in the best interest of the community? How is the informal power structure used to the detriment of the community? These types of questions form the basis of analysis that will assist you in practice with communities.

Relationships

All communities, regardless of type (i.e., location, identification, interest, or virtual) are dependent on relationships, which we will broadly define as connections within and among systems created through the course of daily activities and functions. As with almost any topic, there are a variety of ways to frame or talk about relationships, including the degree of formality (*gemeinschaft* and *gesellschaft*), the manner in which they are developed (civic and political engagement), the ways in which they are leveraged to accomplish tasks (social capital), and the intersection of social capital, civic engagement and political engagement (civic and moral responsibility). We can also characterize them as internal or external to the community.

Gemeinschaft and Gesellschaft.   One of the most common approaches to thinking about community relationships was offered by German sociologist Ferdinand Toennies in the late 1880s. In his book, *Gemeinschaft Und Gesellschaft*, he proposed that relationships were changing from *gemeinschaft* to *gesellschaft*. *Gemeinschaft* relationships are based on shared traditions and experiences, which foster interdependence and mutual respect. *Gemeinschaft* relationships are most often associated with small communities, such as rural towns, where a large proportion of the members are more likely to interact with one another on a regular basis. Conversely, *gesellschaft* relationships are more formal, task-oriented, impersonal, and often based on a contractual exchange. The formal nature of these relationships may encourage dehumanization or the tendency to view others as objects or assets to be used for gain, rather than as human beings (Brueggeman, 2006). *Gesellschaft* relationships tend to be associated with relationships in urban communities, where intimate interaction at the community level is more difficult. It is also important to note that Toennies attributed the shift from *gemeinschaft* to *gesellschaft* to urbanization. Based on what you have learned in other classes, how would urbanization, immigration, and industrialization contribute to this shift?

Civic and Moral Responsibility.   In more recent times, a significant amount of attention has been given to social capital, civic engagement and political engagement, all of which are elements of a larger concept, civic and moral responsibility. Colby, Ehrlich, Beaumont, & Stephens (2003) describe a civically and morally responsible individual as one who:

> recognizes himself or herself as a member of a larger social fabric and therefore considers social problems to be at least partly his or her own; such an individual is willing to see the moral and civic dimensions of issues, to make and justify informed moral and civic judgments, and to take action when appropriate. A fully developed individual must have the ability to think clearly and in an appropriately complex and sophisticated way about moral and civic issues; he or she must possess the moral commitment and sense of personal responsibility to act, which may include having moral emotions such as empathy and concern for others; moral and civic values, interests, and habits; and knowledge and experience in the relevant domains of life. (pp. 18-19)

In other words, in order to be civically and morally responsible you must recognize your responsibility to the greater community, be willing to engage actively in problem solving, and value democratic and collective action. Such activities require social capital, civic engagement, and political engagement.

The concept of social capital is grounded in the belief that the networks formed by our social relationships have value (Putnam, 2000). Social capital is defined as the "connections among individuals," which include "social networks and the norms of reciprocity and trustworthiness that arise from them" (Putnam, 2000, p.19). Hyman (2002) adds to this definition by recognizing social capital as an asset that can be used to bring about change. Specifically, he states that "social capital is an asset representing actionable resources that are contained in, and accessible through, a system of relationships" (p. 197). One of the most important elements of social capital is reciprocity, or the expectation that a favor given will be returned at a later date. Someone must take the first step, trusting that the favor will be returned. Whereas each returned favor builds trust, each unreturned favor erodes it.

You can use your use social capital for your own benefit, as well as for the benefit of others and the larger community. For instance, let us assume you have agreed to serve on a board of directors for a local nonprofit organization. Through your service you are able to develop several key relationships that result in you securing your dream job. At the same time, you develop new relationships that help the nonprofit organization obtain a significant grant for service delivery. Whereas both of these examples are positive, social capital also has a negative or "dark" side (Hyman, 2002 Portes & Landolt, 1996; Putnam, 2000; Raab & Millward, 2003; Schulman & Anderson, 1999). For example, it can be used to benefit an individual to the detriment of others, exclude individuals and groups from decision making, force conformity, and control access to social and economic resources.

Social networks can be based on bridging or bonding social capital. Social networks based on bridging social capital tend to have a diverse membership and are open to anyone with similar interests. Examples include PTAs (Parent–Teacher Association), Boys Scouts, Girl Scouts, and social movements. The inclusive nature of bridging networks helps to broaden our perspectives by connecting us with others that we are not likely to meet through our regular social structures (Putnam, 2000). On the other hand, networks based on bonding social capital are exclusive in nature and tend to lack diversity. Bonding social networks offer members support, security, familiarity, and solidarity and serve as a source of mutual support. Putnam (2000) likens bonding social capital to "superglue," because it provides the ties that hold the group together. Examples of bonding social networks include country clubs, ethnic neighborhoods, and groups who limit membership to a specific ethnicity (Putnam, 2000). When examining networks, you need to keep in mind that bridging and bonding are not mutually exclusive, a network can possess characteristics of both (Putnam, 2000). For example, an organization could limit its membership to women, but have diversity in terms of socioeconomic class and ethnicity.

Competency Connection

Communities in Social Welfare History

Cesar Chavez and the Rural and Immigrant Worker's Movement

In the 1960s, Cesar Chavez sought social justice for migrant and immigrant farm workers who picked produce in the hot, 100-degree-plus temperatures of the California fields. Most of the workers were illegal Mexican nationals, and many of them did not speak any English. Because they either needed money, or feared deportation, these workers were powerless to approach agribusiness companies. Initially, Chavez found community organizing to be a difficult task. Aside from attending the Catholic Church, the workers were unable to form ties with community agencies, and they had a hard time building cohesive relationships with one another. Chavez began to form clubs where workers could purchase gas and food (Brueggemann, 2002, p. 213). These clubs afforded the workers the opportunity to form social ties and solidarity with one another. Eventually, Chavez was successful in empowering the farm workers to elect club leaders, and to form alliances with community churches and labor unions (Brueggemann, 2002, p. 213). Together the workers were able to stage marches, boycotts, and pickets protesting low wages, long work hours, poor housing, and deplorable working conditions.

Brueggemann, W.G. (2002). Becoming a community organizer. In: *The practice of macro social work*. Belmont, CA: Wadsworth/Thomson Learning, pp 196–220.

Social capital is closely related to civic engagement, which can be broadly defined as your dedication of time and resources to improving your community. Hyman (2002) suggests that civic engagement is a catalyst for the development of social capital. In order to become civically engaged, you must act on your sense of responsibility to the greater community or common good. Vehicles for civic engagement might include mutual support (formal and informal), participation in volunteer organizations, social activities, and political activities. In addition to providing an opportunity to enhance social capital, civic engagement encourages tolerance for gender equality and racial diversity (Putnam, 2000). Unfortunately, there is evidence to suggest that in the United States, we are steadily losing our sense of civic responsibility and concern for the common good (Colby et al., 2003).

Political engagement—active participation in local, regional, state, and national politics—can be exercised in a variety of ways, such as voting, lobbying, and advocating. Sanchez-Jankowski (2002) highlights the importance of such engagement:

> if a country is to maintain its democratic appeal it must teach young people what it means to be both civic minded (knowledgeable and attitudinally supportive of the political system) and engaged (actively involved).... in the case of the latter, they must participate in a way that sustains the health of the body politic (p. 239).

Political engagement in the United States has declined steadily since the mid-1960s, as evidenced by a 25% drop in voter turnout for presidential elections over the 36 years leading up to Putnam's book in 2000. Despite the overall decline, it is important to note there was a sharp increase in voter turnout for the 2008 general election, as evidenced by a turnout rate of 61.7% (U.S. Election Project, 2009).

Why are U.S. citizens so politically disengaged? While there are a variety of factors, trust and influence stand out. For example, during the 1990s, 75% of Americans reported not trusting the government to take the right course of action (Putnam, 2000). Furthermore, U.S. voters tend to believe that voting does not impact government decisions (Dionne, 1992). Simply, many of us have lost faith in the democratic political system and our ability to influence it. As Putman (2000) explains, "We remain, in short, reasonably well-informed spectators of public affairs, but many fewer of us actually partake in the game" (p. 46).

Political and civic engagement provides us with important opportunities to bring about change in policies, organizations, government, communities, and society. Withdrawal only ensures that our voice will not be heard and that the decision-making process will not be representative of the community. Representation is especially important when working with disenfranchised populations. Civic and political engagement is also influenced by one's socioeconomic status and ethnicity (Sanchez-Jankowski, 2002). Despite our understanding of diversity, current models of social capital and civic engagement tend to overlook factors specific to minority communities, such as prejudice, dilution of minority votes, and exclusion from politics (Segura, Pachon, & Woods, 2001). These factors impede the development of interpersonal trust and subsequent formation of relationships within groups, among groups, and with the greater society (Segura et al., 2001). Given that such relationships foster civic engagement, which is critical to resolving macro issues, it is important for us to understand the patterns of civic engagement of specific ethnic groups. We must also be aware of the similarities and differences among such groups.

Internal and External Relationships. To this point, our discussion of relationships has focused primarily on relationships among individuals within the community. While interpersonal relationships are very important, communities are also dependent on both internal and external relationships among families, groups, organizations, and communities. Internal relationships hold the community together and external relationships connect the community to its environment. With this in mind, please take a moment to think about Warren's (1978) five functions of a community outlined above and then identify at least two relationships for each function. Also, try to identify relationships that involve at least one larger system (families, groups, organizations, and communities), as well as internal and external relationships.

Now that you have revisited Warren's community functions, let us explore the example of the lumber-manufacturing plant provided in the section on "Economy." What relationships are necessary to production, distribution, and consumption? Potential internal relationships may include those between the company and employees, local consumers, local businesses, and local government (taxes, regulations, etc.). Potential external relationships include regional timber growers, outside buyers (consumers and businesses), and government (state and federal). How are these relationships important to the overall community? How could the loss of one or more of these relationships affect the community?

VIEWING COMMUNITIES FROM A STRENGTHS PERSPECTIVE

It is human nature to focus on deficits when assessing a situation or issue. That holds true for social workers when assessing a client system. The deficit model is not inherently bad, although there are drawbacks. For example, the deficit model encourages one to overlook strengths or assets and accept deficits and can affect the process of service delivery as well as outcomes (Alcorn & Morrison, 1994; Graybeal, 2001; Templeman & Mitchell, 2004). In other words, the deficit model may encourage clients to view themselves as hopeless, helpless, and not in control. The deficit model also allocates more funding to service providers than the community (Kretzman & McKnight, 1993). A strong focus on service providers could encourage the belief that only the experts have the solutions, limiting the involvement and empowerment of the clients. Finally, the deficit model, often equated with urban social work, tends to overlook important characteristics of the rural community, such as tradition, independence, strong relationships, informal helping networks, and avoidance of formal services or assistance.

In contrast, a strengths or asset model focuses on positive characteristics and how they can be used in a preventive manner, while also addressing current deficits or issues. The underlying philosophy of the strengths/asset approach includes the belief that all clients possess the ability to address their needs, that success is based on client involvement and investment, and that such an approach has longer-lasting results (Blundo, 2001; Brun & Rapp, 2001; Cox, 2001; Graybeal, 2001). Other important themes include importance of positive relationships, development of youth, a common vision, continuous attention and maintenance, and continued use of effective methods (Templeman & Mitchell, 2004). At the community level, residents are viewed as holding the resources and solutions to overcome problems and prevent future issues. The focus then becomes the process of using the assets to strengthen the community, with the role of professionals being one of support and facilitation. Such an approach is congruent with many social work values, including empowerment, self-determination, and education.

The strengths perspective is not without opposition. Critics allege that it merely attempts to maintain positive thinking or view misery from a different context (Saleebey, 1996; Graybeal, 2001). The strengths perspective has also been accused of ignoring objective reality (Brun & Rapp, 2001). Furthermore, the philosophical shift from a deficit model to a strengths perspective is often difficult for students and practitioners (Blundo, 2001). Cox (2001) suggests that some of the difficulty comes from the tendency to view client populations as unable to help themselves. Such a perspective places responsibility for resolving the issues on the practitioner rather than the client. Despite the noted drawbacks to the strengths perspective, at the very least it provides students with a positive alternative to the deficit model that is consistent with social work values and ethics.

Using the Strengths Perspective:
Rural Communities as a Case Example

Based on the above information, one could conclude that the strengths/asset approach to communities is beneficial, but does that hold true for rural as well as urban communities? Each rural area has a unique combination of characteristics, circumstances, and issues and each community is different, but rural areas tend to possess factors that exacerbate the social issues and interfere with efforts to alleviate them. These characteristics may include lack of economic opportunity, limited resources, geographical isolation, lack of public transportation, cultural resistance to outsiders, archaic technology, and scarcity of trained professionals. (Carlton-LaNey, Edwards & Reid, 1999; Daley & Avant, 1999, 2004; Ginsberg, 1993, 1998; Scales & Streeter, 2004). Conversely, rural areas also possess unique characteristics that serve as strengths or assets. Examples of such include natural helping networks, a strong "sense of community," emphasis on self-sufficiency, abundance of personal space, strong family ties, faith-based organizations, interdependence, and intergenerational thinking (Aker & Scales, 2004; Daley & Avant, 2004; Davis, 2004; Murty, 2004; Nooe & Bolitho, 1982). Finally, some characteristics may serve as either strengths or deficits, depending on the situation. Examples include informal decision making, informal power structures, slower pace of life, emphasis on traditional values, preference for acceptance of peers over individuality, geographical isolation, and being closed to outside influence. For instance, is it geographical isolation or plenty of personal space? Is it independence or resistance to outsiders? The strengths perspective appears to be valuable for rural social work practice and rural social work education (Alcorn & Morrison, 1994; Martinez-Brawley, 1980, 1985; Nooe & Bolitho, 1982; Scales & Streeter, 2004; Sherraden, 1993).

CONNECTING THEORY AND PRACTICE

To this point we have discussed the different types of communities, various aspects of communities of location, and viewing communities from a strengths perspective. A thorough understanding of each of these concepts is essential to developing the knowledge necessary for competent community practice. Of particular importance is their relationship to assessment and choosing an intervention. As with any system, the process of assessment requires you to gather information or data about the community that will inform your development of a comprehensive community assessment. Since the assessment will serve as the basis for the intervention(s), it must be accurate, otherwise the intervention is at greater risk of failure.

Given the importance of the assessment process, we want to focus on how the information in this chapter will help you understand a community and develop an assessment. First, consider all of the elements of the community that could be related to the issue. Such elements may include demographics (population, ethnicity, social class, etc.), neighborhoods, housing, infrastructure, economy, values, power structures, civic responsibility, civic responsibility, internal and external relationships, and community strengths. As you gather and analyze this information, it is important to look for the presence of other social issues in the community and their impact. All of this information allows you to determine the degree to which the community is able to function or meet the needs of all its members. In addition, you must identify the community's strengths and begin thinking about how those strengths can be incorporated into the intervention.

Let us revisit the scenario provided in the introduction, in which you are a case manager whose clients are experiencing issues related to loss of employment. You find that the underlying causes are related to the local and regional economy. Therefore, you have two concerns, the immediate situation your clients find themselves in and the larger community issue. Assume that you are able to temporarily assist your clients via case management and referrals to local programs. However, local resources are limited and the current workforce is unable to absorb the newly unemployed workers. Thus, your intervention must also focus on increasing local resources and economic development, both of which will require community-level interventions.

Whereas we have an idea of what our intervention will entail, we cannot tailor the intervention to the local community without more information. For example, suppose we find that the community's core values include an emphasis on mutual support and government involvement in providing for the welfare of its members. In this case, more than likely the community would be willing to take appropriate action to address the issues. This makes the intervention process much easier. How might your intervention differ from the first scenario if the core values included self-reliance and limited government involvement? In general, we would have to begin with activities to educate community members about the importance of developing the economy and resources. What would happen if you assumed the first scenario was the case when in reality it was closer to the second? What other pitfalls might you avoid by possessing a solid understanding of the community before planning an intervention?

In addition to providing an overview of the local community, an assessment gives us a basis to make comparisons to other communities with similar characteristics and issues, thereby helping with the process of identifying an intervention. Using our earlier example, suppose that we found a community that had been successful in addressing issues similar to ours, could we use their intervention in our community? If the two communities are similar, we should be able to transport interventions with minimal modifications. This is important because "reinventing the wheel" wastes time and other important resources. If they are different, we should consider the differences when transporting the interventions. If the differences are significant, we may need to design a completely different intervention.

Whereas this section has focused on assessment, this is just one element of community practice. In order to further assist you with making the connection between theory and practice and to provide a historical view of social work's development of community practice, we have included in our unit an article by Roland Warren. Warren was a sociologist writing in the 1960s and 1970s, when an increasing number of social workers were taking an interest in community practice and community organizing. "A Good Community—What Would It Be?" will introduce you to the theoretical underpinnings, base largely in sociology, that social workers use to understand community contexts.

Competency Connection

Ethics in Community Practice

Ethical Decision-Making for Community Organizers
Social workers serving as community organizers must honor ethical practice principles such as self-determination, informed consent, and protection of confidentiality, all identified in the Code of Ethics of the National Association of Social Workers. However, as Hardina (2004) points out, situational factors inherent in community practice may make application of these principles different than in direct practice. Organizers may use a decision-making framework suggested by Reisch and Lowe (2000) to resolving ethical dilemmas. This framework presents a series of questions to help social workers identify applicable ethical principles, relevant information, and ethical values, as well as potential conflicts of interest. Then, ethical rules are applied and prioritized. Here is the series of questions posed by Reisch and Lowe:

- What are the ethical issues within this practice situation (i.e., issues of principle, rights, duties, and obligations)?

- What additional information is needed to properly identify the ethical implications of the problem under scrutiny?

- What are the relevant ethical rules or ethical criteria that might be employed to help resolve this dilemma?

- If the situation involves a conflict of interest, who should be the principal beneficiary?

- What rank ordering of ethical rules should be used to assist in the resolution of the dilemma?

- What would be the consequences if different ethical rules or a different ranking were used?

- Must the organizer be the one to resolve this ethical dilemma? Under what circumstances could the obligation to make an ethical decision be transferred to another person? To whom might it be transferred in this situation and with what potential consequences? (Reisch & Lowe, 2000, p. 26).

After a thorough examination of these factors, the community organizer determines an appropriate decision. In this way the best interventions are selected while considering social work ethics.

Reisch, M., & Lowe, J.I. (2000). "'Of ends and means" revisited: Teaching ethical community organizing in an unethical society. *Journal of Community Practice, 7*(1):19–38; and Hardina, D. (2004). Guidelines for ethical practice in community organization. *Social Work, 49*(4), 595–604.

Reading 2

The Good Community—What Would It Be?

Roland Warren was one of the foremost sociologists thinking about communities in the 1960s, and 1970s, as community development became a concern of more and more social workers. In this article, Warren describes a good community and nine issues for social workers and other community developers to consider. How do Warren's descriptions reflect the historical times in which this article was written? Consider how social workers might use the work of sociologists like Warren in their practice with communities.

THE GOOD COMMUNITY—WHAT WOULD IT BE?

ROLAND L. WARREN

Although social scientists have been active in addressing themselves to community problems and in engaging in community development efforts, they have produced little systematic thinking regarding the characteristics of a "good" community. Nine issues confront anyone who seeks to formulate a model of a good community under today's circumstances. These are: primary group relationships, autonomy, viability, power distribution, participation, degree of commitment, degree of heterogeneity, extent of neighborhood control, and the extent of conflict.

Not only is there extensive disagreement on what resolution of these individual issues a "good" community would embody, but some research findings indicate that certain commonly-accepted characteristics of a good community—autonomy, viability, and broad distribution of power—may be incompatible. Research regarding such interrelationships can illuminate political decision-making, though it cannot replace it.

From Warren, R., "The Good Community-What Would It Be?" *Journal of the Community Development Society* 1(1), 14-24. Copyright (c) 2000 Taylor & Francis. Reprinted by permission.

When I was writing *Studying Your Community* about 15 years ago, I came across a passage from Josiah Royce which had a great deal of meaning for me so I included it on a separate page at the beginning of the book. It read: "I believe in the beloved community and in the spirit which makes it beloved, and in the communion of all who are, in will and in deed, its members. I see no such community as yet, but nonetheless my rule of life is: Act so as to hasten its coming."

The statement was appealing in its suggestion that there is a good way for us to live together; there is a regard for the whole and a compassion for the individual, a way in which we can treat each other as brothers, a sense of caring and being cared about. I found the image very moving; and I still do. I suppose it is another way of getting at what some of our young people are also seeking to express: that there must be a way to love and to care, but our local communities today fail miserably in measuring up to this simple image of what human life really might be, if we took it—and some of our other professed aspirations—seriously.

In these days when riots break out in our cities, when parents find it difficult to maintain a meaningful relationship with their children, when fluoridation creates violent controversy, when part of the people think that the local community is too conservative and another part think that the old values are being undermined by liberalism and the welfare state, when neither whites nor blacks can agree among themselves or with each other on desegregation or separatism, when the call is for greater federal involvement at the same time as more neighborhood control, and greater rationality and systems analysis for efficiency are demanded at the same time as increased citizen participation in policy-making—few people are thinking in any systematic fashion about what a good community would be if we had one.

How is it possible for citizens working to improve their own communities, or for professional community development workers, to operate effectively? How can they set realistic goals, and measure progress toward them, unless they have, even in general terms, a clear conception of what the community would be like that they are striving for? Let us examine the nine issues mentioned earlier.

1. PRIMARY GROUP RELATIONSHIPS

By way of illustrating the problems involved, let us take the question of the extent to which people may or should really know each other in the community, and should interact with each other on a personal basis. The very ambiguity of the term "community" allows us to sustain some extremely implausible images of what communities should be. For example, when we read in Baker Brownell's *The Human Community* that "A community is a group of people who know one another well," we nod our heads in agreement (1). He goes on to point out that "knowing well" must mean "the full pattern of functional social relationships which people may have with one another." To put this another way, we must know the grocer or lawyer not only as such, but also as persons—whether or not they go to church, how they feel about politics, where they live, how they get along with their family, what they think about the local school, and so on.

At the same time we nod our heads in assent, however, we realize, when reminded, that such *personal acquaintance* among all community people is impossible in all but the very smallest communities. And since more than 70 per cent of our people in this country live in large metropolitan areas, this component of the community—so important that Brownell makes it a criterion of community—becomes largely irrelevant. Brownell acknowledges this situation—but he doesn't have to like it. He writes:

> The great city rises; the human community declines. The stability of
> little places and the ordered rhythm of rural life are lost. The intimate
> faith that this man belongs here in the little group of people known well
> calls only for a "wisecrack" or contemptuous indifference (2).

Three questions may be useful as we examine Brownell's prescription, or prescriptions by others regarding desirable characteristics of a community.

To what extent is the desired characteristic possible under the circumstances of the 20th century living?

How much of any particular good thing do we want?

What is its price in terms of other values?

Brownell's conception of a desirable community does not do well in answering our first criterion: To what extent is it possible under circumstances of 20th Century living? But even if it did, there are those who question whether this small community, where everyone knows his own and everyone else's place, actually is or ever was quite so desirable as many people assume.

Yet the issue is more complex. If both advantages and disadvantages exist in the primary relationships of a tightly-knit neighborhood, this can be extremely important. For example, Zorbaugh pointed out four decades ago that in Chicago it was in the "World of Furnished Rooms," a neighborhood characterized by little primary group contact, where neighbor did not know neighbor, where one was truly anonymous, that there was the greatest freedom from the prying eyes of neighbors, the greatest liberation from small town gossip and back-biting, the freedom to be oneself. At the same time, there was the highest suicide rate of any area in the city, and other social indicators suggested that a price was paid for this freedom. There was little gossip because people didn't care enough to gossip about each other. They also didn't care enough to help out a person if he got sick, or even to know who the neighbor was, let alone knowing or caring if he was sick (11).

The question of how well people should be expected to know each other has relevance today to what may be called the revival of the neighborhood movement, and increased emphasis on neighborhood self-determination. These neighborhoods are each comprised of many components, including the movement toward decentralization, emphasized by the present federal administration, the movement for participatory democracy, and the Black Power movement. The question of how well people should know each other not only illustrates the complexity of the problem of what sort of communities we want, but it illustrates the relevance of the three questions raised concerning any proposed characteristic of the good community.

2. AUTONOMY

The next issue to be considered is autonomy. It is often said that a community should, insofar as possible, be "master of its own fate." Decisions as to what goes on in the community should be made by local people. They should not be made by federal officials, or in the state house, or in the headquarters offices of a national corporation or voluntary association. Rather, local people should have the principal say about business, governmental, and voluntary associations operating in the local community.

Unless the talk about *local community autonomy* is to be empty rhetoric, we must be willing to follow some of its implications. A community which was serious about its own local autonomy would tend to be rather resistant to things which make definite encroachments on local autonomy. Since federal and state grant-in-aid programs often place considerable limitations on such local freedom of choice, a community that was serious about its autonomy would turn them down—at great financial expense to itself, incidentally.

It would also shy away from voluntary organizations such as some of the national health associations, whose local units are merely branches whose policies are determined at state or national headquarters. Likewise, it would hesitate to attract branch plants of national industrial firms, since decisions as to whether the local plant is to be expanded or not; whether local workers will be hired or laid off, would likewise be made by absentee owners, not local people.

These may seem like extreme examples. But if we mean anything at all when we say that local communities should insofar as possible direct their own affairs, what do we mean? We mean these things, and we may mean other things. My point is not which ones we should mean, but rather that we are not at all clear about this business of local autonomy, and if we want to be clear about what kind of community we really want, we have to think it through.

3. VIABILITY

A third important issue with which we have to grapple in conceiving of the good community is that of *viability*. By viability I refer to the capacity of local people to confront their problems effectively through some type of concerted action. Much of the community development movement, much of voluntary community work and professional community organization has been devoted to this goal of helping communities to assess their problems and take action with respect to them. I shall return to this matter of viability later.

4. POWER DISTRIBUTION

Another issue with which we must come to grips if we are serious about our communities is the issue of *power*. Although numerous studies of community power structure have followed upon Floyd Hunter's ground-breaking book published in 1953, (7) not a single study finds power over decision-making to be equally distributed throughout the population. To the contrary, although differing in degree, all the studies find that the power over community decisions is unevenly distributed, with a relatively small minority of people exercising inordinate power in decision-making.

The numerous studies of community power distribution have been conducted by sociologists and political scientists. They have directed themselves at how power is actually distributed, rather than at how it should be distributed. Yet, in many of the study reports it is quite clear that the author has a frankly "democratic" bias in the sense of believing that community power should actually be distributed more broadly than it is. The concentration of power, in other words, is looked upon with diffidence—sometimes, as in Hunter, to the point of alleging that it constitutes a conspiracy to subvert democracy. The relative "powerlessness" of poor and Black groups constitutes an important current issue. But I do not know of a study which attempts to answer the question of how power should be distributed in the good community, beyond the simple and unexamined admonition: "More broadly than now."

Should all people have equal power? Can they? And if they can, at what price in terms of other desirable values?

5. PARTICIPATION

The fifth issue raised is *participation*. Most people who concern themselves with the community believe that it would be better if more people participated in community affairs. This has been especially true of community development workers.

Two interrelated circumstances are pertinent. On the one hand, as indicated by various power structure studies, large groups of citizens are systematically excluded from the decision-making process governing some of the most important community decisions. On the other hand, there is often widespread apathy, and many citizens do not participate, even where the opportunity is there for them.

But how widespread should participation be? Should all community people actively pursue all the important decisions that are made in the community? This would be mathematically impossible, for there is not time enough in the day for citizens to keep themselves well informed and fully participating on all issues. Some of them they must leave to others. Where are the limits, here? And if not everyone can participate in everything, what would be a suitable arrangement?

6. DEGREE OF COMMITMENT

A sixth issue closely related to participation, is the matter of *commitment*. How important should my local community be to me? Should it be an overriding preoccupation, or is it purely secondary? Many community workers assume that the community should be an important focus for the individual's life.

Lawrence Haworth, a philosopher who has come as close as anyone I know of to writing a systematic work on the good community, writes:

> If the city is to become a community, then, the inhabitants must identify the settlement itself as the focal point of their individual lives (6).

But in today's differentiated world of continental and intercontinental communications and transportation, and of changes of residence as people move from place to place, how realistic is it to presume that the local community will be the identification of overriding importance? And should it be? Should we all be localities, rather than cosmopolitans, in Merton's terminology (8)? And what of the many people who are very happy being cosmopolitans, equally at home in any community? Is there something deficient about them? Clearly, many people would not want to live in a community where people expected them to make the community the most important focus of their lives. Yet, obviously, there must be some people who consider the local community most important. How many? What proportion? And, how much is too much?

7. DEGREE OF HETEROGENEITY

Let us turn now to a matter which is even more perplexing: the matter of *homogeneity* or *heterogeneity*. How much difference would you have among people in your good community—and how much likeness?

Consider just a few random aspects of this controversial question. In the city planning field, as well as in many other fields, the idea of heterogeneity has long held moral sway. It has simply been accepted as a value that it is better for people to live in communities which are more or less a cross-section of the population than to live in economically or racially or ethnically segregated communities. Yet, interestingly, many of these same city planners show through their behavior that they themselves prefer to live in communities which are segregated, in the sense of being economically, racially, and ethnically homogeneous. They choose to live, according to the standard joke, where the man gets off the commuter train, gets into the wrong station wagon, goes home, spends the night, and gets back onto the train the next morning never having noticed the difference.

Note also the gradual breakdown in the constitutionality of ordinances or covenants which exclude poor people by acreage zoning, and exclude Blacks and other minorities by collusion or covenant. At the same time, note the rise in separatism on the part of Black and Chicano militants, as well as the more long-standing separatism practiced by whites in the form of segregation. Note the different decisions made in various cities in determining the borders of the Model Neighborhood in the Model Cities program, with some deliberately opting for a mixed neighborhood, others for a homogeneous neighborhood—in most instances, all Black.

It is one thing to talk of the values of different life styles, the greater variety caused by a plurality of sub–cultures. But how much heterogeneity can a community stand and still retain some degree of coherence. If we really want a heterogeneous community, if we really want all kinds of people, from John Birchers to socialists, can we expect not to see the sparks fly once in a while? And, in a different vein, how acceptable is the notion, often voiced today in one form or another, of homogeneous neighborhoods within heterogeneous communities?

8. EXTENT OF NEIGHBORHOOD CONTROL

This brings us to the matter of *neighborhoods*, and their relation to the larger local community. Here we have an issue around which there is great controversy today. How much shall we invest in the neighborhood, as an important social unit, as distinguished from investing in the community as a whole. Haworth concludes:

> We would not want to decentralize urban institutions to such an extent that the city becomes a mere confederation of neighborhoods. But this danger appears so remote, at least in American cities, that it seems insignificant (9).

In recent years, however, there has been a tremendous acceleration in the movement toward decentralization and neighborhood control. There are many reasons for this, one being the simple one that the complex larger cities are proving themselves more and more difficult to manage from centralized offices. Another is the increasingly recognized need, in many fields, to have services distributed closer to the recipient in his own neighborhood. Still another is a growing sense, both within racial ghettos and outside them, that control centers are too remote and insensitive, that neighborhood institutions have too long been run by outsiders in the larger community, that neighborhood people must have a larger say in the decisions that govern their lives. In short: "community autonomy," but in this case at the neighborhood level.

An additional underlying reality is that many so-called city neighborhoods are larger than many entire cities, so that in one sense the autonomy that some people demand in the name of an entire community may be demanded with equal logic by the inhabitants of a neighborhood of similar size. If 60 thousand people in a small city can control their own schools through their own board of education, why shouldn't 60 thousand people in one of the many large neighborhoods of a metropolis have the same right? In any case, the question of the relative strength of the neighborhood versus that of the city has to be faced by anyone presuming to become specific about what he means by a good community.

9. EXTENT OF CONFLICT

Only one more knotty issue, last but not least: How much *conflict* will there be in your good community? Up until 10 years or so ago, the answer by most interested Americans would have been virtually: "None." For conflict was simply a dirty word. Conflict was something whose effect can only be destructive. Now, all that has changed, and each of these statements is questioned.

Probably the most identifiable intellectual influence in this change in viewpoint has been Coser's book on *The Functions of Social Conflict* (4). Although this book has a deservedly high reputation, its great impact may be based in part upon a misunderstanding of its contents. Most of the book is devoted to the ways in which conflict is functional for a unit taken as one of the parties to a larger conflict, rather than a unit which is itself torn by conflict. Thus, conflict in Belfast between Catholics and Protestants may be functional for the solidarity of each conflicting group, but I don't think Coser would argue that it promotes solidarity in the city as such.

Another reason for the growing acceptance of conflict is the growing conviction in many quarters that strategies based on consensus play into the hands of the status quo, and permit the continuation of gross injustices. Hence, though conflict may be less desirable as a method of change than collaborative change strategies based on consensus, it is considered by many to be preferable to its alternative, the seeking of consensus and hence the preservation of social injustices in substantially their current form.

It is no longer generally agreed that the good community is a community without conflict—which places conflict on the agenda as one of the issues we must face if we are to speak meaningfully about what a good community would be like.

One possible implication of this list of issues which must be addressed in considering the character of a good community is that there is no such thing as *the* good community. There are *many* good communities, all according to the specific combination of preferences which may be held regarding each of these issues, in an almost infinite variety of combinations. On so many of these issues, there is simply no way to demonstrate that one viewpoint is more valid or more moral than another.

It is perhaps for this reason that social scientists have avoided the pursuit of definitions of the good community. Nevertheless, a review of the issues raised here does substantiate their importance. Such issues must be faced, and unless we face them, we are working in the dark when we seek to build better communities.

Perhaps the most we can aspire to is to give sustained attention to such considerations as have been raised in this paper, especially in connection with the three questions raised:

How much of what we want is actually possible?

How much of what seems desirable do we actually want?

How much of a price are we willing to pay for it when other values are jeopardized by it?

In closing, this last question can be illustrated by examining the relation between the first three values mentioned: Community autonomy, community viability, and a broad distribution of community power. There is some research which indicates that these three values, as desirable as they may be, do not always support each other. In a sense, what you gain in trying to pursue one of them may be paid for in a loss to the others. For example, a considerable number of studies are beginning to show that the broader the distribution of power and the more vigorous the public participation in a city, the less likely is a school integration campaign or a fluoridation campaign or an urban renewal proposal or other types of community improvement venture to be successful (5).

Hence, those who accept such measures as indications of a community's viability and its ability to confront and resolve its own problems must recognize that in such cases, viability and broad power distribution are likely to work at cross purposes.

Although other research findings offer almost contradictory conclusions (3), the important point is that one is not justified in simply assuming that such values as these can be maximized simultaneously.

Likewise, there is much theory and research to support the statement that community autonomy and a broad distribution of power are mutually incompatible. In a review of the power structure literature, John Walton found that it was the cities which were the least autonomous which had the broadest distribution of power. Dependence on governmental, business, and political networks extending beyond the community tends to diffuse power, rather than concentrate it (10).

By the same token, community autonomy, if pressed too far, apparently threatens viability, the ability of community people to confront their own problems. Obviously, to the extent that a community deliberately cuts itself off from sources of grant-in-aid programs, whether from state or federal government or from national foundations, it foregoes the access to important financial resources which might help to solve its problems. Likewise, to the extent that it discourages branch plants and other types of absentee-owned industrial activity, it takes on a self-imposed threat to its economic base.

How much of what kind of autonomy do communities want, and how much are they willing to sacrifice for this autonomy in terms of other things they want—like problem-solving ability and a broad distribution of power, rather than a concentrated power structure? These are the kinds of questions that seem relevant when we begin to dig underneath the surface of our conception of what a good community would be like.

I want to return to my earlier quotation from Royce. I believe in the beloved community. But unless this concept is to be a mere poetic expression, a sort of sentimental catharsis, we have to become serious with it and make some difficult choices.

Hence, the question: Do we really agree on what a good community would be like? When we become specific about its qualities, a number of crucial questions arise, about which there is much disagreement. The good community is not a "grab-bag of goodies" to satisfy every conceivable desire. It involves choices and rejections which we make either deliberately or by default.

These choices are worked out in the interplay of political forces, as different groups bring their different combinations of preferences to the arena of community decision-making. A careful analysis of the implications of such choices can help illuminate the political decision-making process, though it cannot replace it.

REFERENCES

1. Brownell, Baker, *The Human Community: Its Philosophy and Practice for a Time of Crisis* (New York: Harper & Brothers, 1950) p. 198.

2. *Ibid.,* p. 289–290.

3. Clark, Terry N., "Community Structure, Decision-Making, Budget Expenditures, and Urban Renewal in 51 American Communities," *American Sociological Review,* Vol. 33 No. 4, August, 1968; Michael Aiken and Robert R. Alford, "Community Structure and Innovation: The Case of Urban Renewal," Institute for Research on Poverty. University of Wisconsin, June, 1969, mimeographed, paper presented at the September, 1969, annual meeting of the American Sociological Society; and Wayne Paulson, Edgar W. Butler, and Hallowell Pope, "Community Power and Public Welfare," *American Journal of Economics and Sociology,* Vol. 28 No. 1, January, 1969.

4. Coser, Lewis, *The Functions of Social Conflict* (New York: The Free Press of Glencoe, 1956).

5. Hawley, Amos H., "Community Power and Urban Renewal Success," in Terry N. Clark, *op. cit.,* p. 405; Donald B. Rosenthal and Robert L. Crain, "Structure and Values in Local Political Systems: The Case of Fluoridation Decisions," in Terry N. Clark, *op. cit.,* pp. 241–242 *et passim.* See also Robert L. Crain, Elihu Katz, and Donald B. Rosenthal, *The Politics of Community Conflict: The Fluoridation Decision* (New York: The Bobbs-Merrill Company, 1969); and Herman Turk, *A Method of Predicting Certain Federal Program Potentials of Large American Cities* (Los Angeles: Laboratory for Organizational Research, University of Southern California, 1967).

6. Haworth, Lawrence, *The Good City* (Bloomington: Indiana University Press, 1963), p. 87.

7. Hunter, Floyd, *Community Power Structure: A Study of Decision Makers* (Chapel Hill: University of North Carolina Press, 1953).

8. Merton, Robert, "Patterns of Influence: A Study of Interpersonal Influence and of Communications Behavior in a Local Community," in Paul F. Lazarsfeld and Frank N. Stanton, eds., *Communications Research 1948–1949* (New York: Harper & Brothers, 1949).

9. *Ibid.,* p. 72.

10. Walton, John, "The Vertical Axis of Community Organization and the structure of Power," *Southwestern Social Science Quarterly,* Vol. 48 No. 3, December, 1967.

11. Zorbaugh, Harvey W. *The Gold Coast and the Slum* (Chicago: University of Chicago Press, 1929).

Reading 3

Photographic Essay: Thriving Communities of Northeastern Africa

BY AMANDA COX, BSW

In many parts of Africa, a strong sense of community is at the core of how people function in society. While poverty, violence and disease are taking too many lives in northeastern Africa, family and community remain vital. These images from Eritrea, Ethiopia, and Uganda capture the spirit of what community means.

From these images, what expressions of community do you see? How might various definitions of community emerge from an artistic expression such as a photograph? You have read many words in this chapter about community. What do the photographs express about community that words cannot say?

Amanda Cox

Amanda Cox

Amanda Cox

Amanda Cox

Catherine McMahon

Amanda Cox

Amanda Cox

Amanda Cox

Amanda Cox

Amanda Cox

Reading 4

Taking Theory to Practice

The following decision case has been included in this unit to give you practice applying the concepts presented. The case is based on an actual practice situation gathered by interviewing a master-level social worker. When exploring the case, try formulating the problems, analyzing the information you have, and deciding on potential courses of action. This exploration can be done on your own or in study groups, discussing parts or the entirety of the case, according to how your instructor may guide you. The point is to help you learn to apply theory to practice and to develop important problem-solving and critical-thinking skills. Although this case is located within the unit on communities it may intersect with other areas of practice as well, such as groups, organizations, social movements, individuals, and families.

JIM'S LICENSE TO DRIVE

KAREN A. GRAY & TERRY A. WOLFER

Standing on the street corner, the November evening air was chilly. But to Jim Miller, social work student and agency director, the reception felt colder. Facing him, some 20 Latino men crossed their arms and lowered their faces, and some turned to walk away. Jim could feel the trust being sucked away. Without asking, Jim knew they felt he had let them down.

Jim had had such high hopes for The Friendship Center, the community center that he helped found. Now it seemed to be crumbling around him, and he wondered if any of his efforts were salvageable. *What, if anything, can I do to keep the Center alive? My word is no longer good*, he thought to himself.

JIM MILLER

Jim Miller was a first year MSW student when, in fall 2001, he began a field placement at a teen-pregnancy program in Monroe, North Carolina. Because he was bilingual, speaking both English and Spanish, he was constantly asked to interpret both in and outside the agency. As a result, he met many community members and, as he later recalled, he "inadvertently became a voice for the [Latino] community."

Jim came to the MSW program with several years of macro-type experience. After obtaining his undergraduate degree, Jim worked as a community development specialist for two years. Then he worked for three years as a Women In Development Coordinator in Small Project Assistance programming with the Peace Corps and US AID in Ecuador. He also worked one year for the North Carolina Department of Juvenile Justice and Delinquency Prevention (DJJDP) and another year in a Job Training Partnership Act (JTPA) program.

The many social injustices Jim had observed while working were the impetus for his return to school. He clearly had the "fire in the belly" that activists say is required to do community organizing or other activist work; he felt passionate about fighting oppression. As an Anglo man, he had learned to be culturally sensitive in his international work. This, combined with his intelligence and his fluency in Spanish meant he brought important assets to practice. During his first year in Monroe, Jim developed good relationships with various community groups, agencies, and politicians. Initially, many in this small Southern town were suspicious of him. Because he was an outsider who became involved with the recent Latino population, Jim continually had to assure people that he had no intentions of organizing the Latino population for union membership. Soon enough, people trusted him, and he was invited by a community liaison at the local hospital to sit on the Latino immigrant health task force. The task force obtained grant money to conduct a health survey and the results suggested that there were a wide variety of untreated health needs. Further, the task force learned that Latinos in Monroe were not receiving adequate health care for a number of reasons, including social isolation, and financial and language barriers. There was grant money left over from the implementation of the survey, and the task force decided to give Jim $8,000 to start a community center. The founding purpose of the community center was to provide health services.

As a result, while still a first year MSW student, Jim served as the founding director of The Friendship Center. Jim did not lack for things to do. In addition to his responsibility as director, Jim juggled the usual classes, a two-day field placement, and a one-day graduate assistantship at the university.

Jim's personal investments in the community surrounding The Friendship Center were complex and multi-faceted. Because he was bi-lingual, the police frequently called upon Jim to interpret for Spanish-speaking community members who were under arrest. As a student, he used community data for a research project and wrote papers about the community. He presented this research and two papers at several statewide conferences. He felt that the community gave him a great deal, and he felt obligated to return the favors.

He also hoped that the Latino community would gain a voice. Whether or not the Latinos who resided in Monroe had the proper documents, Jim believed strongly that they did not deserve deplorable work conditions nor to be taken advantage of by unscrupulous employers. They had basic human rights. And they were contributing members of the community. His ultimate dream was to build an environment where children could prosper and be safe.

THE "NEW JACK CITY" COMMUNITY

The community surrounding The Friendship Center was nicknamed "New Jack City," or simply "New Jack," by people living outside the community. Locally, New Jack was famous for being the first neighborhood in Monroe to have drive-by shootings, crack dealers, and gang activity. For more than a decade, it had been considered a dangerous place to live, work, or simply pass through.

The composition of the community had changed dramatically in the last two years. While it used to be 100% African American, it was now 80% Latino. A labor contractor recruited the Latinos to work at Wilson's, the local chicken processing plant, in low-wage, low-skill jobs.

When Jim arrived in Monroe, racial tensions were running high. Most of the workers who were fired from Wilson's over the previous two years were African American. Most of the replacement workers were Latino because, as the Wilson CEO allegedly claimed, "The workers we had before were addled with drugs and they were an unreliable labor force. They were unable to meet our production demands. We were at the brink of closing the plant." The CEO was quick to explain that Wilson's didn't hire the Latinos, but simply contracted with Key Employment, a labor contractor.

Key Employment had contracts all over North Carolina. Its owner, Bob Slusser, hired a *coyote* to recruit and transport potential workers from Mexico. Bob also set up a pyramid system to run his business. He hired Latino *contratistas*, like Antonio Cruz, to supervise. In exchange for arranging and supervising employment, a *contratista* took a cut of the worker's pay (typically $1 per hour) and Bob took a cut, too (another $1 per hour).

In Monroe, many members of the Latino community worked at Wilson's, where they earned $5.50 per hour (before the withholdings noted above). They often worked six days per week. Wilson's paid rent and utilities for the workers to live in some run-down apartments in New Jack, and they paid Antonio to manage the apartment complex. Although Wilson's paid the rent, workers had to buy their own work supplies such as boots.

Wilson's was located within walking distance of New Jack, so people had no problem getting to work. But because there was no public transportation in Monroe, and because cabs were expensive, owning a car or carpooling were the only reasonable means of transportation to the grocery store and church. But getting a license posed a particular problem for the Latinos, as most were undocumented. As a result, they just drove without licenses. Driving without a license might not have caught so much attention except for an elevated rate of DUIs within Monroe's Latino community.

Latinos arrested for driving without a license and without automobile insurance were typically fined $800 and jailed until they could pay the fine or a bond. If arrested for DUI, the penalties were even stiffer. In any case, because they received low wages, the Latinos found it nearly impossible to pay these fines and get out of jail. And most did not have family members nearby who could help them out.

But the Latinos had more serious legal concerns. Because most did not have the proper documents, they were always looking over their shoulders for *la migra*. In 1997, the INS deported 172 people from another community with a Wilson's chicken processing plant. The Latinos believed that Wilson's made the call to INS because workers were beginning to organize a union.

THE FRIENDSHIP CENTER

"With the $8,000," Jim recalled, "We rented an apartment in the neighborhood and BOOM! We started going. We just did whatever we could get together, with mostly in-kind resources." But he soon secured new funding from several sources, mostly from a local, private foundation.

The initial mission of the center was fourfold: 1) English as a Second Language (ESL) classes, 2) after school and other children's activities, 3) monthly health screenings, including pap smears, and 4) community development.

Instead of a board of directors, the center had an advisory board. The board chair, Jane Long, was a sociology professor from the local community college. As board chair, she was Jim's boss. Although the agencies represented at the advisory board meetings were fairly constant, different agency representatives attended the meetings. In other words, each agency was a member of the board, with representatives revolving. Typically, about 15 people attended. The number and diversity of the members were impressive. The advisory board meetings usually consisted of religious leaders, like Reverend Al Smith (who ran an anti-gang program), a Chamber of Commerce representative, a representative of the Mayor's Office, Sgt. Tom Johnson from the Monroe Police Department, a Literacy Council member, a Memorial Hospital representative, a City Council representative, a Parks and Recreation employee, a Free Medical Clinic employee, Immigrant Health Task Force members, the director of the Monroe County Department of Social Services, and five core community people, like Antonio Cruz (some had lived in New Jack for years and some were new). Jim had invited most community members face-to-face.

COMMUNITY MEETINGS

To fulfill the community development mission of the Friendship Center, Jim organized the first general community meeting in August 2001. It was a cookout with Leland Jordan, the African American mayor of Monroe. Because he was dressed in shorts and cooked hot dogs and hamburgers, the Latinos didn't believe Jim when he said this was the mayor. In Latin American countries, they said, the mayor always wore a suit and tie and would never "serve" constituents by cooking.

Several weeks prior to the September community meeting, at a meeting of the Advisory board, Jim mentioned his concern about the number of unlicensed drivers and DUIs in the Latino community, and wondered what prevention tactics could be set in place. As a result, Reverend Smith introduced Jim to Everett Blue, a community education specialist with the North Carolina Department of Alcohol and Substance Abuse. Everett said he had a fantastic brochure that addressed Jim's concerns, but it would need to be translated into Spanish. Jim agreed to do this. The brochure was not just about DUIs. It also explained North Carolina driving laws and how to get a driver's license—a sort of "Welcome, Neighbor" brochure that Jim thought would be a wonderful "Welcome, Neighbor from Mexico" brochure once translated into Spanish. Without waiting for permission from the state Department of Transportation, Jim started making copies and handing out the brochure in the community.

The brochure said that if one brought a birth certificate and picture identification card to the Department of Motor Vehicles, and a letter from the Social Security Office stating why a Social Security number could not be assigned, one could get a driver's license, even without a Social Security number. With this information, Antonio started translating birth certificates for $25 per person.

Jim convinced Mayor Jordan to return to the second community meeting. This was no small task. Jim knew Mayor Jordan had taken some flack from African American citizens for being "too cozy" with the Latino population. Several community leaders insisted that because he was African American, the mayor should be helping African Americans, not Latinos.

Besides getting the mayor to attend again, Jim arranged for Manuel Ramos, the owner of an unlicensed weekend restaurant, to cook his famous, delicious chicken. Latinos curious about this American mayor came to the September community meeting. At least 75 people attended to socialize and to present their concerns about their inability to obtain a driver's license. Mayor Jordan said he would talk to the Police Department, the Social Security office, and the Department of Motor Vehicles, and find out how to get drivers licenses. He promised to report this information at the October community meeting. Naturally, this excited folks.

Before the October community meeting, Jim mentioned to Jane, "The local Social Security office is not providing the services it is required to provide. 'Jim Crow' is being replaced by 'Juan Crow' laws." He explained the office was to provide anyone who requested a social security number either a number or a letter explaining why she or he did not qualify. Such a letter could be used to obtain a driver's license without a social security number. Instead, he reported, Director Anita Williams, an African American, posted a yellow flyer at the Social Security office that stated without correct papers from the INS, one could not be served by Social Security.

Incensed by this information, Jane took a video camera and some Latinos to the local Department of Motor Vehicles office. She filmed an African American man in line in front of them obtaining a driver's license without a Social Security number. When Jane and the Latinos' turn came, the Latinos were denied a license because they had no Social Security number.

At the October community meeting, Mayor Jordan sent a representative in his place. The representative, an African American woman, did not know anything about the drivers' license issue, and therefore had nothing to report. The 40–50 Latinos at the meeting grumbled a bit, but Jim tried to appease them by saying, "This kind of thing takes time."

Jim decided to move the November community meeting to a more central part of the neighborhood, in hopes that more African American community members would show up. He selected a laundry mat parking lot. It was late on a Sunday afternoon, almost dark and quite chilly when the meeting began. Only when the meeting began, did Jim remember that the local drug dealers occupied an adjacent corner of the block.

Nevertheless, Jim was pleased to see several new African American faces in the crowd, and went to introduce himself and offer dinner. There was no famous chicken this time but the cook's famous *posole* instead. When the new attendees introduced themselves as Black Muslims, however, Jim was embarrassed that he had nothing but pork to offer them.

The other 20 people present were Latino men. Some women and children had stopped by earlier, but they appeared uncomfortable and left before Jim could extend a welcome.

Twenty minutes after the scheduled start time, Jane had not yet arrived. In addition, there was no mayor and no representative. Jim felt abandoned by his colleagues. People were getting antsy, so Jim reluctantly began the meeting alone. The Latinos wanted to know about drivers' licenses but Jim had no news to give them. Facing him, the men crossed their arms and lowered their faces, the disappointment evident. Quickly, some turned to walk away. But even with those who hesitated, Jim could feel the trust being sucked away. Without asking, Jim knew they felt he had let them down.

As the meeting ended, Jim felt stumped about what to do next, and how to understand what was going wrong. He had held such high hopes for the community center that he helped found but now it seemed to be crumbling around him. Discouraging questions tumbled through his mind. *Now what? What, if anything, can I do to keep the center alive? Can we salvage any of our efforts here? Is my word any good in this community? How can I still be a community leader and regain people's trust? Do I have to suck up to the mayor? What do I do first?*

SUMMARY

Our goal for this unit was to assist you in developing your understanding of the types, functions, elements, and strengths of communities. We began with an overview of the basic concepts, including definitions, community types,

community functions, population, social class, ethnicity, neighborhoods, economy, values, power structures, relationships, and strengths.

We presented the idea of a community as a system in an environment consisting of systems (local, county/parish, state, national, and international systems)
which directly and/or indirectly impact its functioning. In other words, international, national, state, and county/parish issues can affect the local community's
ability to function. Given this, when we examine a local community, we must
consider the subsystems that constitute the community, as well as the larger systems that form its environment. We reviewed Roland Warren's five specific
community functions: production, distribution, and consumption; socialization;
social control; social participation; and mutual support.

Our discussion of the strengths or assets model in examining communities
emphasized keeping your focus on positive characteristics and how they can be
used in a preventive manner, while also addressing current deficits or issues. The
underlying philosophy of the strengths/assets approach includes the beliefs that all
clients possess the ability to address their needs, that success is based on client
involvement and investment, and that such an approach has longer-lasting results.
Throughout Reading 1 we urged you to draw connections to other courses in
social work curriculum through the "Competency Connections" feature.

To deepen your understanding of communities, we presented a photo essay
for you to explore the themes of community in a more creative and visual way.
Each photo provides a visual image of some aspect of community in a context
that may be less familiar to our readers. The case "Jim's License to Drive" gave
you an opportunity to apply the concepts and theories presented to an actual
practice situation.

We hope you now have a solid foundation on which you can begin to build
your macro practice knowledge and skills, including an understanding of the
importance of communities and community practice in reversing the inequities
in access to social and economic resources. Whereas many of you will not
engage in macro practice on a regular basis, this foundation is still essential, especially since we approach our clients holistically. Such an understanding will assist
you in recognizing the community's impact on your clients, and your clients'
impact on the community. It will also assist you in formulating interventions to
improve the quality of life in our communities.

REFERENCES

Aker, R., & Scales, T.L. (2004). Charitable choice, social workers, and rural congrega-
tions: Partnering to build community assets. In: T.L. Scales & C. Streeter (Eds.),
Rural social work: Building assets to sustain rural communities. Belmont, CA: Brooks/
Cole, pp. 226–239.

Alcorn, S., & Morrison, J.D. (1994). Community planning that is "caught" and "taught":
Experiential learning from town meetings. *Journal of Community Practice, 1*(4), 27–43.

Barker, R.L. (1999). *The social work dictionary* (4th ed.). Washington, D.C.: NASW Press.

Blundo, R. (2001). Learning strengths-based practice: Challenging our personal and professional frames. *Families in Society, 82*(3), 296–304.

Brueggemann, W.G. (2002). Becoming a community organizer. In: *The practice of macro social work*. Belmont, CA: Wadsworth/Thomson Learning, pp 196–220.

Brueggeman, W.G. (2006). *The practice of macro social work* (3rd ed.). Belmont, CA: Thomson Brooks/Cole.

Brun, C., & Rapp, R.C. (2001). Strengths-based case management: Individuals' perspectives on strengths and the case manager relationship. *Social Work, 46*(3), 278–288.

Carlton-LaNey, I.B., Edwards, R.B., & Reid, P.N., Eds. (1999). Small towns and rural communities: From romantic notions to harsh realities. In: *Preserving and strengthening small towns and rural communities*. Washington, DC: NASW Press, pp 5–11.

Cisneros, A. (2001). Texas colonias: Housing and infrastructure issues. In: M. Yücel (Ed.), *The border economy*. Dallas, TX: Federal Reserve Bank of Dallas.

Colby, A., Ehrlich, T., Beaumont, E. & Stephens, J. (2003). *Educating citizens: Preparing America's future for lives of moral and civic responsibility*. San Francisco: Jossey-Bass.

Cox, A. (2008). *Thriving communities of Northeastern Africa*, Unpublished photographic essay, Waco, TX.

Cox, A.L. (2001). BSW students favor strengths/empowerment-based generalist practice. *Families in Society, 82*(3), 305–313.

Daley, M., & Avant, F.L. (1999). Attracting and retaining professionals for social work practice in rural areas: An example from East Texas. In: I.B. Carlton-LaNey, R.L. Edwards, & P.N. Reid (Eds.), *Preserving and strengthening small towns and rural communities*. Washington, DC: NASW Press, pp 335–345.

Daley, M., & Avant, F.L. (2004). Rural social work: Reconceptualizing the framework for practice. In: T.L. Scales & C. Streeter (Eds.), *Rural social work: Building and sustaining community assets*. Belmont, CA: Brooks/Cole, pp 34–42.

Davis, T.S. (2004). Using wraparound to build rural communities of care for children with serious emotional disturbance and their families. In: T.L. Scales & C. Streeter (Eds.), *Rural social work: Building and sustaining community assets*. Belmont, CA: Brooks/Cole, pp 132–146.

Dionne, E.J. (1992). *Why Americans hate politics*. New York: Simon & Schuster.

Elliot, J., & Smith, R. (2004). Race, gender, and workplace power. *American Sociological Review, 69*(2), 365–386.

Fellin, P. (2001). *The community and the social worker* (3rd ed.). Itasca, IL: Peacock.

Ginsberg, L.H., Ed. (1993). Introduction: An overview of rural social work. In: *Social work in rural communities* (2nd ed.). Alexandria, VA: Council on Social Work Education, pp 2–17.

Ginsberg, L.H., Ed. (1998). Introduction: An overview of rural social work. In: *Social work in rural communities* (3rd ed.). Alexandria, VA: Council on Social Work Education, pp 3–22.

Gray, K.A. & Wolfer, T.A. (2006). Jim's license to drive. T.A. Wolfer, & T.L. Scales, eds. *Decision cases for advanced social work practice: Thinking like a social worker*. Monterey, CA: Brooks/Cole, pp 29–42.

Graybeal, C. (2001). Strengths-based social work assessment: Transforming the dominant paradigm. *Families in Society, 82*(3), 233–242.

Hardina, D. (2004). Guidelines for ethical practice in community organization. *Social Work*, *49*(4), 595–604.

Hilfiker, D. (2004, May). Still separate, still unequal. *Sojourners Magazine*.

Hylton, T. (2003, January 19). Discourage sprawl: Segregation in Milwaukee. *Milwaukee Journal Sentinel*.

Hyman, J.B. (2002). Exploring social capital and civic engagement to create a framework for community building. *Applied Developmental Science*, *6*(4), 196–202.

Kretzman, J.P., & McKnight, J.L. (1993). *Building communities from the inside out: A path toward finding and mobilizing a community's assets*. Chicago: ACTA.

Longres, J. (2008). Diversity in community life. In: J. Rothman, J.L. Erlich, & J.E. Tropman (Eds.), *Strategies of community intervention* (7th ed.). Peosta, IA: Eddie Bowers, pp 77–106.

Martinez-Brawley, E.E. (1980). Historical perspectives on rural social work: Implications for curriculum development. *Journal of Education for Social Work*, *16*(3), 43–50.

Martinez-Brawley, E.E. (1985). Rural social work as a contextual specialty: Undergraduate focus or graduate concentration? *Journal of Social Work Education*, *21*(3), 36–42.

Mattessich, P., & Monsey, B. (2001). *Community building: What makes it work. A review of the factors influencing successful community building*. St. Paul, MN: Wilder Foundation.

May, M.L., Ramos, I., & Ramos, K.S. (2002). Promotoras and environmental health awareness in the colonias [electronic version]. *Rural Voices* 7(4).

Mizrahi, T. (2002). Community organizing principles and practice guidelines. In: A.R. Roberts & G.J. Greene, *Social worker's desk reference*. New York: Oxford University Press, pp 517–534.

Murty, S. (2004). Mapping community assets: The key to effective rural social work. In: T.L. Scales & C. Streeter (Eds.), *Rural social work: Building assets to sustain rural communities*. Belmont, CA: Brooks/Cole, pp 278–289.

Netting, F.E., Kettner, P.M., & McMurtry, S.L. (2004). *Social work macro practice* (3rd ed.). Boston: Pearson.

Nooe, R.M., & Bolitho, F.L. (1982). An examination of rural social work literature. *Human Services in the Rural Environment* 7(1), 11–18.

Olaveson, J., Conway, P., & Shaver, C. (2004). Defining *rural* for social work practice and research. In: T.L. Scales & C. Streeter (Eds.), *Rural social work: Building and sustaining community assets*. Belmont, CA: Brooks/Cole, pp 9–20.

Portes, A. & Landolt, P. (1996). The downside of social capital. *The American Prospect*, *21*, 18–21.

Putnam, R.D. (2000). *Bowling alone: The collapse and revival of American community*. New York: Simon & Schuster.

Queralt, M. (1996). *The social environment and human behavior: a diversity perspective*. Boston: Allyn & Bacon.

Raab, J. & Milward, H.B. (2003). Dark networks as problems. *Journal of Public Administration Research and Theory*, *13*(4), 413–439.

Reisch, M., & Lowe, J.I. (2000). "'Of ends and means" revisited: Teaching ethical community organizing in an unethical society. *Journal of Community Practice*, 7(1):19–38.

Richardson, C. (1999). *Batos, bolillos, pochos, & pelados: Class and culture on the South Texas border*. Austin: University of Texas Press.

Saleebey, D. (1996). The strengths perspective in social work practice: Extensions and cautions. *Social Work, 41*, 296–305.

Sanchez-Jankowski, M. (2002). Minority youth and civic engagement: The impact of group relations. *Applied Developmental Science 6*(4), 237–245.

Scales, T.L., & Streeter, C. (2004). *Rural social work: Building assets to sustain rural communities*. Belmont, CA: Brooks/Cole.

Schriver, J.M. (1998). *Human behavior and the social environment: shifting paradigms in essential knowledge for social work practice* (2nd ed.). Boston: Allyn & Bacon.

Schulman, M.D., & Anderson, C. (1999). The dark side of the force: A case study of restructuring and social capital. *Rural Sociology, 64*(3), 351–372.

Segura, G.M., Pachon, H., & Woods, N.A. (2001). Hispanics, social capital, and civic engagement. *National Civic Review, 90*(1), 85–96.

Sherraden, M.S. (1993). Community studies in the baccalaureate social work curriculum. *Journal of Teaching in Social Work, 7*(1), 75–88.

Takei, I., & Sakamoto, A. (2008). Do college-educated, native-born Asian Americans face a glass ceiling in obtaining managerial authority. *Asian American Policy Review, 17*, 73–85.

Templeman, S.B., & Mitchell, L. (2004). Utilizing strengths and assets in service delivery within rural communities: One size does not fit all. In: T.L. Scales & C. Streeter (Eds.), *Rural social work: Building assets to sustain rural communities*. Belmont, CA: Brooks/Cole, 196–205.

Texas Comptroller of Public Accounts (1999). *Challenging the status quo: Toward smaller, smarter government*. Austin, TX: Author.

Texas Department of Human Services (1998). *Colonias factbook summary*. Retrieved April 11, 2004, from http://chud.tamu.edu/files/factbook.html.

Texas Health and Human Services Commission (2003). *Colonias initiative: Bringing access to those in need*. Retrieved October 6, 2003, from http://www.hhsc.state.tx.us/hhsc_projects/colonias/colonia_home.html.

Thio, A. (1992). *Sociology: An introduction* (3rd ed.). New York: HarperCollins.

Toennies, F. (1887). Gemeinschaft Und Gesellschaft.: Abhandlung des Communismus und des Socialismus als empirischer Culturformen. Leipzig: Reisland.

U.S. Census Bureau (2000). *Appendix A. Census 2000 geographic terms and concepts*. Retrieved February 7, 2009, from http://www.census.gov/geo/www/tiger/glossry2.pdf.

U.S. Census Bureau (2002). *Census 2000 urban and rural classification*. Retrieved December 21, 2006, from http://www.census.gov/geo/www/ua/ua_2k.html.

U.S. Census Bureau (2005). *Geographic changes for census 2000 + glossary*. Retrieved February 7, 2009, from http://www.census.gov/geo/www/tiger/glossary.html.

U.S. Department of Housing and Urban Development (2003). *What are colonias?* Retrieved October 6, 2003, from http://www.hud.gov:80/groups/frmwrkcoln/whatcol.cfm.

U.S. Election Project (2009). 2008 general election turnout rates. Retrieved February 28, 2009, from http://elections.gmu.edu/Turnout_2008G.html.

Ward, P.M. (1999). *Colonias and public policy in Texas and Mexico: Urbanization by stealth.* Austin: University of Texas Press.

Warren, R. (1970). The good community—What would it be? *Journal of Community Development Society 1*(1), 14–24.

Warren, R.L. (1978). *The community in America* (3rd ed.). Chicago: Rand McNally.

Yamane, L. (2002). Native-born Filipina/o Americans and labor market discrimination. *Feminist Economics, 8,* 125–144.

Social Movements

LEARNING OBJECTIVE

To expose students to the theories and concepts needed to understand social movements, including historical information and social workers' roles in them, so that they may connect knowledge about human behavior in social movements to other areas of the social work curriculum.

INTRODUCTION

The purpose of Unit 4 is to assist you in developing an understanding of social movements as an important aspect of human behavior. Social workers may encounter movements in a variety of contexts. They may found a movement as a response to injustices. They may serve as allies and supporters of organizations or communities involved in social movements, or they may fight against a movement that they perceive will have a negative impact on their client systems. Unit 4 begins with an overview of social movements and an opportunity to connect theory to practice.

We have included three additional elements to supplement and illustrate key aspects of Unit 4. First, we want you to understand the role and impact of social movements around the world, but draw your attention to movements in United States history by including "The Seneca Falls Declaration of Sentiments and Resolutions," which provides historical insight into the early stages of the women's rights movement to promote basic rights and freedoms, including the right to vote. The spoken word poetry, written by a 14-year-old African-American woman, encourages you to apply "right brain thinking" to how the next generation of leaders may respond to our nation's social problems; the next social movements to emerge will engage this generation in new and unique ways. A decision case, "How Can Everyone Get a Just Share?," will engage you in applying the theories and concepts presented in this unit and give you practice "thinking like a social worker" about client systems that may engage social movements. Finally, the *Curriculum Connections* commentaries will assist you in understanding how the topic of social movements relates to other areas of your social work education.

We anticipate that through this unit you will have an opportunity to deepen your understanding of human behavior as it relates to social movements. A strong theoretical foundation is essential for you to begin building your practice knowledge and skills. It is very likely that at some point in your practice, whether you practice primarily with individuals, families, groups, organizations, communities, or all of these client systems, you will encounter a social movement that will impact your practice in some way.

Reading 1

Human Behavior in Social Movements

The final system in the social environment that we discuss is in many ways most relevant to the roots of the profession. As you may remember, the profession of social work was born out of the settlement house movement and the charity organizations movement. This history of social work in the United States, rooted in the Progressive Era of the early 20th century, includes care for individuals and families affected by poverty as well as social reform of the conditions contributing to poverty. We see the role of social reform in the story of Jane Addams and Hull House and the many others involved in the settlement house movement in other parts of the country. This movement inspired the professional mission of social service and social justice that continues to be central to social work today. It is important to understand this history and our mission so that we can better understand social movements and their role in practice.

The relevance of social movements to social work is seen throughout our profession's history. The Progressive Era of the early 20th century and the Great Depression era, efforts to create the modern American welfare state in the 1930s, the War on Poverty and Civil Rights Movement of the 1960s, and the efforts to address extreme poverty around the world at the beginning of the 21st century through the Millennium Development Goals, show us people participating together for social change and carrying out the social justice mandate of the profession.

The preamble to the National Association of Social Workers (NASW) Code of Ethics emphasizes the need to promote social justice and social change. It calls us to do so in our focus on individual well-being in a social context as well as on the well-being of our communities and our world. The profession itself functions as a social movement; we can serve as a force for social justice and liberating social change. The profession takes into consideration cultural and structural factors as we challenge injustice, discrimination, and oppression.

So how do we define these efforts for social change? Social movements have been defined in many ways. Here's how we define this area of practice. A social movement is a form of group action, perhaps through the work of a formal organization or perhaps through community members who have come together for a common cause that seeks to promote or to resist social change. Social movements are a meaningful component of this text because of their impact on individual behavior, groups, communities, and organizations.

We begin this chapter with a review of concepts and frameworks that form the foundations for understanding social movements.

THEORETICAL APPROACHES TO SOCIAL MOVEMENTS

Early writings in the field of sociology focused on a general theory of social movements. Over the years, literature about social movements has expanded to include a focus on understanding collective behavior, fostering the mobilization of resources, and a broadened focus on identity and cultural movements, new social movements, that shifts the focus from economic understanding of society to a criticism of its social order (Fisher & Kling, 1994; Wenocur & Soifer, 1997). Each of these represents a theory we will consider in more detail below.

As we said earlier, the progressive era gave birth to the profession of social work as a part of the movement to address urban social problems in the wake of the industrial revolution. From working for peace to the war on poverty, and from women's rights to rights for people with different abilities, social workers have actively led social movements throughout this country's history. Other contemporary movements that have had social work support include immigration rights and living wage movements. While these practical efforts are focused on social change, they reflect theoretical foundations that help us understand how social movements bring about change.

Social movement theories include both the concepts and the frameworks for understanding how social movements develop and what they strive to accomplish, but these theories also help us to understand human behavior and social environments (Holst, 2002). Starting in Europe in 1896, Gustave LeBon's publication of *The Crowd* put him in the position of "grandfather" of social movements (Berk, 1974; Lyman, 1994; Turner & Killian, 1957). Of course, sociologists such as Herbert Spencer and Emile Durkheim addressed collective human behavior and Karl Marx proposed the economic foundations of social

Competency Connections

Social Movements and Social Welfare History

Jane Addams and Settlement Leaders Organized to Improve Conditions for Immigrants

Jane Addams and the social settlement workers sought social justice for immigrants and the urban poor who lived in a community located on Chicago's West side. The settlement workers believed that environmental factors such as poor housing and sanitation conditions contributed to the lowly status of the community members. The settlement workers established the Hull House in the late 1800s, a central location where community members could develop skills in art, music, and drama (Brieland, 1990, p. 135). Hull House had a "welcoming spirit" that broke down communication

barriers, connected two social classes, and helped form a partnership between the workers and the residents, which was critical to challenging landlords and lawmakers to improve housing and address other social concerns in Chicago (Brieland, 1990, pp. 134–135).

Like other social movements, the settlement movement involved people of varying social status. Settlements established communication between wealthy citizens and the working classes and was based on a democratic ideal. As Jane Addams stated, settlements demonstrated that "the dependence of classes on each other is reciprocal" (Davis, 1984, p. 19).

behavior. Each one of these theoretical perspectives of social movements taught us a little bit more about human behavior in their social environments and helped to present what became a general theory of social movements. In time, this led to the array of social movement theories that we have come to see in more recent decades.

There are many ways we could present theories of social movements. Here, we present contemporary concepts and theories social workers can use in practice. These concepts can be grouped into three theoretical perspectives: collective behavior, resource mobilization, and new social movements (della Porta & Diani, 1998 Holst, 2002). We choose these three because of their presence in social work and sociological literature. Also, we believe they most clearly present ideas that can help us see our role in social movements today.

COLLECTIVE BEHAVIOR: FROM GENERAL THEORY OF SOCIAL MOVEMENTS TO A THEORY OF COLLECTIVE ACTION

In *The Crowd*, Gustave LeBon (1896) describes collective behavior as the way crowds act when they gather; he says they have their own psychological behaviors. Sadly, his classic text offers a largely negative and even stereotypical perspective of human behavior. LeBon shares his view of people gathering collectively for social change and forming what he identifies as the "mental unity" of "psychological crowds" (LeBon, 1896). His negative view of social movements incorporates social Darwinism and other negative perspectives on race and class that can be expected of popular writings of European imperialism at the end of the 19th century (Dickens, 2000). His bourgeois perspective sees a threat in collective behavior, particularly among what he describes as "inferior races" (LeBon, 1894, p. 26). He says that as crowds organize, the result is that people "descend several rungs in the ladder of civilization" (LeBon, 1896, p. 36).

Given our strengths perspective, social workers would likely have a different understanding of the value of people organizing for social change. Despite LeBon's support for the power of people who are privileged, he does offer a critical assessment of human behavior in social environments. LeBon gives us three principles of human behavior. His "law of the mental unity of crowds" recognizes that there is great power in human unity; his suggestion that "in a crowd, he is a barbarian" suggests how individual choice, and at times rational and moral decision making, can be lost in collective behavior; and to support this, his view that the "heroism of primitive beings" leads crowds to follow strong leaders, perhaps blindly at times, teaches us about leadership and participation in social change.

How does this relate to how social workers organize for social change? From LeBon, social workers can find themes that are discussed throughout theories of collective behavior. First, we will hear about the relationship between the personal and psychological influences for involvement in a social movement on the one hand, and social and political foundations for social movements on the other. A second theme is the ongoing questions raised about a range of rational and emotional motivations driving people to become involved in collective action. While other theoretical perspectives go further in emphasizing the rational and political perspectives for social movements, collective behavior theories cover a range of perspectives that will be described as spontaneous and nonrational. Even described as such; the collective behavior approach has strength in its emergent and interactive creation and interpretation of meaningful social action.

Collective Behavior in Structural Functionalism.   The dominant sociological perspective of Talcott Parsons (1967) in the mid-20th century affected social movement theory, particularly the structural functionalist approach. In this theory of how society works, social functions are derived from social structures and we hear that society is ordered toward equilibrium even though people function without equality. Parsons' sociology reinforced coercive social norms that govern behavior, but recognized collective action as those efforts that people engage in when social functions break down.

Although structural functionalism fell out of favor by the 1970s, it did contribute to the understandings of collective behavior as seen in the writings of Neil Smelser. *Collective action* is a theory that describes what occurs when two or more people come together to pursue a common goal, even when they do not necessarily have the formal structure of an organization. Smelser (1962) believes collective action is based on beliefs that guide "exaggerated behavior" in response to "extraordinary forces," which is different from ordinary human behavior in communities. He believed collective action had the function of working for stability in light of the rapid change of social structures. However, Smelser was largely critical of such action (della Porta & Diani, 1998; Holst, 2002). Consider his response to industrial protests in England, which he says were "accompanied by many extravagant claims" and compounded by "anxiety, hostility, and fantasy" (quoted in Currie & Skolnick, 1970).

Smelser, like Parsons, assumed that social structures allow for essential and normal functions. In contrast, Smelser writes that collective behavior offers non-institutional or non-traditional reactions to normal social functions. He describes it as spontaneous, short-lived, disorganized, and deviant responses to stress and strain.

Structural functionalists discuss these reactions and the beliefs that bring them about as inherently irrational and characterize them by the forms the beliefs take, such as hysteria, wishful or magical thinking, and even hostility (Smelser, 1962; Holst, 2002). In turn, these beliefs are said to give rise to specific forms of collective behaviors: panics, crazes, fads, and outbursts.

Here, as we see in Smelser (1962) and others, existing social structures are privileged and departures from the status quo are deviant at best and perhaps even described as dangerous, irrational, and extremist (della Porta & Diani, 1998; Holst, 2002). Critics of this theoretical approach recognize that collective behavior cannot be reduced to micro-level deviant behaviors as they point out macro-level political dimensions to collective behavior (McAdam, 1982).

The structural functionalist approach often describes the collective action of social movements as a crisis behavior that seeks to deal with change. Other approaches to collective behavior provide grounds for new norms and new expressions of social solidarity based on social and political meanings of actions. Before turning to symbolic interactionism as an alternative way to understand collective behavior, let us look at an example of where these characteristics can be seen.

In recent years, student movements have organized at American universities to address the issue of a living wage. These movements have come under criticisms that describe their efforts as collective fads that are irrational in light of the economic functions at work in the structures of university life. The clearest example is the response to a hunger strike that took place at Harvard University. The students' decision not to eat was seen as dangerously naïve and immature in light of the explanations given by the administration that university wages reflected normal economic practices in the region. While other theoretical factors were at play in the success of the movement at Harvard, there is value to be seen in the collective behaviors exhibited there, for their symbolic meaning, but also, perhaps, for people living in poverty and the social strain created as students raised awareness about these matters.

Collective Behavior in Symbolic Interactionism.   We have discussed elements of the theory of symbolic interactionism in earlier chapters. These elements can be applied to collective behavior as well. Whereas the structural functionalists described above see collective behavior as merely abnormal, symbolic interactionists discuss how social strains foster the creation of shared beliefs that shape people's responses. Elizabeth Cady Stanton helped lead the young feminist movement of the early 20th century and her writing, including the Declaration printed later in this unit, offers an example of the sentiments of those who shared a belief that women have basic rights as human beings.

Herbert Blumer (1951), as part of the Chicago School of Social Thought, represents this perspective on collective behavior. He describes collective behavior as an expression of social change and social movements as a natural experience in times of social transformation. The meaning participants assign to social movements is essential to understanding their collective behavior. This symbolic interactionism is at the core of Blumer's perspective.

Social organizing for social change is based on the social meanings people associate with social structures (Buechler, 2000). In other words, the conflict of value systems and the way people understand these differences motivates then to organize in meaningful ways that can drive social change (della Porta & Diani, 1998; Turner & Killian, 1987). This view emphasizes the creativity of individuals making meaning of their world. It recognizes that people behave based on meaning-making processes that may be spontaneous, but may also be based on rational communication of interpreted symbols that drive social action.

Perceptions, feelings, and ideas give rise to fluid social processes that are created, sustained, and transformed in an ongoing interpretive manner (Blumer, 1951).

Turner and Killian (1987) reflect this perspective in describing the spontaneous developments that arise in contradiction to those of the larger society when there is a shared image of a better future and a feeling of participation in working toward this imagined future. Groups develop and interpret symbols to guide their actions. These processes may still be largely unstructured, but Turner and Killian do emphasize more rational communication than Blumer through their notion that collective action is based on the translation of perceptions, feelings, and ideas into action (Turner & Killian, 1987).

As an example, let us consider another university-based living wage movement. The experiences at Baylor University show the use of local shared meanings as well as resistance to them. In 2007, a student social justice organization had been working on a campaign for several months before having a conversation about what motivated their involvement. Several participants had relationships with low-wage staff members from their churches and had deep feelings about the matter. This led to the recognition that most students involved in the effort were shaped by biblical themes of justice. On this largely evangelical, Christian campus, students knew they must interpret symbols of their faith in light of its message of compassion for brothers and sisters living in need. This helped in recruiting other students, in developing relationships with other staff members, and in sustaining their involvement over time, but has not been strong enough to overcome shared economic beliefs, which have proven to be stronger than shared beliefs of Baylor's religious faith.

The shared meaning of a faith-based sense of justice and the collective grievance of students and staff has not yet been enough to foster social change at Baylor. Key resources, organization, and allies may be what are needed to make the difference. This is a part of McCarthy & Zald's (1973, 1977) argument for the turn to resource mobilization theory. The negative connotations of irrational collective behaviors on the one hand and the potential strength of shared meaning for collective action on the other have led to empirical studies of behavior. These studies reflect a shift by some critics to the economic and political forces that can mobilize resources for action. After discussing resource mobilization theory, we will turn to other recent efforts that emphasize the construction of identity in working for change, as seen in writings identified as new social movement theory.

Resource Mobilization: From Spontaneous Crowds in Crisis to Rational Sociopolitical Structures

In contrast to the arguments above, which say that collective behavior and social movements are disorganized and irrational, at worst, and meaningful, but still emotional, reactive symbolic experiences, at best, research begun in the 1970s suggested that social movements were a normal part of economic and political struggles for social change (della Porta & Diani, 1998; Holst, 2002; McAdam, 1982). As a result, social movements and collective protests have been presented

Competency Connections

Social Movements Using Research

The Role of Research in Support of the International Fair Trade Movement

Research reports and fact sheets support the International Fair Trade Movement by addressing the unfair trading of coffee and exporting of handicrafts from poor developing countries to the wealthy nations of North America. According to the Oxfam America website, "75% of the world's coffee is produced by small-scale farmers, who sell their beans for less than they cost to produce" (http://oxfamamerica.org). Oxfam America plays a vital role in producing research and fact sheets that demonstrate the economic inequalities that farmers experience, while also producing reports outlining strategies that would allow farmers to get a better deal for their products. Research papers, like "Mugged: Poverty in Your Coffee Cup," which analyzes the results of collapsed coffee prices, play a vital role in educating Americans about how fair trade would impact farmers.

In addition to research, Oxfam America advocates for farmers by asking consumers to pressure their local supermarkets to stock Fair Trade Certified™ products. If farmers could get a fair price for their product, their lives would be forever changed. They would have more wages to obtain the basic necessities of food, clothing, and shelter, and they would be empowered to live a better quality of life.

As agencies like Oxfam America demonstrate, research provides a very important advocacy tool for social workers and others seeking involvement in social movements.

Oxfam America website. Retrieved March 3, 2010 from http://oxfamamerica.org.

---

by this perspective as rational, goal-oriented experiences of working for the collective social good (McCarthy & Zald, 1973).

According to proponents of this view, if political and economic resources are mobilized for change, then social movements look much more like conventional politics. People organize when they disagree with the direction current leaders are going. When shown that the benefits of their efforts outweigh the costs, new recruits will be motivated to join them. They can form organizations and alliances and with enough resources collected and enough political will, the participants of the movement will have created change (McAdam, 1982; McCarthy & Zald, 1973).

Entrepreneurial Approach to Resources.   McCarthy and Zald (1973), as pioneers of this perspective, focus on a rational choice. In this perspective, potential participants in the social movements conduct a personal cost–benefit analysis. If it benefits an individual more than it costs her, then why would she not join? And, if there is no clear gain, why would an individual participate? In the view of resource mobilization theory, social movements include these kind of calculated expressions based on the presence of individuals, as well as the resources that can be strategically organized and mobilized for their cause (Holst, 2002; Oberschall, 1993; Zald & McCarthy, 1987).

Because grievances and frustrations are not enough to bring about social change, individuals, also known as "entrepreneurs," and organizations work to maximize resources that can help them communicate a vision to foster change. These resources include relationships with influential individuals and organizations, finances, services, and benefits that others might bring, the support of media, and a general understanding that the benefits of change outweigh the costs (Buechler, 2000). Obtaining these resources implies that the benefits of participation outweigh the costs. With these material and nonmaterial resources at hand, the tension of social discontentedness can be purposefully transformed into mobilization for change (della Porta & Diani, 1998). Here, conscious actors make rational choices for change in a system.

There is an entrepreneurial spirit to this approach, and this economic perspective lends itself to an organizational perspective. To sustain movements, maximize benefits, maintain involvement of allies, and promote change, entrepreneurs develop social movement organizations (SMOs) as key mobilizing structures (McCarthy & Zald, 1977). As a mobilizing structure, these organizations formalize the mission and the goals of the movement and help to bring about collective action. For some movements and organizations, we see social movement industries arise as the next step. Here, multiple SMOs work together toward the common goals of a social movement.

Eve Ensler provides an example of entrepreneurial spirit from a feminist theoretical perspective. V-Day is a global social movement organization that Ensler helped to create to stop violence against women and girls. V-Day "generates broad attention for the fight to stop violence against women and girls, including rape, battery, incest, female genital mutilation and sexual slavery" (V-Day, 2008).

Through V-Day campaigns that the organization has created, local volunteers and college students produce benefit performances of "The Vagina Monologues" to raise awareness and funds for antiviolence groups in local communities. V-Day strengthens local antiviolence organizations through the money, volunteer interest, and general awareness raised through performances.

Political Approach to Resources.   The rational choice economic theory of resource mobilization theory has been criticized for being so rationally focused that it ignores structural and political factors, as well as the emotional force of people who desire change. In recognizing the "political process" of a social movement, value is seen not only in financial resources, but also in relational factors, particularly if elite political actors become involved in working for change (della Porta & Diani, 1998; McAdam, 1982).

Elite allies represent great value to a movement; social movements also have to consider free-riders. The economists in resource mobilization theory suggest that it is rational to have free-riders who reap the benefits of a movement while reducing the costs to themselves. Another argument the political approach suggests is that there are also people who will participate without a full consideration of costs and benefits (Fireman & Gamson, 1979). One result is that some social movement organizations offer incentives to encourage full participation, incentives "nonmembers" may not be able to receive even if there are widely available social benefits.

McAdam (1982) suggests that elites and entrepreneurs within a movement do not really have as much power as some say that they do; rather, social movements are mass movements, and even without key human resources, the collective grievances of people is an invaluable resource. Political opportunities arise where the will of the people, or their "cognitive liberation," is a vital force for change, even without key leaders.

Resource mobilization theory has often suggested that the organization of social movements is a natural part of the experience of social systems rather than the result of a strain, grievance, crisis, or malfunction in a social system. The people who participate in collective action may be conscious, rational participants in conventional activities of "normal politics" (Tilly, Tilly, & Tilly, 1975). Piven & Cloward (1995) have criticized this perspective for its tendency to normalize collective protest as a part of rational, institutional processes. They argue that the dynamics of privilege and the struggles for power point to a level of conflict that is, in fact, beyond the scope of everyday political processes.

There may be a rational and even calculated dimension to social movements, strengthened by the presence of resources, but there is an emotional dimension and a force as well. This emotional aspect may help to motivate solidarity and resistance that may be nonconformist and nonrational. Piven and Cloward (1995) make their point: "A riot is clearly not an electoral rally, and both the participants and the authorities know the difference" (p. 139).

An clear example of Piven and Cloward's statement occurred in 2002, when the United States was fighting in Afghanistan and preparing for war in Iraq: dissent was labeled "un-American." Americans United for Peace and Justice came together as the result of a meeting of 70 organizations working for peace. Together, they initiated hundreds of protests around the nation and the two largest demonstrations as the war was beginning, including the "The World Says No to War," a rally at the United Nations headquarters in New York City that drew more than 500,000 participants. In President George W. Bush's hometown of Crawford, Texas, several small groups came together to hold rallies. This small, conservative community was very patient, but it was clear that collective action against the war was outside the realm of normative politics. Bush acknowledged the events, yet responded that public opinion would not shape his leadership around matters of foreign policy.

Recognition of logical and linear approaches to organizing a movement has been the value of resource mobilization theory. Similarly, this theory has shown how methods used by social movements can be a part of the normal political process. However, whether struggling for peace or for human rights, there are those who recognize that sometimes the issues are not so clear and simple. More often than not, culture is among the factors that call into question the norms of resource mobilization theory. We now turn to new social movement theories, an array of perspectives that consider the diversity of approaches to working for change in society.

NEW SOCIAL MOVEMENT THEORIES: FROM MODERN ECONOMIC ARGUMENTS TO POSTMODERN PLURALISTIC PRACTICES

Most of the interpretations of social movements discussed so far point to economic and political factors driving social movements. With movements arising that have addressed peacemaking—as well as access to education, support for the environment, and the role of women and sexual minorities—scholarship began to look beyond the dominant Marxist lens used in social movement theories (della Porta & Diani, 1998; Holst, 2002). Furthermore, in the same way resource mobilization theories were critical of the collective behavior theories for not being rational and linear in their development, new social movement theories are critical of resource mobilization for not being attentive to the role of culture and diversity. The diversity of movements, of participants in movements, and of research about movements has provided a wider range of emphases in the past few decades. Whether or not everyone agrees on the issue of how much theoretical content is actually "new," there is something distinct in the emphasis on diverse cultural processes in working for change (Buechler, 2000).

With roots in Europe and a worldview that is critical of modern, economic progress and growth, there are some questions and issues being raised that seem to be new, namely the primacy of focus on independent identities and cultural autonomy (Holst, 2002). Individual identity and personal rights have been central to these writings (Larana, Johnston, & Gusfield, 1994; Melucci, 1989).

Competency Connections

Social Movements and Policy

Recent Legislation Related to Sexual Minorities

The Human Rights Campaign rallies against state and federal laws that deny equal rights to lesbian, gay, bisexual, and transgender (LGBT) people. This 750,000 member grassroots movement founded in 1980 seeks rights related to marriage and relationship recognition, employment laws, hate crimes, the military, religion and faith, and other issues of concern for LGBT people.

In the 21st century, one of the most intense debates in the United States is how each state will define marriage and domestic partnerships In 1996, Congress passed the Defense of Marriage Act (DOMA), which defined marriage on a federal level as a union between one man and one woman and proclaimed unions of same sex couples as being null and void. As of 2010, five states and the District of Columbia have recognized same-sex marriages (Massachusetts, Connecticut, Iowa, New Hampshire, Vermont, and DC). However, under DOMA, even if a state recognizes same-sex marriages, the federal government does not. Consequently, same-sex couples may not access federal benefits such as those related to Social Security, survivorship, and inheritance. The Human Rights Campaign has been advocating for the equal rights of federal LGBT employees by appealing to legislative members to implement The Domestic Partnership and Obligations Act, which would define a domestic partner as "an adult person living with, but not married to, another adult person in a committed, intimate relationship" for partners to filing an affidavit of eligibility for benefits.

Human Rights Campaign website. Retrieved March 2010 from http://www.hrc.org.

Desiring more than simply material gain, participants in new social movements challenge social and political norms and desire personal freedom and autonomy. New social movements are distinct not only in that they are not rooted in economics, but also that they are less conventional in the actions their participants use (Klandermans, 1991).

New social movement theories have emerged as the dominant approach to understanding social movements in Europe because of the rise of peace, environmental, women's, and other identity movements. The characteristics of these movements may or may not be all that new, but this title has remained, as there seems to be some distinction from the class-related movement theories, such as those rooted in trade union and working-class political party efforts of the industrial movement (Holst, 2002). What does seem to be new is the attention given to social movement theory in a wide variety of disciplines and the focus of the literature, which includes traditional economic and Marxist themes, but also foci that include race, ethnicity, gender, sexual orientation, age, citizenship, and many others (Buechler, 2000; Holst, 2002). Others have stated that the pluralism of values and ideas is what makes these theories new (Larana, Johnston, & Gusfield, 1994).

New movements for change are still social, but in new ways. There is both increased attention on the needs, opportunities, and roles of individual participants and at the same time a renewed focus on characteristics of larger systems. Buechler (2000) describes this as having a backdrop of "societal totality." Buechler (2002) is perhaps most clear in stating that "the most distinctive feature of new social movement theories is their attempt to identify the links between (new) social structures or societal totalities and (new) forms of collective action" (p. 50).

The environmental movement, as well as the deep ecology movement, are both recent value-laden movements that promote wide-scale (global) social change but whose primary emphasis is not economic. The ecological movement began with the book *Silent Spring*, by Rachel Carson (1962). Environmentalists work with anyone interested in protecting the environment, yet the efforts of leaders in the movement are not always based on rational methods or normalized politics. Deep ecology as a movement goes even further, placing an even greater value on nonhuman species, ecosystems, and processes in nature than established environmental movements. The basis of deep ecology is founded in Arne Næss's (1989) teachings that, like humanity, every entity in the living environment as a whole has the same right to live and flourish. Deep ecology has led to a new system of environmental ethics.

THE STATE OF THEORY AND PRACTICE TODAY

A contemporary perspective that may deserve its own category is seen in the role that social constructionist theory offers to new social movement theories. Social constructionism is an interpretive theory that serves as an alternative to the functionalist resource mobilization paradigm and a return to some of the concepts of symbolic interactionist approaches to collective behavior theory (Buechler, 2002; Gamson, 1995; Gusfield, 1994). As with new social movement theories, social constructionist theory does not give preference to the role of rationalism, but recognizes the roles that individuals and organizations play in a movement, while also emphasizing the meaning that is formed by these participants working together. This also recognizes the social, emotional, and cognitive role of politics, and not just economics, in movements.

Social constructionist approaches to collective action are based on negotiated interactions among participants and between participants and opponents. The shared meaning among participants is described using the concept of "framing" (Goffman, 1974). The social construction of a social movement begins to take shape as individuals and organizations create and adapt "frames," or the concepts and ideas that can unite and incite movement participants. If a concept is framed well, it will have meaning that motivates people to be involved in social activism and fosters a collective identity.

Assessing the costs and benefits of resources is important; however, equally important is the shift from vague dissatisfactions to the social construction of well-defined grievances (Buechler, 2000). As these grievances are framed among multiple stakeholders, then consensus and solidarity can be formed among participants, motivating people to join the movement and work for change.

With so many diverse approaches to understanding social movements, the questions can be asked: Are we returning to a general theory of social movements? Is there some synthesis of theoretical perspectives available? McAdam, McCarthy, and Zald (1996) promote a synthesis that includes the concepts of political opportunities, mobilizing structures, and framing processes. This model has been criticized as a revival of resource mobilization theory with some recognition of social constructionism, but with firm roots in a functionalist, perspective. Social constructionism and new social movements argue that diverse cultures develop a sense of multiple perspectives for their involvement and that these are political and social and not just economic, are not always valued in a world where social movement organizations and elite allies control the way a movement is framed (Buechler, 2000; Giugni, 1998).

Attempts at a unified understanding of a general social movement theory can have value, but it is just as important to understand the similarities and differences between the multiple theories mentioned above. The following implications point to what the theories may have in common, but also to where they diverge.

CONNECTING THEORY AND PRACTICE

Having access to knowledge about social movements can be of value as social workers function in their role as change agents. For example, Oberschall (1992), representing resource mobilization theory, argues that for movements to grow and make a difference, there have to be changes in the ability to work for change together (increased group size, better communications, group cohesion, etc.), as well as a weakness in the opposition, support from powerful allies, and the success of other social movements in the context.

However, others have argued that increased capacity and opportunity do not determine actions or outcomes. Piven and Cloward (1995), promoting collective action theory, write, "capacity does not predict anything" (p. 150). McNair, Fowler, and Harris (2000), promoting new social movement theories, state that the diversity functions of a movement as a whole, and not simply the organizations they form or the people they employ, create change.

Social workers need not know which perspective is right in order to be involved, but it can be helpful to know which theory relates to their view of the issues at hand. Knowledge of these theories may help inform how a social worker chooses to be involved.

How do we see these theories in practice today? In social work, there are a variety of ways practitioners are involved in social movements. In considering social work practice in social movements, there are several questions to be asked that reflect the theoretical perspectives above. Social movement practice suggests some macro-level interaction of people, many of whom are passionate at the microlevel of practice. Social workers involved in clinical practice participate in movements to promote mental health parity. In health care settings, social workers are often engaged in addressing a lack of affordable quality health care options. Practitioners offering case management may also join community-wide efforts to address the social forces impacting the individuals they serve. For each opportunity to join in on a social movement, there is an opportunity to consider how you participate. Is the effort the collective action of individuals and small groups, or does it represent the work of an organization? Are people joining in because of specific ways they stand to gain, or is there a deeper meaning driving their involvement? Is the movement based on a common social experience or economic factors? These questions likely have more complex answers, but the discussions they prompt are reflective of the different theories addressed above. Let us consider these in more detail.

For example, if dedicated individuals come together to work for peace, to fight poverty, or to challenge racism, to what extent do they function as individuals with shared beliefs working in solidarity or as individuals joining a more formal organization? Some will see both options as equally appropriate means to an end. For some, reflecting symbolic interactionism or social constructionism, collective action may include meaningful, but less formal efforts to build unity in a way that is transformative. It may not be a step toward a formal organization that is mobilized for change, but it could include social workers who meet regularly and work faithfully for change in a variety of ways as volunteers or as representatives of other agencies. Reflecting resource mobilization theory, social workers may organize toward a more formal organization, or at least toward a calculated consideration of resources, may include social workers in planning and development, and may hire social workers in administration as well as in organizing activities in a new organization that may come about. Others might argue that the same time spent mobilizing resources could be spent developing shared meaning and identity. From a social constructionist or a new social movement perspective, the administration and planning of a new organization is not as important as the process of developing shared meanings and seeing how this contributes to change. This may not lead to the hiring of professional organizers, but it certainly reflects a process whereby social workers in multiple roles can be of value.

Another difference in theoretical perspective is seen in the question of whether social movements tend to be matters of political participation or public protest. The issue here is one of power, and the questions about use of power are similar to the issues above. Some people involved may address power through creating a formal organization and others through consensus-building activities. Furthermore, some may feel that power is addressed through conventional political participation. Social workers involved from a resource mobilization perspective may hire lobbyists to work for legislative change or encourage the creation of procedures as a way to implement social policy. Meanwhile, others, from a

Competency Connections

Ethical Decision Making and Social Movements

The NASW Code: Ethical Principles for Social and Political Action

Social workers involved in social movements must practice ethical decision making. The Code of Ethics of the National Association of Social Workers (Approved by the 1996 NASW Delegate Assembly and revised by the 2008 NASW Delegate Assembly) reminds us that all social workers may not agree on every social issue.

Ethical decision making is a process. There are many instances in social work in which simple answers are not available to resolve complex ethical issues. Social workers should take into consideration all the values, principles, and standards in this Code that are relevant to any situation in which ethical judgment is warranted. Social workers' decisions and actions should be consistent with the spirit as well as the letter of this Code (see section on the "Purpose of the NASW Code of Ethics").

In section 6.04 the Code outlines ethical principles for social and political action. As you read them, consider the complexity of decision making for social workers involved in social movements.

(a) Social workers should engage in social and political action that seeks to ensure that all people have equal access to the resources, employment, services, and opportunities they require to meet their basic human needs and to develop fully.

Social workers should be aware of the impact of the political arena on practice and should advocate for changes in policy and legislation to improve social conditions in order to meet basic human needs and promote social justice.

(b) Social workers should act to expand choice and opportunity for all people, with special regard for vulnerable, disadvantaged, oppressed, and exploited people and groups.

(c) Social workers should promote conditions that encourage respect for cultural and social diversity within the United States and globally. Social workers should promote policies and practices that demonstrate respect for difference, support the expansion of cultural knowledge and resources, advocate for programs and institutions that demonstrate cultural competence, and promote policies that safeguard the rights of and confirm equity and social justice for all people.

(d) Social workers should act to prevent and eliminate domination of, exploitation of, and discrimination against any person, group, or class on the basis of race, ethnicity, national origin, color, sex, sexual orientation, gender identity or expression, age, marital status, political belief, religion, immigration status, or mental or physical disability.

collective action perspective, may practice in such a way that goes against the status quo political process. Here, social workers may lead a rally that disrupts "business as usual" when policies are not implemented or when legislators fail to act. Again, there seems to be a clear difference between social workers meeting with the city council to discuss homelessness and social workers uniting to live with the homeless on the steps outside city hall.

Different movements may use different tactics reflecting different theories. For example, a local living wage movement may always reflect a collective action approach and a women's rights movement may use concepts from new social movement theories. On the other hand, as a movement develops, we may see leaders use actions that reflect different theories. The hunger movement may shift from collective action, in which people seem to gather for marches and rallies for a shared purpose that seems unclear, into a resource mobilization perspective when, for example, influential allies are on board whose financing contributes to an organization. As multiple, diverse stakeholders are equally involved, the movement may then again shift to a social constructionist perspective when there are shifts in the meaning of "hunger."

The theories contribute to a diversity of practice. Social workers can be involved in many different ways and we hope that you have a greater appreciation of social movement theories and the ways those can be lived in your professional life.

Reading 2

Declaration of Sentiments and Resolutions, Seneca Falls Convention

This classic document, written at the Women's Rights Conference in 1848, launched the fight for women's rights, especially women's right to vote. It discussed the many abuses women have historically suffered at the hands of a male-dominated society and focuses on the truth that women and men inherently have equal worth and value. Therefore, they should posses the same rights as men in how they are treated and what they are permitted to do in society. It marks the launch of the women's rights movement in the United States in the 19th century. Consider the rhetoric (tools of language) used in this declaration. How can social workers use language to promote and enhance social movements of all kinds?

THE SENECA FALLS DECLARATION OF SENTIMENTS AND RESOLUTIONS SENECA FALLS, NEW YORK, 1848

When, in the course of human events, it becomes necessary for one portion of the family of man to assume among the people of the earth a position different from that which they have hitherto occupied, but to one which the laws of nature and of nature's God entitle them, a decent respect to the opinions of mankind requires that they should declare the causes that impel them to such a course.

We hold these truths to be self-evident: that all men and women are created equal; that they are endowed by their Creator with certain inalienable rights; that among these are life, liberty, and the pursuit of happiness; that to secure these rights governments are instituted, deriving their just powers from the consent of the governed. Whenever any form of government becomes destructive of these ends, it is the right of those who suffer from it to refuse allegiance to it, and to insist upon the institution of a new government, laying its foundations on such principles, and organizing its powers in such form, as to them shall seem most likely to effect their safety and happiness. Prudence, indeed, will dictate

Stanton, E.C. (1848). *Declaration of sentiments and resolutions*. New York: Seneca Falls Convention.

that governments long established should not be changed for light and transient causes; and accordingly all experience hath shown that mankind are more disposed to suffer, while evils are sufferable, than to right themselves by abolishing the forms to which they were accustomed. But when a long train of abuses and usurpations, pursuing invariably the same object evinces a design to reduce them under absolute despotism, it is their duty to throw off such a government, and to provide new guards for their future security. Such has been the patient sufferance of the women under this government, and such is now the necessity which constrains them to demand the equal station to which they are entitled.

The history of mankind is a history, of repeated injuries and usurpations on the part of man toward woman, having in direct object the establishment of an absolute tyranny over her. To prove this, let facts be submitted to a candid world.

He has never permitted her to exercise her inalienable right to the elective franchise.

He has compelled her to submit to laws, in the formation of which she had no voice.

He has withheld from her rights which are given to the most ignorant and degraded men—both natives and foreigners.

Having deprived her of this first right of a citizen, the elective franchise, thereby leaving her without representation in the halls of legislation, he has opposed her on all sides.

He has made her, if married, in the eye of the law, civilly dead.

He has taken from her all right in property, even to the wages she earns.

He has made her, morally, an irresponsible being, as she can commit many crimes with impunity, provided they be done in the presence of her husband. In the covenant of marriage, she is compelled to promise obedience to her husband, he becoming, to all intents and purposes, her master—the law giving him power to deprive her of her liberty, and to administer chastisement.

He has so framed the laws of divorce, as to what shall be the proper causes, and in case of separation, to whom the guardianship of the children shall be given, as to be wholly regardless of the happiness of women—the law, in all cases, going upon a false supposition of the supremacy of man, and giving all power into his hands.

After depriving her of all rights as a married woman, if single, and the owner of property, he has taxed her to support a government which recognizes her only when her property can be made profitable to it.

He has monopolized nearly all the profitable employments, and from those she is permitted to follow, she receives but a scanty remuneration. He closes against her all the avenues to wealth and distinction which he considers most honorable to himself. As a teacher of theology, medicine, or law, she is not known.

He has denied her the facilities for obtaining a thorough education, all colleges being closed against her.

He allows her in Church, as well as State, but a subordinate position, claiming Apostolic authority for her exclusion from the ministry, and, with some exceptions, from any public participation in the affairs of the Church.

He has created a false public sentiment by giving to the world a different code of morals for men and women, by which moral delinquencies which exclude women from society, are not only tolerated, but deemed of little account in man.

He has usurped the prerogative of Jehovah himself, claiming it as his right to assign for her a sphere of action, when that belongs to her conscience and to her God.

He has endeavored, in every way that he could, to destroy her confidence in her own powers, to lessen her self-respect, and to make her willing to lead a dependent and abject life.

Now, in view of this entire disfranchisement of one-half the people of this country, their social and religious degradation in view of the unjust laws above mentioned, and because women do not feet themselves aggrieved, oppressed, and fraudulently deprived of their most sacred rights, we insist that they have immediate admission to all the rights and privileges which belong to them as citizens of the United States.

In entering upon the great work before us, we anticipate no small amount of misconception, misrepresentation, and ridicule; but we shall use every instrumentality, within our power to effect our object. We shall employ agents, circulate tracts, petition the State and National legislatures, and endeavor to enlist the pulpit and the press in our behalf. We hope this Convention will be followed by a series of Conventions embracing every part of the country.

RESOLUTIONS

WHEREAS, The great precept of nature is conceded to be, that "man shall pursue his own true and substantial happiness." Blackstone in his Commentaries remarks, that this law of Nature being coequal with mankind, and dictated by God himself, is of course superior in obligation to any other. It is binding over all the globe, in all countries and at all times; no human laws are of any validity if contrary to this, and such of them as are valid, derive all their force, and all their validity, and all their authority, mediately and immediately, from this original; therefore,

Resolved, That such laws as conflict, in any way, with the true and substantial happiness of woman, are contrary to the great precept of nature and of no validity, for this is "superior in obligation to any other."

Resolved, That all laws which prevent woman from occupying such a station in society as her conscience shall dictate, or which place her in a position inferior to that of man, are contrary to the great precept of nature, and therefore of no force or authority.

Resolved, That woman is man's equal was intended to be so by the Creator, and the highest good of the race demands that she should be recognized as such.

Resolved, That the women of this country ought to be enlightened in regard to the laws under which they live, that they may no longer publish their degradation by declaring themselves satisfied with their present position, nor their ignorance, by asserting that they have all the rights they want.

Resolved, That inasmuch as man, while claiming for himself intellectual superiority, does accord to woman moral superiority, it is preeminently his duty to encourage her to speak and teach, as she has an opportunity, in all religious assemblies.

Resolved, That the same amount of virtue, delicacy, and refinement of behavior that is required of woman in the social state, should also be required of man, and the same transgressions should be visited with equal severity on both man and woman.

Resolved, That the objection of indelicacy and impropriety, which is so often brought against women when she addresses a public audience, comes with a very ill-grace from those who encourage, by their attendance, her appearance on the stage, in the concert, or in feats of the circus.

Resolved, That woman has too long rested satisfied in the circumscribed limits which corrupt customs and a perverted application of the Scriptures have marked out for her, and that it is time she should move in the enlarged sphere which her great Creator has assigned her.

Resolved, That it is the duty of the women of this country to secure to themselves their sacred right to the elective franchise.

Resolved, That the equality of human rights results necessarily from the fact of the identity of the race in capabilities and responsibilities.

Resolved, therefore, That, being invested by the Creator with the same capabilities, and the same consciousness of responsibility for their exercise, it is demonstrably the right and duty of woman, equally with man, to promote every righteous cause by every righteous means; and especially in regard to the great subjects of morals and religion, it is self-evidently her right to participate with her brother in teaching them, both in private and in public, by writing and by speaking, by any instrumentalities proper to be used, and in any assemblies proper to be held, and this being a self-evident truth growing out of the divinely implanted principles of human nature, any custom or authority adverse to it, whether modern, or wearing the hoary sanction of antiquity, is to be regarded as a self-evident falsehood, and at war with mankind.

Reading 3

Social movements arise out of a desire for change. In this poem, written in the wake of 9/11 as our nation went to war, a young African-American woman expresses her frustration with our nation's focus. As she expressed it, "everyone seemed to be focused on war, and missing the big picture: we needed to fix us." Social movements often inspire music and poetry, from "Where Have All the Flowers Gone?," protesting war in the 1960s, to "We Are the World," written in the 1980s calling citizens to address the world's social problems. Artists like this young woman can contribute to social movements of their times by calling our attention to social issues.

Patriotic Observation

Reprinted by permission of Whitney Morris

Psychiatrist on TV
Trying to tell me
What I need to be
But what they can't see
Is what's inside of me
This is who I am
Time for me to take a stand
So that you will understand
This is me

People killin'
People dyin'
All around be folks is lyin'
People hurtin'
People cryin'
All I is this is mine
Where's the love
Where's the care
Hate is here
Hate is there
All around me no one's near
No one's there to calm my fear
No one seems to give a care
All I here is life's not fair

My friends are hanging from the trees
Rotting flesh comes on the breeze
They still can't seem to get a care
Though people see them hanging there
We turn our heads the other way
Tomorrow is another day
But tell me this, what can we say
Babies born everyday
As if that makes it all okay
For children to die everyday
For mothers to cry everyday
For fathers to say everyday
"I saw my baby die today"

Stop the pain
Stop the shame
We've ruined the American name
Someone famous once did say
We are our own worst enemy
But tell me this, who is to blame
No it's not Bush and his campaign
And Clinton's got his own shame
No Iraq is not to blame
It's not Bin Laden or Hussein
We're the only ones to blame
We wallow in our own shame
We have created our own pain

Yes our country still is one
But look at what we have become
We are one in pain
One in shame
The one's that are hurt
And the ones to blame

Reading 4

Taking Theory to Practice

The following decision case has been included in this unit to give you practice applying the concepts presented. The case is based on an actual practice situation gathered by interviewing a social worker at the master of social work level. When exploring the case, try formulating the problems, analyzing the information you have, and deciding on potential courses of action. This exploration can be done on your own or in study groups, discussing parts or the entirety of the case, according to how your instructor may guide you. The point is to help you learn to apply theory to practice and to develop important problem-solving and critical-thinking skills. Although this case is located within the unit on social movements it may intersect with other areas of practice as well, such as groups, organizations, communities, individuals, and families.

HOW CAN EVERYONE GET A JUST SHARE?

KAREN A. GRAY & TERRY A. WOLFER

In late January 2002, Anton Gunn, executive director of Just Share, left the House Ways and Means Health and Human Services subcommittee meeting feeling heavyhearted. With South Carolina's $320 million revenue shortfall, agencies were being forced to cut their budgets once again. For Health and Human Services, this meant deciding whether to cut Medicaid services for children or for the elderly. Frustration and anger welled up, as Anton reflected, "This is the second year of budget cuts, and most agencies have cut what little fat they had from their budgets. More cuts will mean cutting muscle. That 'muscle' is vital services to citizens of our state. We need to decide how Just Share can weigh in on the issues, and quick, while there's still time to exert some influence. Children and elderly folks' lives might be literally on the line."

JUST SHARE

Just Share, a statewide consumer advocacy organization, was founded 15 years before to protect the everyday citizen/consumer in South Carolina. A "consumer" was defined as anyone who consumed governmental services, pharmaceuticals, utilities, public transportation, or financial services. However, Just Share focused on low- and moderate-income families because they spend such a large portion of their income on essential goods and services (i.e., food and utilities). As Anton described it, "Our mission is to enhance the health, safety, and well-being of everyday people in the Palmetto state; which is a very bland way to say that we're about building the infrastructure for a social change movement in South Carolina."

In order of organizational priority, Just Share's activities included community organizing, policy advocacy that included lobbying on behalf of low-income consumers, and training for grassroots community organizations. Although Just Share did not do casework, they routinely received phone calls from individual consumers. In such cases, they typically referred people to appropriate agencies or to an attorney. As Anton explained, the organization's activities and issues "are more staff directed than board directed."

According to Anton, "Our bylaws state that it is imperative that the majority of our board should be people of color and women. Currently, we only have one white male, a local trial lawyer." There were 11 board members; they included the SC executive director of the AFL-CIO, the director of Interfaith Community Services, two professors from the University of South Carolina, and 4 consumers, such as an uninsured undergraduate student at Columbia College.

Although Just Share had developed an effective presence with state government, the state legislature, and local communities, it was a small organization. The other three staff members included John Ruoff, Ph.D., Research Director (part-time), who had been with the organization from the beginning; Gwen Hampton, MSW, Program Associate who had been on staff for nearly 2 years; and Rainie Jueschke, Development Director, a fund-raiser who was also a recent addition. According to Anton, raising money was sometimes difficult because, "We piss people off. We usually take the position that others are afraid to take, such as advocating for same sex marriages and outlawing marital rape." Most funding (80%) came from national foundations (outside of South Carolina). The remaining funds came from a local foundation and individual contributions by 350 in-state members of Just Share. The annual budget was approximately $200,000.

ANTON GUNN, MSW

Not quite 30 years old, Anton had several years' experience in community organizing and advocacy in South Carolina and other states. An ex-football player for the University of South Carolina, he had an imposing physical presence. This, coupled with his charisma, intelligence, and warmth, made him someone that people remembered long after meeting him. As an African-American man from a working-class background, several experiences had contributed to his passion for social justice. While Anton was growing up, his father was in the Navy and his mother was a teacher. Nevertheless, his family still qualified for food stamps. It angered Anton that his parents worked so hard and were so woefully underpaid. Anton recounted how his undergraduate years helped form his feelings about justice: "I was oppressed and exploited as a Division I college football player. I participated in a sport that generated several million dollars a week for a university, but I personally didn't have money to buy toothpaste, deodorant, clothes, or shoes for myself. Other black men and I were physically, emotionally, and financially exploited by big-money college athletics and given little to nothing in return. We were left with a degree, if we got one at all, that wasn't even worth the paper it was printed on. After I graduated from college, I worked for minimum wage for 18 months."

Although very good at building relationships, Anton wasn't afraid of confrontation. His curiosity, imagination, and passion—other qualities important for a community organizer and policy advocate—sometimes led him to take on too much. Anton knew this limited his effectiveness because he didn't always have enough time to devote to all of Just Share's projects.

THE STATE OF THE STATE

In the 1990s, during an extended period of relative prosperity and budget surpluses, South Carolina legislators passed, and a Democratic governor signed, several major tax cuts. But in late 2001, for the second year in a row, South Carolina experienced a budget crisis when shrinking tax revenues from a slumping economy could not keep pace with state budget needs.

Therefore, this year coming up with a budget was going to be a painful, arduous, and dividing process. All budget bills originated in the solidly Republican House; if passed, the bills move on to the Senate. In November 2001, all state agency directors were given specific directives before presenting their budgets to the House Ways and Means subcommittees: "Don't show up with a big budget. Trim as much as possible, and then more will be trimmed."

Rick Quinn, a Republican, the House Majority leader, and chairman of the Ways and Means subcommittee on health care said that $100 million of the cuts had to come from health care, specifically the Department of Health and Human Services that administered Medicaid. This $100 million cut would cost South Carolina approximately $400 million in reduced expenditures, because the state would lose matching federal dollars.

The total Medicaid budget for the state of South Carolina was $2.9 billion. Most of it was spent on two populations: children and elderly or disabled adults. In South Carolina, less than 6% of the current Medicaid population received Temporary Assistance for Needy Families (TANF). More than 370,000 (44%)

of all children in South Carolina received Medicaid. Medicaid paid for two-thirds of all nursing home beds and half of the births in South Carolina. If the proposed budget cuts targeted both children and the elderly or disabled adults, it could result in up to 42,000 children losing Medicaid and up to 46,000 elderly or disabled adults losing coverage for prescription drugs.

The director of the Department of Health and Human Services was Bill Prince. In light of the budget crisis, he offered several proposals for the General Assembly to consider. First, he suggested that South Carolina could reduce optional Medicaid services. One conservative legislator liked to call South Carolina's Medicaid program "the Cadillac version of health care," because it provided several optional services. South Carolina Medicaid covered some services because federal regulations required it to do so, and some because it chose to do so. Bill Prince suggested that the state could save money by going to a bare bones Medicaid program, which meant eliminating optional services such as prescription drugs, adult day care, and Meals on Wheels. It could continue to cover hospitalization, emergency room care, and other core services as required by federal policy. Alternatively, he proposed that the state could reduce the number of people eligible for Medicaid by reducing eligibility levels from 150% of the federal poverty level to 100% or by reducing nursing home coverage. But Bill Prince *did not* want to reduce the amount that providers (i.e., physicians) were reimbursed for treating Medicaid patients. Because there were already too few providers, he feared a cut in reimbursement rates would prompt some providers to leave the system, thus reducing recipients' access to services.

As reported by Crumbo (2002) in *The State* newspaper (p. A1), "Some say the cuts are politically motivated." In television ads, Democratic governor Hodges touted the Silver Card program, a prescription drug program for seniors he had created the previous year. Although the program required seniors to pay a $500 deductible before they could get these prescription drug benefits, it relied on substantial funding by the state. This program was funded by part of the tobacco settlement a few years before. The $20 million from the tobacco settlement used to start the program was a "one-time shot" of funding. Thereafter, the state needed to find money to fund the program. Rick Quinn suggested scrapping the Silver Card program and funneling that $20 million into Medicaid. Under a new federal Health Insurance Portability and Accountability Act (HIPAA) proposal, it was possible to receive matching federal dollars (at a rate of 3:1) if a state extended Medicaid coverage to more seniors. This included prescription drugs and potentially recaptured 40% to 50% of the seniors cut from the Silver Card program.

JUST SHARE'S ALLIANCES AND RELATIONSHIPS

Just Share was in coalition with several nonprofit organizations that have an interest in health care for poor children and elders. However, almost none of these organizations were positioned to act on the current crisis. For instance, the South Carolina chapter of the National Association of Social Workers was heavily involved in promoting a Scope of Practice bill, an effort to protect and promote the social work profession, and had little energy and few resources for other issues. Statewide advocacy groups for children don't advocate for the elderly, and statewide advocacy groups for the elderly don't advocate for children. The one organization that might be in a position to advocate was a statewide legal services organization.

Both Just Share and Anton had a working relationship with Bill Prince. He had been open to meeting with Medicaid and health care advocacy organizations on this and other issues. Anton knew Bill Prince was in a tough position now; he didn't want to make any more cuts.

Although Just Share had productive relationships with many legislators, Rick Quinn was not one of them. As Anton put it, "We have influence and impact with many different legislators who are in key positions on key committees. However, we have a stumbling block with the chair of this subcommittee, Rick Quinn. Most of the organizing work Just Share does is with low- and moderate-income African Americans. Quinn's constituency is moderate- and high-income whites, most of whom don't see themselves in the same class as poor and middle-class black people, even though their need for quality health care is exactly the same."

FUNDING FOR HEALTH CARE

Anton explained Just Share's position on health care: "Health care is very important to our work at Just Share. We hung our hat on that issue in 1993 when Bill Clinton was talking about universal coverage and reforming health care. Our recent work has mainly been to cover low-income people under Medicaid. Our primary concern is covering low-income children and their working-poor parents. We have raised money for that advocacy work. A lot of our grant proposals are tied in to us having some success in organizing and affecting public policy on health care issues, which means improving public policy or changing public policy around health care. Therefore, if we don't make any positive changes in health care policy this year, if seniors' and children's Medicaid services get cut, then we basically have not accomplished what we were trying to do in those proposals. People understand that it is difficult to make change in that regard and that sometimes that there are 4- or 5-year fights, but funders don't fund in 4- or 5-year cycles. They fund in 1-, 2-, or possibly 3-year cycles. After the first or second year, if you haven't made significant progress towards your goal then they will give the money to somebody else. Once you lose the money, you lose the momentum that you gained because you don't have money to have meetings and pay for food and child care for these low-income people who come out in the evening and miss time off of work to come to actions or other things that we ask them to do. It puts us in a more difficult situation in order to be able to achieve anything because this is movement-building. We start with our base and build; but it takes resources to do that. It takes time to make those changes and so without the resources and without having the time to make the changes, you lose. We get a lot of our money for health care, close to $75,000. So this budget crisis is a very important issue for us, both for our constituency and for our organization."

"Do we have to decide who is more valuable—children or the elderly? Can we think outside the box? Do we have enough time and resources to think outside the box?"

Anton mulled over his choices of actions. To him, "The choice between children and elders is a choice between primary and tertiary care, both of which are necessary for the health of South Carolina. This is the choice the subcommittee wants to make. Just Share sees other options, but these options are not palatable to many South Carolina legislators. So do we play by their rules or do we make up new rules?" The subcommittees would soon be presenting to the full committee.

Just Share thought an increase in the tobacco tax would be a good source for new revenue. A tobacco-producing state, South Carolina charged the fourth lowest amount of taxes per pack of cigarettes, only 7 cents per pack. Other states charged from 5 cents to $1.11. If South Carolina raised its tobacco tax from 7 cents per pack to 17 cents per pack, it would create $40 million in new state revenue. If South Carolina used that $40 million for a Medicaid match, it could draw down $92 million in federal dollars, for a total of $130 million for Medicaid. The added benefit of increasing tobacco taxes is the inverse correlation between increased prices and decreased smoking by children. But Anton knew that tobacco farmers had successfully defeated such tax increases before. In addition, legislators opposed to any kind of tax increase would attempt to shoot this one down, too.

Anton needed to decide quickly how Just Share should weigh in.

SUMMARY

Our objective for this unit was for you to see the value of social movements and the role social workers can serve within them. A social movement is a form of group action, perhaps through the work of a formal organization or perhaps through community members who have come together for a common cause, which seeks to promote or to resist social change. In some ways, the profession itself functions as a social movement; we can serve as a force for social justice and liberating social change. The profession takes into consideration cultural and structural factors as we challenge injustice, discrimination, and oppression. Social workers have actively led social movements throughout our history. Other contemporary movements that have had social work support include immigration rights and living-wage movements.

Early social movements focused on collective behavior and resource mobilization, while more recently, newer views of social movements recognize the diversity of movements and of participants in movements. Whereas earlier movements were economically driven, more recent value-laden movements such as the environmental movement, as well as the deep ecology movement, promote global social change, for which the primary emphasis is not economic.

Readings 2, 3, and 4 were designed to deepen your understanding of social movements and provide opportunities to apply what you have learned. We included the famous "Seneca Falls Declaration of Sentiments and Resolutions" (Stanton, 1848) to provide you with historical insight into the early stages of the women's rights movement to promote basic rights and freedoms, including the right to vote. In order to examine the passions of young people, we included a poetry selection addressing our nation's social problems; the next social movements to emerge will engage this generation in new and unique ways. Finally, you had an opportunity to apply these theories to a real practice situation in the decision case, "How Can Everyone Get a Just Share?"

Social workers are involved in social movements in myriad ways: they may lead a rally that disrupts "business as usual" when policies aren't implemented or when legislators fail to act, or they may unite to live with the homeless on the steps outside city hall.

Social movements form as the result of social struggles over values, resources, and claims to power and privilege. They function to form shared perspectives, mobilize resources for change, and confront oppression. As they are forming and their functions are underway, people typically are not stopping to ask what theory they will use; nevertheless, there is great value in asking ourselves questions that may draw from these readings, and as a result, we may strengthen the movements that face current and future generations.

REFERENCES

Berk, R. (1974). *Collective Behavior*. Dubuque, IA: Brown.

Blumer, H. (1951). The field of collective behavior. In A.M. Lee, A. M. (Ed.), *Principles of sociology*. New York: Barnes & Noble.

Brieland, D. (1990, March). The Hull-House tradition and the contemporary social worker: Was Jane Addams really a social worker. *Social Work*, 134–138.

Buechler, S. (2000). *Social movements in advanced capitalism: The political economy and cultural construction of social activism*. New York: Oxford University Press.

Buechler, S. (2002). Toward a structural approach to social movements. In: B. Dobratz, T. Buzzell, & L. Waldner (Eds.), *Research in political sociology* (vol. 10). Oxford, England: Elsevier.

Carson, R. (1962). *Silent spring*. Boston: Houghton Mifflin.

Crumbo, C. (2002, March 12). First step advocates plan fight. *The State*, pp. A1, A7.

Currie, E., & Skolnick, J. (1970). A critical note on conceptions of collective behavior. *American Academy of Political and Social Science, 391*, 34–45.

Davis, A.F. (1984) *Spearheads of reform: The Social Settlements and the Progressive Movement 1890–1914*. New Brunswick, NJ: Rutgers University Press.

della Porta, D., & Diani, M. (1998). *Social movements: An introduction*. Malden, MA: Blackwell.

Dickens, P. (2000). *Social Darwinism: Linking evolutionary thought to social theory*. Philadelphia: Open University Press.

Fireman, B., & Gamson, W. (1979). Utilitarian logic in the resource mobilization perspective. In: Zald, M., & McCarthy, J., *The dynamics of social movements*. Cambridge, MA: Winthrop, pp 8–44.

Fisher , R., & Kling, J. (1994). *Mobilizing the community: Local politics in the era of the global city*. Newbury Park, CA: Sage.

Gamson, W. A. (1995) Constructing social protest. In H. Johnston & B. Klandermans (Eds.) *Social movements and culture*. London: UCL Press.

Gray, K.A., & Wolfer, T.A. (2005). How can everyone get a just share? In: T.A. Wolfer & T.L. Scales (Eds.), *Decision cases for advanced practice: Thinking like a social worker*. Monterey, CA: Brooks/Cole, pp 107–112.

Giugni, M. (1998). Structure and culture in social movement theory. *Sociological Forum 13*, 365–375.

Goffman, E. (1974). *Frame analysis: An essay on the organization of experience*. London: Harper and Row.

Gusfield, J. (1994). The reflexivity of social movements: Collective behavior and mass society theory revisited. In H. Johnson, E. Larana, & J. Gusfield, (Eds.) *New social movements: From ideology to identity*. Philadelphia: Temple University Press.

Holst, J. (2002). *Social movements, civil society, and radical adult education*. Westport, CT: Bergin & Garvey.

Human Rights Campaign website. Retrieved March 2010 from http://www.hrc.org.

Klandermans, B. (1991). New social movements and resource mobilization: The European and American approach revisited. In: D. Rucht (Ed.) *Research on social movements: The state of the art in Western Europe and the USA*. Boulder, CO: Westview Press.

Laraña, E., Johnston, H., & Gusfield, J. (1994). *New social movements: From ideology to identity*. Philadelphia: Temple.

LeBon, G. (1896). *The crowd*. London: Ernest Benn.

Lyman, S. (1994). *Social movements: Critiques, concepts, case studies*. New York: New York University Press.

McAdam, D. (1982). *The political process and the development of black insurgency*. Chicago: University of Chicago.

McAdam, D., McCarthy, J., & Zald, M. (1996). *Comparative perspectives on social movements: Political opportunities, mobilizing structures, and cultural framings*. New York: Cambridge University Press.

McCarthy, J., & Zald, M. (1973). *The trends of social movements in America: Professionalization and resource mobilization*. Morristown, NJ: General Learning Press.

McCarthy, J., & Zald, M. (1977). Resource mobilization and social movements. *American Journal of Sociology 82*(6), 12–12.

McNair, R., Fowler, L. & Harris, J. (2000). The diversity function of organizations that confront oppression: The evolution of three social movements. *Journal of Community Practice 7*(2), 71–88.

Melucci, A. (1989). *Nomads of the present: Social movements and individual needs in contemporary society*. Philadelphia: Temple University Press.

Meyer, D., & Tarrow, S. (1998). *The social movement society: Contentious politics for a new century*. Lanham, MD: Rowman & Littlefield.

Morris, W. (2005). Patriotic observation. Unpublished poem, Houston, TX.

Næss, A. (1989). *Ecology, community and lifestyle*. Cambridge: Cambridge University Press.

Oberschall, A. (1993). *Social movements: Ideologies, interests, and identities*. New Brunswick, NJ: Transaction.

Oxfam America website. Retrieved March 3, 2010 from http://oxfamamerica.org.

Parsons, T. (1967). *Sociological theory and modern society*. New York: Free Press.

Piven, F.F., & Cloward, R.A. (1995). Collective protest: A critique of resource-mobilization theory. In: S.M. Lyman (Ed.), *Social movements: Critiques, concepts, and case studies*. New York: New York University Press.

Smelser, N. (1962). *Theory of Collective Behavior*. New York: Free Press.

Stanton, E.C. (1848). *Declaration of sentiments and resolutions*. New York: The Seneca Falls Convention.

Tilly, C., Tilly, L. & Tilly, R. (1975). *The rebellious century: 1830–1975*. Cambridge: Harvard University Press.

Turner, R., & Killian, L. (1987). *Collective behavior*. Englewood Cliffs, NJ: Prentice Hall.

V-Day (2008). About V-Day. http://www.vday.org/about/more-about.

Wenocur, S., & Soifer, S.D. (1997). Prospects for community organization. In: M. Reisch & E. Gambrill (Eds.), *Social work in the 21st century*. Thousand Oaks, CA: Pine Forge Press.

Zald, M. & McCarthy, J. (1987). *Social movements in an organization society*. New Brunswick, NJ: Transaction.

Index